Opera and the Built Environment

Opera Lab: Explorations in History, Technology, and Performance

A series edited by David J. Levin and Mary Ann Smart

ADVISORY BOARD

Carolyn Abbate
Gundula Kreuzer
Emanuele Senici
Benjamin Walton
Emily Wilbourne

ALSO PUBLISHED IN THE SERIES

*Music in the Present Tense:
Rossini's Italian Operas in Their Time*
Emanuele Senici

*Singing Sappho: Improvisation and Authority
in Nineteenth-Century Italian Opera*
Melina Esse

Networking Operatic Italy
Francesca Vella

*"Don Giovanni" Captured:
Performance, Media, Myth*
Richard Will

*New Orleans and the Creation of
Transatlantic Opera, 1819–1859*
Charlotte Bentley

*Screening the Operatic Stage:
Television and Beyond*
Christopher Morris

*Lyric Personhood: On the Aesthetics of
Being Someone in the West*
Dan Wang

Opera and the Built Environment

Laura Vasilyeva

The University of Chicago Press   Chicago and London

This book is freely available in an open access edition thanks to the generous support of Johns Hopkins University. Learn more at JH Libraries Open Monograph Initiative website, available at: https://www.library.jhu.edu/library-services/scholarly-communication/tome-grant/.

The terms of the license for the open access digital edition are Creative Commons Attribution-Non-Commercial-No-Derivatives 4.0 International License (CC BY-NC-ND 4.0). To view a copy of this license, visit https://creativecommons.org/licenses/by-nc-nd/4.0/. *Note to users:* A Creative Commons license is only valid when applied by the person or entity that holds rights to the licensed work. This work may contain components to which the rightsholder in the work cannot apply the license. It is ultimately your responsibility to independently evaluate the copyright status of any work or component part of a work you use in light of your intended use.

The University of Chicago Press, Chicago 60637
The University of Chicago Press, Ltd., London
© 2025 by Laura Vasilyeva

Subject to the exception mentioned above, no part of this book may be used or reproduced in any manner whatsoever without written permission, except in the case of brief quotations in critical articles and reviews. For more information, contact the University of Chicago Press, 1427 E. 60th St., Chicago, IL 60637.
Published 2025

34 33 32 31 30 29 28 27 26 25   1 2 3 4 5

ISBN-13: 978-0-226-84444-2 (cloth)
ISBN-13: 978-0-226-84446-6 (paper)
ISBN-13: 978-0-226-84445-9 (ebook)
DOI: https://doi.org/10.7208/chicago/9780226844459.001.0001

Library of Congress Cataloging-in-Publication Data

Names: Vasilyeva, Laura, author.
Title: Opera and the built environment / Laura Vasilyeva.
Other titles: Opera lab.
Description: Chicago : The University of Chicago Press, 2025. | Series: Opera lab: explorations in history, technology, and performance | Includes bibliographical references and index.
Identifiers: LCCN 2025009540 | ISBN 9780226844442 (cloth) | ISBN 9780226844466 (paperback) | ISBN 9780226844459 (ebook)
Subjects: LCSH: Music and architecture. | Opera. | Theaters—History.
Classification: LCC ML3849 .V37 2025 | DDC 780/.072—dc23/eng/20250304
LC record available at https://lccn.loc.gov/2025009540

CONTENTS

List of Illustrations and Tables vii

1. ARCHITECTURE 1
Divisive Architecture 11
Distributed Architecture 13
Blueprint 15

2. SURFACES 22
(Chromo)phobia 26
Red 33
Sur-Face 37
Erasure 42

3. ATMOSPHERE 46
Ransacked Earth 49
Pure Air 54
Dirty Opera 58
Escapist Fantasies 62

4. ACOUSTICS 66
Orchestra Chamber 69
Calibrating Acoustics 72
Protected Space 77
Acoustic Signatures 80
Pure Sound? 82

5. THRESHOLDS 87
Ethics of Boundaries 88
Colonial Metal 96
Cellular Expansion 103

Acknowledgments 111
Appendix 115
Notes 121
Bibliography 149
Index 165

ILLUSTRATIONS AND TABLES

Musical Example

1.1 Puccini, *Manon Lescaut*, act 4, "Sei tu che piangi?," Manon and Des Grieux. 6

Figures

1.1 The Gran Teatre del Liceu in Barcelona filled its nearly 2300 seats with plants for a June 22, 2020 concert. 2
1.2 Teatro SS. Giovanni e Paolo, Venice, digital reconstruction of longitudinal section. 2
2.1 Exterior of Le Corbusier's Villa Savoye in Poissy, France, completed in 1931. 31
2.2 Exterior of Giuseppe Terragni's Casa del Fascio in Como, Italy, completed in 1936. 32
2.3 Scene at the inn, as described in Goethe's *Theory of Colors*. 39
2.4 Color wheel demonstrating the complementarity of color according to Goethe (1809). 40
2.5 World production and exports of raw silk, 1872–1936. 43
3.1 Illustration of the carbon cycle. 51
3.2 The Gran Teatre del Liceu destroyed by fire in 1994. 55
3.3 Ventilation at the Vienna Court Opera in 1891. 56
3.4 The Duomo in Milan, with the fifty-two-meter chimney of the central power station in Via Santa Radegonda visible on the right, c. 1900–1920. 61
4.1 Cross-section of the Bayreuth Festspielhaus. Note the deep orchestra pit and double proscenium arches. 67
4.2 Architectural blueprint from 1913 showing a cross-section of the orchestra pit at the Teatro alla Scala. 71

4.3 "To lower or not to lower...," caricature of four commissioners involved in the decision about whether to lower the orchestra at La Scala (*left to right*: Gatti-Casazza, Puccini, Toscanini, and Boito), 1907. 74

4.4 "The hollow of the seals," caricature of the orchestra pit at La Scala, 1907. 79

4.5 Fonotipia advertisement, 1906. 83

5.1 Drawing of the exterior architecture of the facade of the Teatro alla Scala in Milan, realized by architect Giuseppe Piermarini (1734–1908). 99

5.2 Photograph of the Palais Garnier facade, August 15, 1867. 100

5.3 Photograph of the Theatro Municipal, Rio de Janeiro facade, c. 1909–15. 100

5.4 Photograph showing the cramped conditions behind the stage at La Scala just prior to the 1920s renovations. 106

5.5 Video still of promotional material for "La Scala green," 2021. 110

Tables

2.1. Summary of responses from theater directors to the question "What is the background color of the boxes [at your theater]?" 34

5.1. Table summarizing the ratio of surface area in the wings versus the stage of various teatri all'italiana. 105

ONE

Architecture

This book begins from a central question: what would it mean to write an account of opera that attends to architecture? A recent event can serve as a heuristic to understand how the two are imbricated. In June 2020 a concert was held at the Gran Teatre del Liceu in Barcelona, not for humans but for an audience of some 2300 plants, one placed in each seat of the auditorium (fig. 1.1). Four musicians walked onto the theater stage, bowed to their verdant audience, and performed Giacomo Puccini's string quartet "Crisantemi." In the video recording circulated on the internet it is possible to view each section of the theater in succession. When the music starts, the camera advances from behind the musicians into the auditorium, scans the initial rows of the orchestra stalls, then moves into the boxes and balconies. All the while beatific shrubs bask in the sounds of Puccini's quartet. The scene is so serene that the proliferation of foliage in the theater starts to seem natural, as if the auditorium held the whole world within it, as if there were no outside to this windowless world.[1]

Although it was built in the 1990s, the Liceu seems much older because it is modeled on an architectural form that dates back centuries: the *teatro all'italiana*.[2] The fact that this architectural designation is also a label for the provenance of the design is a marker of how successful this theatrical form was even beyond the Italian peninsula, where it originated. Indeed, thousands of such architectural forms were built in the 1800s alone across five continents.[3] The scale of this construction is so considerable that it has been likened to the replication of life itself.[4]

These were venues built to accommodate a host of entertainments, and one above all others: opera. Their main characteristics were already in evidence at the first theater built *ex novo* for operatic spectacle, the SS. Giovanni e Paolo in Venice. Constructed in 1639, its windowless

FIGURE 1.1. The Gran Teatre del Liceu in Barcelona filled its nearly 2300 seats with plants for a June 22, 2020 concert that was also broadcast online. AP Photo / Emilio Morenatti.

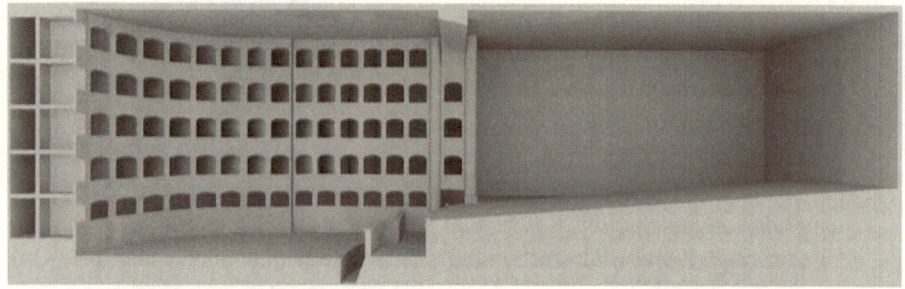

FIGURE 1.2. Teatro SS. Giovanni e Paolo, Venice, digital reconstruction of longitudinal section. Drawing: Benjamin Hoyle. In Johnson, *Inventing the Opera House*, 220. Reproduced with permission of the Licensor through PLSclear.

auditorium featured a vast distance between floor and ceiling, rows of stacked boxes around its horseshoe-shaped perimeter which dramatized that distance, and a proscenium arch that divided the auditorium from the stage.[5] In addition to these "hard" architectural features, shown in figure 1.2, there were elements of interior architecture that remain constant at teatri all'italiana even now, not least their swaths of silk and velvet.[6]

Such theaters induce a sense of aesthetic wonder and sensuous pleasure continuous with the dramas that unfold within them, sensations enhanced by their construction as self-enclosed worlds. Indeed, for much of their history, theaters were microcosms to which one could retreat. At the court of Ercole I d'Este, Duke of Ferrara, in the late 1400s, a room was repurposed for drama in which curtains were drawn over the windows to make the hall dark and torches were lit to illuminate the scene.[7] At Mantua in 1501, a theater was built ex novo that featured a turquoise cloth "starred with those signs which that very evening were appearing in [the] hemisphere" pinned across the ceiling, thus creating the illusion that the theater indeed contained the whole world within it.[8] In the decades that followed, theaters were constructed that did sometimes have windows in their auditoriums, but these were usually added for ventilation purposes and covered with cloth during performances. In the absence of natural light, theater designers have experimented with various means of illumination and various ways of distributing light between the auditorium and the stage. By the late 1800s, however, most artificial illumination in the auditorium during performances had been eliminated, while audiences had been lured into a new, attentive silence. With near-total darkness and silence comes disorientation, the sensation that it is almost impossible to measure where one is in relation to another. In the most extreme cases, leaning forward in the auditorium can feel like slipping into a pool of ink.[9]

The Liceu concert nonetheless takes the idea of the world-within-the theater to a new level altogether, revealing how completely these rarefied environments condition our existence when we are in them. Crucially, the installation was conceived as an artistic response to COVID-19. The auditorium filled with all those plants meanwhile cleansed the air of accumulated toxins in the form of carbon dioxide (CO_2) and infused it with oxygen (O_2), the substance so desperately depleted in those claimed by the coronavirus. The hall is turned into one enormous ventilator—one that does not feature the whirring and beeping of an intensive care setting, but operates with the silent assurance of nature, the ultimate breathing apparatus. In an Eden such as the Liceu's auditorium, it even seems conceivable that the sick could breathe once more.

One valuable lesson to be learned from this installation is that built environments can set the conditions for life itself, at least while one is inside them. However extreme this sounds, a prominent strain of architecture scholarship is oriented around the notion that built environments are the original source of daydreaming, of imagination. For Gaston Bachelard, the house was "one of the greatest powers of integration for the thoughts, memories and dreams of mankind." As he put it: "thrust[ing] aside contingencies, its councils of continuity are unceasing. Without it, man would be a dispersed being. It maintains him through the storms of the heavens and through those of life. It is body and soul. It is the human being's first world."[10] Although the house is foremost a "geometrical object," dominated as it is by "straight lines" and "well hewn solids," it is experienced phenomenologically: all those elaborate components also furnish humans with images that are lived directly and open up new worlds.[11] It is in this same intellectual territory that we find one of the finest books on the teatro all'italiana. In *Le rouge et or: Une poétique du théâtre à l'italienne* (Red and gold: A poetics of the teatro all'italiana), Georges Banu takes the impact of these theaters on the imagination with unprecedented seriousness.[12] For Banu, as for Bachelard, built environments are indissolubly connected with the horizons of being.

Opera and the Built Environment continues this work, beginning with the central claim that there can be no histories of opera that are not also histories of the built environment—that we cannot adequately contemplate or comprehend opera detached from its architectural settings.[13] For a taste of what this approach can yield, we might consider how the much drier acoustic of the teatro all'italiana relative to other theaters of the period—including the Bayreuth Festspielhaus, the theater opened in 1876 for the exclusive performance of Richard Wagner's music dramas—set the parameters within which composers worked. The distinctive feature of the Festspielhaus was (and remains) its long reverberation time: it took some 1.55 seconds for sound there to decay to the point that it was inaudible to most listeners, relative to the 1.2 seconds at the Teatro alla Scala in Milan, a theater that opened in 1778 and soon became a model for thousands of other teatri all'italiana.[14] As the architectural historian Joseph L. Clarke has proposed, the Festspielhaus's reverberation—a product of the especially pronounced distance between the floor and the ceiling—seems to have fascinated Wagner, who went on to score sounds that would reverberate for some time in this space.[15] Indeed, to understand *Parsifal* (1882) is in an important sense to understand how the acoustics of the Festspielhaus left their mark on the composition. (Whether either the theater's architect, Otto Brückwald, or Wagner wanted or anticipated such an acoustic is unclear; reverberation is, however, what they got.) La Scala has a much drier acoustic, and it is no coincidence that the music written for it sounds quite different. One wonders whether the sounds of operas composed for teatri all'italiana, such as Gioachino Rossini's *Semiramide* (Teatro La Fenice, 1823) or Puccini's *Manon Lescaut* (Teatro Regio, Turin, 1893) would have been conceivable had these composers had different theaters at their disposal.

To think of the theater as a stable medium that conditioned how sound was designed is to hear moments when the theater was instrumentalized as an extension of the orchestration itself, to hear the architectural environment within the music.[16] To examine this in practice, we could consider the abundant use of *violinata*—the doubling of the vocal line by the orchestra—in the musical aesthetic that Puccini, Umberto Giordano, and other members of the so-called *giovane scuola* cultivated in the later nineteenth century. Such reliance on the orchestra to double the voice has, over the decades, been dismissed as lazy overstatement, a crass means of creating affective immediacy. But this fails to take into account what violinata achieved at teatri all'italiana. To have both the voice and the instruments of the orchestra issue the same melodic line from their separate locations was to set in motion distinct reverberative patterns: it created a minuscule mismatch between the reverberation of the melodic line in the voice and in the orchestra. These doublings generated a small amount of immersive sonic confusion that countered the nonreverberative tendencies of the Italian opera house. They also became a means of rendering visceral the extreme conditions of characters within the narrative. To cite just one example: in the final act of *Manon Lescaut*, the heroine, Manon, banished to the New World for her sexual transgressions, crawls across the Louisiana desert (!) in search of water in a desperate attempt to save herself from certain death. As her vocal line is doubled in the violins, violas, cellos, flute, and English horn, her disorientation briefly becomes our own; at a perceptual level, the mismatch ties our somatic experience to hers (ex. 1.1).

To hear the built environment within orchestration is one way of listening to the entwined histories of music and architecture. It is, in tandem, to embrace the material conditions within which sound is created. As scholars of sound studies have been keen to emphasize, the minimum criterion for music to come into existence is that there must be spatial coordinates within which it does so: until vibrations in the air come into contact with the ears of listeners, there is no music.[17] Under the influence of a hermeneutic bent within the humanities, music historians have long tended to stress the endpoint in this process—how the listener extracts meaning from music—while skimming over the actual mechanisms that enable us to receive information in the first place.[18] There have been decades of resistance in the humanities to the simple notion that information is received in material form—that existence, as Martin Heidegger articulated it, is "always already in a substantial and therefore in a spatial contact with the things of the world."[19]

But the interwoven histories of music and architecture do not begin and end within the microcosm of the teatro all'italiana, in the

EXAMPLE 1.1. Puccini, *Manon Lescaut*, act 4, "Sei tu che piangi?," Manon and Des Grieux.

EXAMPLE 1.1. (continued)

EXAMPLE 1.1. (continued)

EXAMPLE 1.1. (*continued*)

reverberative space between its walls. *Opera and the Built Environment* insists instead that however powerful such constitutive conditions can be, they are always curated and as such have social histories that must not be erased.

In this sense, my book both proceeds from what is arguably the most famous attempt to connect opera and the built environment—the media scholar Friedrich Kittler's description of the Festspielhaus—and distances itself from it.[20] For Kittler, music drama at the Festspielhaus was one of the earliest instances of a modern mass medium, in which individual data streams were isolated, perfected, and then combined: the audience heard orchestral sound but did not see the orchestra (which was concealed in a sunken orchestra pit), and they could view the fictional world but had the rest of their field of vision obscured (because the auditorium was in near darkness during the performance). If this isolation of the senses made it modern, so too did the nature of the data communicated. Kittler understood media as material channels that carried information but also nonsense; the ratio between the two characterized the medium. In *Discourse Networks 1800/1900* (1985), he made the bold claim that the network of materials, institutions, and individuals around 1900 had abandoned the noematic world, the world of intention, since its media had ceased to differentiate between noise and everything else.[21] Literature had cultivated souls, with its insistence that letters and words bore meaning; in contrast, modern media did no more than encode, store, and deliver data to the user. The form of the shellac (or vinyl) record is the perfect demonstration of Kittler's thesis: the grooves in the surface of the disc capture all variations in air vibration during the recording process, not only those deemed "musical." When Kittler cast the Festspielhaus as the first modern mass medium, he celebrated the fact that it foreshadowed the dissolution of the noematic world. These were not so much music dramas in which words and leitmotif-laden music reached the listener and awaited the extraction of meaning in a single communicative action, but immersive and unruly experiences in which reverberation, resonance, and air swells reached the senses and surrounded them with direct data.[22] This was their triumph.

Kittler in this sense reinscribed the Festspielhaus as a wondrous medium that could recalibrate how the senses received and processed information. But Kittler was not the first to orient discussion of the architectural structure in this direction. If the Festspielhaus is the sole theater to have attracted the attention of music historians on a routine basis—its architectural features usually the only ones to be noted in survey courses—this status can be traced to a specific composer who towers over this narrative.[23] In his voluminous prose, Wagner limned the built environment in intricate detail: even beams and trusses are described for the reader. But he also ensured that all those architectural elements would be understood as mechanisms for the total immersion of the audience member in the music drama, for their consummate submission to art. Architectural elements materialize in his texts only to dissolve into one transcendent vision, as the theater is rendered as nothing less than a site for the salvation of man.[24]

I need not force the case that there are issues with this. But I do want to sketch a route out of such seductive architectural microcosms; in fact, doing so is the central project of this book. In what follows, I consider what it would look like to stand within the microcosm of a teatro all'italiana, to rest at its thresholds, and to follow the distributed and atomized forms these architectural structures take. I do this with a focus on the teatro all'italiana in the 1800s and early 1900s, that curious time when its architectural form was constructed thousands of times over.

Divisive Architecture

As we begin this journey, the Liceu installation serves once more as a heuristic. However much the camera seems to lure us into a terrestrial paradise within its auditorium, there is an out-of-placeness about these plants that cannot be overlooked: the shrubs no more belong there than lions at a childcare center. Plants are almost never welcomed into auditoriums. This would not even be worth commenting upon if we had not banished so much besides flora. The odd intrusion of the outside inside at the Liceu is a bold reminder that there are always rules about what—and who—should remain outside the doors of the opera house, rules that have become natural over time. (How else could we have reached a situation in which the remark "the homeless? Aren't they the people you step over when you come out of the opera house?" could be bandied about by a member of the British Parliament in the 1990s?)[25]

Opera and the Built Environment theorizes architectural boundaries and thresholds at teatri all'italiana: those elements used to naturalize exclusion.[26] I consider, for instance, how these theaters used for their facades monumental, polished blocks of stone, and how, in this sense, their architectural skins announced particular sensibilities that limited who would be likely even to approach their thresholds in the first place. The vast amount of stone used for teatri all'italiana often made them stand out within their local environments. When the Teatro Amazonas in Manaus, Brazil, was constructed in the 1890s, for instance, it cast its shadow over built environments made from straw, paxiúba palm, and other native woods.[27] Stone dominated both because stone-faced teatri loomed tallest in their immediate environments and because stone was so laden with racialized values. For Charles Garnier, the French architect of the iconic new home of the Paris Opéra constructed between 1861 and 1875, stone stood alone in its abilities to narrate the beauties of the human condition.[28]

One conclusion to be drawn from this example is that accounts which focus on the subliminal lessons encoded in opera overlook the much less subtle lessons about who we are and how we relate to one another; lessons that are internalized—and indeed naturalized—before we have even entered a theater or a note has ever sounded. Aside from a few important exceptions, music historians have tended not to notice the values that lie at the surface of these teatri all'italiana, even though they exert disproportionate force on all of us.

Rules also limit who can move with freedom inside a theater. To divide classes and sexes from one another, barriers and divisions were used in the earliest models of theatrical architecture, those constructed well before the heyday of the teatro all'italiana. These earlier theaters, built for dramatic and musical performance within the Italian peninsula, featured endless permutations of how audience members were seated. Such manifold transformations became possible because architects exploited the full vertical and horizontal extensions of a theater: internal structures such as floors, risers, steps, and balconies afforded the possibility of fracturing the audience. If the most characteristic feature of the teatro all'italiana is its stacked boxes, it is notable that from the start, such boxes allowed the noblest audience members to formalize claims to dedicated areas of the theater and even afforded them the ability to move around undetected, to become invisible, cloaked amid the masses. At the Teatro di Baldracca in Florence, constructed around 1576 behind the Palazzo degli Uffizi, for commedia dell'arte, a series of small rooms or *stanzini* were each under the permanent control of an individual with a key. Although considerably larger than the typical private boxes in later teatri all'italiana, these were probably the earliest boxlike structures. A private corridor seems to have communicated with these rooms so that those who possessed the keys—the Medicis and their inner circle—could enter them without encountering the wider audience.[29]

Boxes used at the SS. Giovanni e Paolo, built some six decades later, retained many of these same features, as do those at most teatri all'italiana now. The theater's 150-plus boxes would have been accessed via individual doors, and curtains might have been drawn across them. Even if the secret corridor had been dispensed with and means of access made more communal, these boxes functioned as private domestic spaces within an otherwise public realm.[30] Even now these remain some of the most exclusive areas of the auditorium, alongside the orchestra stalls, whose value soared in the later 1800s.

Opera and the Built Environment is as interested in the manner that architectural boundaries nurture connections as the ways these foreclose social relations, however. It is at and across the boundaries of our selves—our skin—and the material world that relations are formed; as the architectural scholar Giuliana Bruno reminds us, boundaries such as walls, doors, and staircases are as much sites of interaction as they are obstacles.[31] Indeed, when we consider what audiences demanded of touchable surfaces at teatri all'italiana around 1800, a new set of social connections comes into focus. True, this was a time of important transformations at opera houses, as audiences learned to sit in that reverent silence and near-darkness during performances. As this book reveals, however, the fabrics selected to line auditorium walls at teatri all'italiana were chosen with the conviction that these would animate faces, in defiance of the room's discipline and hermeticism. All this said, those fabrics were destined to enliven one set of faces alone: those of white females. Across one curated surface, social distance was at once erased and created. As this book demonstrates, there was—and remains—a racial and gendered dimension to theatrical decoration.[32]

Distributed Architecture

Opera and the Built Environment, finally, conceives of architecture in a third sense: as atomized and distributed. It is conventional to think of built environments as delineated structures with clear coordinates. But architecture is never so neat and coherent. For one, built environments are not inert. They crumble, become weathered, and are otherwise altered by natural processes. Furthermore, all inhabited built environments are modified as a result of interactions with them. This is obvious when renovations are involved, as when an addition such as an annex is made to a home. But inhabitants also move items in and out of built environments all the time. And even though items such as furniture could be classed as accessories rather than architecture, they are in fact constitutive of the fundamental experience of the built environment. Following the architectural scholar Lois Weinthal, I think of the interior as "experienced from elements closest to us in scale and intimacy, such as clothing, to those farther away, such as perimeter walls that divide interior from exterior, and their interrelatedness at different scales and atmospheres." Advocating for a more seamless understanding of architectural elements—one that has not been characteristic of architectural studies, with its divide between architecture on the one hand and interior design on the other—Weinthal calls for readers to "move toward a new interior," in which "thinking that stems from how we integrally experience the interior realm between these scales" predominates.[33] In this sense, *Opera and the Built Environment* has more in common with important works such as Gundula Kreuzer's *Curtain, Gong, Steam: Wagnerian Technologies of Nineteenth-Century Opera* than is at first obvious. Although Kreuzer does not frame her discussion as architectural, the conclusions she reaches nonetheless illustrate much about the lived interiors of the theater.[34]

If the notion of interior architecture forces us to think about the built environment as being in continual flux, it is the distributed nature of architecture that interests me here, the manner in which built environments draw locations far removed in time and distance into contact. This sometimes occurs before a particular structure is even conceived, when construction materials that have been formed across millennia—such as elemental minerals and fossil fuels—are extracted from the Earth. It continues as the built environment is constructed and then inhabited or utilized, as items are moved in and out of it, and it occurs once more with its ultimate destruction. In each case, some of the processes employed will cause climate deterioration; in each case, harmful emissions from the built environment also transform and degrade the planet.

Opera and the Built Environment thus heeds calls from architecture scholars such as Esther da Costa Meyer and Daniel A. Barber to rethink how built environments and climate connect. As da Costa Meyer would have it, "we build in the Anthropocene, and write as if in the Holocene." We build in an era in which humans exert untold influence on climate, but write as if we live in a time in which humans leave minimal trace on the planet[35]—despite the fact that in the United States alone the built environment is said to account for up for 50 percent of greenhouse gas emissions.[36]

To heed these calls is also to build on the momentum of studies that understand music in relation to the global.[37] As Jürgen Osterhammel has noted, opera is a genre that "underwent globalization early on."[38] As such, it has long involved circulation—of musicians, instruments, audiences—around the Earth. Some of the most innovative current work in opera studies examines this movement.[39] But all that operatic activity also entailed movement of the Earth itself, movement that was no less social. Accumulation of timber or stone construction materials demanded movement of materials over sometimes improbable distances, placing people in locations where they otherwise would not be and, in the case of forced labor, did not choose to be. Each time a theater was redecorated, meanwhile, vast amounts of fabric had to flow into it, fabric that needed to be both woven and dyed. Until the establishment of chemical coloration industries in the mid-1800s, the dyeing of fabric entailed the extraction of color from animal, mineral, or plant sources drawn from across and beneath a vulnerable Earth. The list goes on, but the important point here is that these are stories that still need to be told, stories focused not on what opera means to us—or how it has moved us—but on how we have moved the Earth and people for opera.[40] In this sense, to heed these calls is to understand opera within the inextricable histories of environmental catastrophe and empire.

Blueprint

Few books centered on opera in the 1800s and early 1900s have directed sustained attention to the architectural features of teatri all'italiana. There are of course exceptions, not least James H. Johnson's *Listening in Paris: A Cultural History* and Jennifer Hall-Witt's *Fashionable Acts: Opera and Elite Culture in London, 1780-1880*. For these authors, architecture had an important role in the creation of conditions under which once-distracted listeners were lured into that attentive, silent state across the 1800s.[41] Johnson, for instance, describes the structure of the boxes, the comfort of the seat cushions, and the feel of the illumination at the Salle Le Peletier—the home to the Paris Opéra from 1821 to 1873—as essential factors in how well middle-class audience members, keen to announce their musical and social credentials, could concentrate. In the hands of these authors, architectural details are integral to the class tensions that shook the nineteenth century.[42]

Opera and the Built Environment could not have been written without the crucial grounding provided by this important scholarship. But this book pursues a different kind of narrative and adopts different methods from those examples. For one, this book makes a case for the teatro all'italiana as an architectural form whose instantiations were so similar from one theater to the next that broad claims can be made about them. Another means to put this is that I understand teatri all'italiana in infrastructural terms, as built environments whose standardization across a theatrical network lent them collective force.[43] This does not, of course, mean that all these theaters were identical, from one to the next, nor that there has been no evolution over time. But when theater architects such as Leo Beranek claim that the teatro all'italiana is "the most stable space for music ever designed," or when the theater historian Carlotta Sorba describes these theaters as "clones" of one another, they are pointing to a standardization and replication that carries considerable historical force and that cries out for scholarly attention.[44]

Italian opera was conceived from the start with circulation in mind, and continuities between theaters made such movement smoother. Standardization reached its pinnacle during the 1800s and early 1900s as innovations were introduced to them (either as theaters were constructed or when these were renovated) and then became standard.[45] As the book reveals, we are beholden to these architectural characteristics even now: we trust in norms established in times far removed, for reasons that have continued to elude us. That those standards became tradition, and that tradition became sacrosanct, makes it all the harder to do otherwise. Those standards, however, have histories that have still to be told.

Although this book makes a case for the teatro all'italiana as an architectural form whose manifestations were similar enough to allow us to think of them in collective terms, it is built on a foundation of research about the Teatro alla Scala in Milan. There are several reasons for this. Erected on the model of the architect Giuseppe Piermarini, it was constructed to contribute to the prominence of this notable urban center, then under the control of the Austrian Empire, and the dozens of Milanese families who funded its construction. Contemporaries were shocked that its auditorium could deliver such clear sound even at extreme limits. It was the largest theater of its time: between its 260 boxes across five tiers and other areas of the auditorium it could accommodate more than two thousand audience members. As resources were directed toward musical life in this dynamic city—the Conservatory was founded in 1807, and a vigorous musical press developed afterward—the theater continued to attract some of the world's best musicians. The numerous visitors to Milan who went to the theater commented on more than its artistic fare, while architects would visit it as a matter of course before they began work on other teatri. As one of the most talked-about teatri all'italiana, it served as a crucial—if not the crucial—model in the theatrical construction boom of the 1800s. The theater, moreover, became a model twice over: as the chapters that follow will show, material innovations introduced at the theater across the 1800s and early 1900s would be widely replicated.[46]

Opera and the Built Environment also charts a new course in that architecture lends momentum to the narrative told here, rather than musical matters or portrayals more common to nineteenth-century studies. Each chapter of the book is centered on a fundamental characteristic of the teatro all'italiana's built environment, from surfaces, to atmosphere, to acoustics, to thresholds. This architectural focus enables me to consider the operatic experience in broader terms than usual; the book does not revolve around the audiovisual dimensions of the music and drama mounted at these theaters, but all the other sensations induced within them, ones almost never mentioned, however central these were. The architectural focus in turn allows me to resolve some fundamental unknowns about teatri all'italiana, such as: Whence the idea that theater auditoriums should be decorated in red, rather than some other color? Or whence the notion that orchestras within these theaters should be seated in a lowered chamber, rather than at the level of the auditorium floor/stalls? And on what timeline were these innovations embraced? Perhaps most foundationally, however, the architectural focus—with the consideration it enables of the microcosm of the teatro all'italiana, its thresholds, and the scattered locations on the Earth imbricated in its construction and operation—enables me to rethink the scales on which we understand opera and in turn the communities to which it is connected.

In chapter 2, "Surfaces," for instance, I consider what drives attachment to architectural surfaces. Whence red silk textiles at teatri all'italiana? How did they become inviolable architectural skins within theater auditoriums? The theaters built in the construction boom were almost all redecorated several times across the 1800s, in no small measure because there was a novel convergence at the time between newness and cleanliness.[47] Swatches of fabrics conserved in the notes of theatrical commissioners make clear that decoration and redecoration were occasions for careful fabric selections to be made.[48] These choices resulted in all manner of colored textiles until around 1850; after that, red silk became the dominant textile. Conversions to this decorative scheme were nonetheless fitful: it was not, for instance, until 1930 that this scheme was introduced at La Scala, and like a true conversion, it elicited intense emotion from those in attendance. Some members of the civic administration even made desperate bids to halt the standardization it would perpetuate.[49]

As alluded to earlier in this chapter, one core reason red silk textiles were selected was the notion that they could animate faces: much as a red tint colored onto black-and-white photos at mid-century imbued faces with hue and motion, a red, silken ambience in an auditorium was believed to intensify the rosiness of flushed cheeks, and thus to instill faces with emotion. Those who advocated for the red theatrical surface did so on the basis that theatrical walls were much like faces themselves: they were sites that allowed inner worlds to spill outward.

As we saw earlier, it was the white, female face that red was believed to best animate. Yet, red was the color of choice across a vast theatrical infrastructure, extending to locations where pale skin was the exception, not the norm. That color in theater auditoriums was used to enact distinctions becomes all the more striking when we consider that, unlike actual skin, architectural skins are not autogenerative. Each time a theater is redecorated, textiles need to be sourced, and scores of decisions have to be made about where and how to do that. Red silks were the end result of interactions that turned insects—their skin, tissue, and secretions—into commodities that were traded in international markets that underwrote entire colonial economies. To inquire into the architectural surface within these theaters is thus to consider how the built environments of opera are connected to the politics of life itself.

In chapter 3, "Atmosphere," I move inward from the surfaces of the auditorium to the air that circulated within its walls. Well before the 1800s it was common across much of the world to talk about music as a moral force that bettered mankind. In 1800s Europe, however, a new mechanism for this improvement came into focus: music was said to cleanse the air we inhale, ridding it of moral sickness. If such a notion was to have any credence, the air in theaters could not be too wretched. In this context, opera houses and concert halls became some of the earliest built environments to have ventilation and climatic controls installed. Climatic controls ensured that not too much carbon dioxide accumulated in an auditorium, which in turn was believed to ensure that the air would neither feel "breathless" nor spread disease. This model relied on recent advances in the science of carbon rotation, in particular the notion that the Earth's carbon cycle ensured that O_2 and CO_2 were in balance.

As James Q. Davies has demonstrated, the combination of music and ventilation mechanisms made the air at such venues seem much more rarefied than in most other environments, not least in relation to outdoor urban air, often described as noxious and foul.[50] Such rarefied air was valued all the more highly because of a dawning awareness that it was not isolated areas alone whose air was impure. Since the Earth had a single continuous atmosphere, vitiated air could never be entirely contained. Indeed, the scholar to whom the term "Anthropocene" is now attributed, the Italian Antonio Stoppani, warned in a series of startlingly prescient articles and lectures in the 1870 and 1880s that as human beings "ransacked the Earth"—above all for fossil fuels—we would create irreversible and catastrophic imbalances in carbon rotation throughout the atmosphere.

Musical venues may have been cast as havens removed from all these concerns, as some of the last frontiers of pure air, yet they played a critical role in the path toward that fossil-fueled modernity. These were some of the first venues to be connected to networked power, even becoming crucial promotional forums for electricity. Indeed, a collaborator of

Stoppani's, Giuseppe Colombo, the founder of the Società Edison Italiana, oversaw the installation of the first electrical network in Europe and ensured that its current was directed to the Teatro alla Scala in Milan.

It would be folly to conclude that electrical networks would have been inconceivable without the opera house, but it is a fact that for a time opera houses and electrical networks were indivisible from one another; in turn, the opera house mobilized modern energy infrastructures as we know them. Given that electricity relies on an initial source of power—typically from combustion—with this came an incalculable expansion in the amount of fossil fuels exhumed, burned, and shunted back into the atmosphere. "Pure," ventilated air at such venues meanwhile became a convenient distraction from their role in this messier, dirtier form of atmospheric alteration. The association between these venues and rarefied air was indeed reinforced in the 1800s as electricity was aestheticized within musical composition, fashioned as a force that leaves almost no trace in the air, something as transcendent and immaterial as music itself was commonly said to be.

Chapter 4, "Acoustics," considers the innovation of the sunken orchestra at teatri all'italiana. Though it is now routine for orchestras to be seated in a lowered chamber, beneath the level of the auditorium stalls, this was not the case at La Scala until 1907, roughly the same time at which various other Italian theaters did likewise. Until then, orchestras had performed at the level of the auditorium floor, a meter or two from the audience in the stalls. Wagner had of course created a lowered orchestra pit at the Bayreuth Festspielhaus in the 1870s and famously described the decision in terms of concealment: an attempt to hide the means of sound production. In view of the modifications made to numerous opera houses in the decades that followed to create orchestra chambers, scholars have tended to assume that the Festspielhaus was both the stimulus and the model for such spaces. This flattens out important variations in architectural design between theaters and also narrates the introduction of orchestra chambers from the perspective of audience members alone. Lowered orchestral platforms may have functioned as "mystical chasms" from which sound floated upward toward awed spectators, but they also had a crucial role in the creation of enclosed, calibrated spaces for musicians and new acoustic environments.

Chapter 5, "Thresholds," continues this book's focus on alterations to the "hard form" of the teatro all'italiana, considering how structural metals were introduced into their frames from the late 1800s onward. This structural innovation is almost never examined in music histories, not least because these metals were largely hidden beneath stone facades and curated interiors. The results will nonetheless be familiar to anyone who has ever entered a teatro all'italiana or even seen one from a distance. First and foremost, metal enabled teatri all'italiana's vertical extension, as it increased the number of stories the theaters could support. Locations such as Garnier's Paris Opéra would have been impossible without structural metal. As *Le fantôme de l'Opéra* (*The Phantom of the Opera*), Gaston Leroux's 1910 detective novel set in this same Opéra, demonstrates so well, with these metals at their core, such built environments could also sustain all manner of uses that would have otherwise overburdened these buildings' foundations, uses that resulted from dramatic new flexibility in the placement of walls and windows. With its 1,942 locked doors, the Opéra was a crime scene with endless narrative possibilities, a teatro all'italiana whose cavernous auditorium was offset by countless corners in which characters could hide.

This novel serves as my entry point into the ethics of the threshold at teatri all'italiana, one that underwent a fundamental shift with the introduction of structural metals. I read *Le fantôme de l'Opéra* as a critical reaction to the new abundance of thresholds at these theaters. The reader is, after all, repeatedly reminded that doors, collapsible walls, and other thresholds control the movement of bodies and create unevenness in what can be heard, seen, or otherwise felt. While, as Thomas Oles has put it, walls and other thresholds "work [themselves] into the fabric of life around [them]," naturalizing rules about who has access and who does not, *Le fantôme de l'Opéra* draws attention to the work that such thresholds do and to the disparate outcomes these can create.[51]

The intersection between structural metals and such ethical matters is, however, much busier than this. Chapter 5 moves outward from the Opéra's internal architecture to examine the routes that metal took. It reveals how much must be reordered—how much of the Earth must move—in order to build a teatro all'italiana in the first place. And it reveals that structural metals were used to build these theaters on a scale that would otherwise have been inconceivable. To trace this is to reckon with how the foundations beneath us—the minerals within the Earth—have been eroded for the sake of creating the built environments that now surround us. And it is to reckon with the colonial dimensions of all this construction. The poetics of these theaters, in the ultimate analysis, are always political.

And yet those poetics are what has drawn audiences to teatri all'italiana. Banu comes closest to the articulation of a vision of these theaters as a network that lives and breathes in his groundbreaking *Le rouge et or*, a work built on tremendous historical research and saturated with evocation. The book is marked by a belief that those thousands of theaters, when inscribed into the landscape, cannot leave those who see and feel them unaltered. There are, to be sure, limitations here, not least that the network Banu describes has circumscribed European boundaries. But the dreamworlds Banu summons across his book, with each discussion of their architectural features, were real. For this alone, the teatro all'italiana merits new attention.

TWO

Surfaces

This chapter is concerned with theatrical surfaces—the textures and colors that form the immediate environment within theater auditoriums. This may seem unusual or niche, but it has in fact been an acute concern for some. That is the least that can be said about a chain of florid letters penned across several months in 1930 concerning the redecoration of the Teatro alla Scala (see the appendix).[1] At the close of that summer, the industrialist Senatore Borletti, then a director of the theater and an Italian senator, oversaw the redecoration within the auditorium. Once the older textiles had been removed and thousands of meters of new fabric ordered, the matter came to the attention of Ettore Modigliani, the superintendent of monuments for the province of Lombardy. This is where the correspondence starts. Since Borletti should have secured authorization from Modigliani before he touched the theater's decor, he attests to his "full commitment to respect the inviolability of . . . the interior of the auditorium at the theater" and reassures him that the work will entail the substitution of older textiles on the walls and chairs with refined silk damask, to create a uniform, consistent look, tailor-made to blend with the rest of the auditorium. To this he adds that the results will constitute a notable improvement, not least in the case of boxes, where individual box owners had each created their own mishmash of styles.[2]

The older condition of the auditorium was precisely what Modigliani had wanted to maintain, however. As he saw it, Borletti had removed valuable fabrics with the intention of introducing a uniform look that was far from desirable. Unable to reverse what had been undertaken without due consultation, he instead advised Borletti to mix and match the silk fabric selected for the auditorium walls—those of the boxes included—with four or five other fabrics to "create a sense of almost accidental variety that will interrupt the monotonous uniformity of a theater decorated with one fabric alone." To do so would ensure that "the Teatro alla Scala, recognized as the most important temple of opera, might continue to emanate a spellbinding, imponderable, aesthetic quality even in its decor."[3]

Much of the passion that lay behind these bold words stemmed from the fact that Borletti's infraction was shameless: he knew he needed to secure authorization. He had even said so to none other than Benito Mussolini, leader of the Fascist state. Mussolini had received the director of the venerable theater earlier in the summer; in a letter sent around a week before the Borletti-Modigliani correspondence started, Borletti informed Mussolini of his "truly courageous decision to renovate the theater without asking anyone anything."[4] But the intensity of Borletti's exchange with Modigliani is also a measure of the extent of their convictions about what a decorative scheme at La Scala should achieve.

For all that divided our correspondents, both subscribed to the same basic notion: that considerable power resided within and between the tensile fibers of textiles. As the full chain of letters makes clear, textiles enchanted these men but also revolted them; were seen as at once desirable and characteristic, monotonous, horrendous, and vile. To be sure, both Borletti and Modigliani had reason to take textiles seriously. The former had been elected head of the Ente Autonomo della Scala—an institution contracted to run La Scala—in 1929, toward the close of a career that had commenced with Borletti's inheritance of a textile empire that dominated Italian linen and hemp production. For several years he had been owner of the broadsheet *Il secolo* (which he transformed into a Fascist outlet) and at the time of this tenure at La Scala was director of SNIA Viscosa, then one of the world leaders in the production of synthetic textiles such as viscose.[5] In 1930 Modigliani was director of the venerable Pinacoteca di Brera, an art museum in Milan.[6] In other words, he was attuned to the visual, if not also the tactile. But their investment in the theater's textiles makes intuitive sense even without these details. Textiles, after all, clothe our bodies, our possessions, our furnishings. They are located at the surface and as such are intimate sites—some of the most intimate that there are. It is—once more—at and across the boundaries of our selves—our skin—and the veneer of the material world where relations occur. Indeed, surfaces are distinct realms of the world around us, vast extensions whose characteristics—visual, tactile, or otherwise—are a continual source of stimulation, one that determines how we see, how we think, and how we conceptualize where we end and the rest of the world starts.[7]

Textiles can also inspire passionate and enduring attachments. In a later letter Borletti indeed conceded that although the old textiles at the theater were "worthy of a delicatessen's back room," he realized Modigliani's attachment to these surfaces was about more than the materials themselves: it was about all that had become bonded to them—memories, traditions, and, in the end, history.[8]

To alter textiles is, moreover, to alter the appearance of a built environment. It is for instance common for the veneers of built environments to be labeled "architectural skins."[9] This term underscores the notion that when architectural veneers are altered, the old is cast aside to make room for the new, as when skin cells are shed and new ones form. The term also underscores the notion that the renewal of architectural surfaces is about a more fundamental shift, one that concerns the identities of built environments and those who associate with them. When we move from the interior of a built environment outward, we encounter—so architects tell us—a series of enfolded skins, from the bedsheets that cocoon us to the fabrics we decorate our houses with, to the external veneers of those houses: surfaces that function as extensions of our own skin, as second or third or fourth skins that shield us from a hostile world and define how we live in and appear within that world. As the philosopher Michel Serres once put it, "Within the house, the bedroom encloses a box within a box.... Sheets add another pocket to the nested series, and rarely do we slide between them naked.... The empiricist is astonished by the number of layers, strata and partitions from rough concrete to bed linen, the number of skins until we reach our real skin.... We do not live as beings in the world in the way books tell us... but rather as a variety of mammal or soft primate which, having lost its fur, invented the house and promptly filled it with boxes inside boxes."[10]

Our correspondents themselves allude to a connection between architectural veneers and skin at critical moments in their discussion. The first sentiment Borletti expresses—"You can rest assured of my full commitment to respect the *inviolability* of... the decor"—makes it seem that the theater has settled into a form that must not be disturbed, as if to do so would constitute an act of violence. Meanwhile, in the peroration of the next letter, Modigliani cautions that the "imponderable" essence of the theater would be lost if the older textiles were cast aside, as if those tensile fabrics somehow held that incalculable essence in situ, beneath and within them.

In both instances these men imbue textiles with characteristics that are normally ascribed only to skin. This delicate membrane has been understood as an outward manifestation of the life within, a surface where the inner and outer worlds meet.[11] But in more basic and much less poetic terms, it is also a sack that contains flesh, blood, and bones all assembled within it. Its essential role as a container raises fears about what occurs when the container is breached. As Steven Connor has proposed, small children are obsessed with cuts and tears to the skin because these stimulate fantasies that, once the skin is compromised, the self will ooze out into an infinitude of time and space.[12] But these are more than childish fantasies. Even a minor cut can lead to loss of life, as when bacteria enters the bloodstream across a minute dermal tear. As the torturer knows well, there is a direct relation between breaches to the skin and breaches of that elusive phenomenon called consciousness. To cut skin, to tear, burn, or flay it, is to toy with the limits of life. It is this loss of "imponderable" essence that our correspondents are discussing here—the idea that once its surfaces are violated, the theater will cease to be what it once was, that its essence will have been annihilated. For Modigliani, this is unthinkable. Borletti, on the other hand, concludes that "all the great traditional theaters, from the Paris Opéra to the Berlin Staatsoper to the Vienna Opera, have had to face this same crisis [of redecoration], but none of them, where the rules of art are venerated and respected, have tried to undertake that which cannot be undertaken. The new cannot stand in for the old and antique."[13] In other words, one has to leave the past behind and move forward, even when that lends an entirely new face, or skin, to the theater.

Far from casual remarks about decor, then, our correspondents are trading in powerful allusions. Their rhetoric should remind us, at a minimum, that textiles matter and have mattered to historical actors. The vigor of their debate is also an invitation to consider the curious, and almost never mentioned, fact that textiles have become standardized across the infrastructure of teatri all'italiana and that we are beholden to those standards even now, for reasons that continue to elude us. These omissions in music histories are continuous with those within the field of architecture studies as a whole. Tales of textiles and those elements of built environments that tend to be renewed at intervals never yield themselves to clean narrativization; the continual substitution of textiles undermines the idea of a stable architectural structure on which the architectural theorist can reflect.[14] Yet textiles nonetheless exert outsized influence on how one moves within the world. The core contention here is that this remains true within teatri all'italiana, and that to trace the use of textiles within them is to recenter within our music histories bodies that have been erased from writing about opera. For if the Borletti-Modigliani debate hints at the connection between textiles and identities, earlier sources also draw explicit connections between the choice of textiles and the identities of individuals within theater auditoriums; indeed, the decorative scheme that is now so standard was founded on such formulations. To put this another way, materials within opera houses have had a central role in narratives about the involvement of opera in the social dramas that shook the nineteenth century, not least since James H. Johnson charted how a new, middle-class audience learned to sit in that absorbed silence, in newly darkened auditoriums, and thereby demonstrate their cultivated credentials.[15] To ask how one main decorative scheme came to be selected at thousands of teatri all'italiana since the nineteenth century, and to consider what was at stake, is to understand the role of materials in still more fundamental matters that structured existence at the time.

In what follows, I consider all this in relation to two inseparable dimensions of textiles—color and texture. The history and reflections that follow stretch back to the early decades of the 1800s since, as we shall see, the broad issues that concerned Borletti and Modigliani had already been under intense consideration for more than a century by the time the two men began their correspondence in 1930.

(Chromo)phobia

The Borletti-Modigliani tussle was not the sole occasion on which decorative choices at theaters occasioned heated debate. If "to live means to leave traces," it is at the surface where such traces first accumulate.[16] Skin, after all, is both alive and dead, the epidermis a collection of deceased cells that have migrated to its outermost layer—in the memorable words of Mark C. Taylor, "where [we] make contact with the world, [we are] always already dead."[17] These cells, moreover, accumulate on surfaces—walls, doorknobs, and the like—as stubborn reminders of our interaction with them, traces that can be lessened but never erased. Since worn architectural skin—covered in an intricate film of interactions across time—does not shed and renew itself, intervention becomes inevitable: architectural skins are removed, new ones are added. Indeed, opera houses have routinely been redecorated across their lifetimes, not least as fumes from combustible illumination accumulated as residues on their surfaces. Until the introduction of electric (and therefore noncombustible) illumination in the 1880s at La Scala, the initial decor from 1778 was replaced in 1830 and 1844; in all likelihood, the auditorium was also redecorated once or twice more during the 1800s.[18] (See chapter 3 for a detailed discussion of illumination at La Scala.)

Each of these redecorations introduced a new look at the theater. The 1930 redecoration was nonetheless unusual, not least because in 1928 box holders had been dispossessed of their boxes. The boxes had been issued to aristocrats in 1778 in exchange for funds used to build the theater and since then had been held in families or traded between them. Other than the era when Milan was under the rule of the Austrian Empire, La Scala's box owners had total control over the decor in their boxes.

Once the theater came into the possession of the state, however, it became a priority for the boxes to blend into the auditorium as a whole. They were to be decorated with the same flooring, wallpaper, lampshades, paint, doors, and even door handles as the rest of the auditorium, and the chairs were all to be upholstered in the same fabric. The textiles ordered were, of course, new in the obvious sense of being unused. But when Borletti insisted that the old must be substituted with the new, it was as much an impulse toward a new surface aesthetic as a desire to rejuvenate the threadbare and the sweat-stained. Historical evidence indicates that textiles had been combined in the boxes with little overarching control, so that when the boxes were reclaimed in 1928, each was as distinctive in color and texture as the drawing rooms of private residences.[19] Borletti found it intolerable that so many contrasting textiles had been thrown together, without control, in the boxes, resulting in a whimsical and unabashed mixture of textures and colors; but there was a time when such an assortment would not have seemed problematic.

Color historians have identified a strain of chromophobia in Western culture, that since ancient times has manifested in a drive to devalue color or position it as inessential, marginal. Aristotle insisted that color was secondary to form, and centuries later Jean-Jacques Rousseau reinforced this bias, remarking "remove [the lines from a painting] and the colors will cease to have any effect."[20] Such declarations might appear to be harmless aesthetic formulations not anchored to real-world concerns. But it becomes harder to sustain this stance when one understands that color has consistently been censored over time, and that there is a broad confluence between those who have most fervidly embraced saturated, varied colors and the voices and communities that have been minoritized and disempowered within Western culture. The art historian David Batchelor has gone so far as to suggest that fear of color historically coincided with a broader and more insidious fear of all that was unknown or could not be controlled.[21] If color has been embraced by cultures outside the West, it has also been considered the domain of children (whose classrooms are often saturated with vivid hues), women (who have often embraced colorful combinations of cosmetics, accessories, and clothes), and those of particular sexual orientations (for whom color can be central to a celebration of identity). Reduction of the chromatic universe has in turn been strategic: diminish the value of color and we diminish those who have been its greatest advocates.

It is in this context that Borletti's aversion to the mismatched textiles in La Scala's boxes must be understood. The last decades of the nineteenth century had seen sustained discussion about the use and combination of colors and colored textiles, founded on the conviction that there were indissoluble connections between color and identities, and thus that color could be radical, subversive, and socially destabilizing. As we shall see, the intensification of these discussions was connected with technical advances in the production of color, advances that soon undermined connections between individual colors and purchasing power.

Until about 1860, in order to render objects in a color that was not inherent to them one had first to extract color from mineral, plant, or animal sources and affix it to them or imbue them with it. Such extraction tended to involve extensive chains of human labor, which came at a cost to the consumer (regardless of whether those monies ever reached the bodies that did the bulk of the labor). The value of individual colors in turn became a function of how hard it was to extract those colors and transport them to a destination. In the earlier decades of the 1800s, reds and especially blues were among the hardest to source and the most valuable hues.[22]

Beginning in the late 1850s, it became possible to create color from a concatenation of chemical reactions in laboratories. The decisive moment is said to have come in 1856, when the English chemist William Henry Perkin, while attempting to manufacture a cure for malaria, cleaned a flask in which he had oxidized aniline and noticed it had become stained a vivid color. This mauve aniline derivate was soon turned into the first commercially successful colorant created from start to finish via a series of chemical reactions and therefore classifiable as wholly synthetic. Marketed under the name "mauve," the colorant had a "glow [about it that] immediately set it apart from . . . dyes commonly used at the time."[23] Other vivid colors were soon derived from aniline—first a fuchsin red (also known as "magenta"), then blues. These colors could be manufactured wherever coal was available, since aniline was a coal tar derivative. Coal tar was meanwhile a common industrial waste product. For some time these aniline colors were manufactured mainly in Europe. Next, in the 1880s, came a series of acid-based colors; combined, these led to an almost endless stream of available colors.

The availability of synthetic dyes soon undid long-standing links between color and cost. The fate of mauve is instructive here: in 1857 Empress Eugénie of France attracted worldwide attention when she wore a brilliant mauve dress. It was a trend few could imitate, since the price of mauve was exorbitant. The same was true for the next few aniline derivates. But as these derivates began to be manufactured on an industrial scale for mass consumption, costs fell. Whereas fuchsin cost around sixteen hundred francs per kilogram when it was first available on the market, by the 1890s the same amount could be obtained for a mere ten francs.[24] Since almost all colors could be manufactured for around the same cost, an ever-widening stream of colors was soon within reach of most consumers.

As Laura Anne Kalba has demonstrated, all this brought about a "shift to a copiously colored world" in which these innovations in color production "heralded ... the democratization of earlier visual experiences" and "the irruption of novel visual experiences."[25] As French manufacturers courted middle-class consumers, markets became structured around endless new trends. For those consumers, access to the latest merchandise, marketed as it was to the class-conscious, came to be understood as a modern—and much-coveted—pleasure. Release of merchandise with ever-new colors, meanwhile, became a sure means to usher in new trends and drive demand for them.

As Kalba tells it, the unmissable colors that became available to the middle and lower classes in modern Paris were a reminder for the elites that industrialization was a threat to their social dominance. But if the irruption of colors warned of an impending "struggle for social order," tastemakers such as fashion writers and decorative arts experts worked hard to contain the color chaos around them. Critical here was their reliance on the earlier pronouncements of the acclaimed chemist Michel Eugène Chevreul (1786–1889). In 1824 he had been made the head of tinting at one of the foremost incubators of European color trends: the historic Gobelins Manufactory in Paris, which had supplied tapestries to French monarchs since Louis XIV. Chevreul also maintained a keen interest in the psychology of color perception and in 1839 had summarized his ideas about how to fashion the colorscape of the world in a seven-hundred-page manual titled *De la loi du contraste simultané des couleurs* (*The Principles of Harmony and Contrast of Colors and Their Applications to the Arts*).[26] In it, Chevreul advised on the coloration of items from furniture to carpets to clothes, all the while articulating a core idea: colors must be combined with care. One color, or a limited number of well-chosen colors, will be the best choice in most circumstances, for this will ensure a unified look. Although his recommendations were not universally adopted, Chevreul's manual had inestimable importance even in the mid-1800s and became a source of solace for tastemakers in the later 1800s, a means for counteracting the chromatic and social chaos around them.[27]

This story of the popularization of vivid colors provides an important context for the purism of the first wave of modernist architecture.

In 1908 Adolf Loos had called for sobriety in the design of new buildings, linking ornamentation—as produced by combinations of colors and patterns—with social degeneracy.[28] Le Corbusier was meanwhile intoxicated with white, as he wrote in a 1925 essay:

> we would perform a moral act: *to love purity*!
>
> we would improve our condition: *to have the power of judgment*!
>
> . . .
>
> Imagine the results of the Law of Ripolin. Every citizen is required to replace his hangings, his damasks, his wall-papers, his stencils, with a plain coat of white ripolin. *His home* is made clean. There are no more dirty, dark corners. *Everything is shown as it is.* Then comes *inner* cleanness. . . . When you are surrounded with shadows and dark corners you are at home only as far as the hazy edges of the darkness your eyes cannot penetrate. You are not master in your own house.
>
> . . .
>
> With ripolin you will throw away what has served its purpose and is now scrap. An important act in life; productive morality. . . . Without the Law of Ripolin we accumulate, we make our houses into museums or temples filled with votive offerings, turning our mind into a concierge or *custodian*.
>
> . . .
>
> On white ripolin walls . . . accretions of dead things from the past would be intolerable: they would leave a mark. Whereas the marks do not show on the medley of our damasks and patterned wall-papers.[29]

Le Corbusier here summons a world that is whitewashed with the then-popular Ripolin brand of paint. But it is not simply white, but an entire realm of whiteness, that is summoned, an architectural universe that is clean, rational, and "untainted." As Batchelor has noted, the basis for Le Corbusier's desperate attachment to whiteness here must be understood in terms of his attitudes about European civilization. For him, the "orient"—as he described it in a series of newspaper articles written in 1911—contained all that he sought to eliminate through his manifesto on Ripolin.[30] It is a site of endless color, but color acts as a narcotic.

FIGURE 2.1. Renato Saboya, exterior of Le Corbusier's Villa Savoye in Poissy, France, completed in 1931. B. O'Kane / Alamy Stock Photo.

It intoxicates. It annihilates. Le Corbusier's whitewashed architectural structures in this context are more than rationalist sites of retreat; they are fortresses that insulate and exclude (fig. 2.1).

It is, moreover, well documented that interest in white—and the realm of whiteness—increased as European colonialists encountered the homelands of other races, peaking in the twentieth century.[31] In Fascist Italy and its colonies, Benito Mussolini would claim that Fascism should be "a glass house into which everyone can gaze freely": unwholesome dark corners had to be eliminated from the home.[32] It is no coincidence that white became the choice for various Italian Fascist Party structures built around the time of the redecoration of La Scala, among them the Casa del Fascio in Como, the local office of the National Fascist Party, completed in 1936 under the architect Giuseppe Terragni (fig. 2.2).[33]

We do not know how conscious either Borletti or Modigliani would have been of the motivations behind a broad intolerance for certain colors and color combinations in their circles, but as the owner of a textile empire, Borletti rubbed shoulders with tastemakers all the time. Neither seems to have been under pressure to renovate the historic theater so

FIGURE 2.2. Exterior of Giuseppe Terragni's Casa del Fascio in Como, Italy, completed in 1936. Alephcomo / Deposit Photos.

that it took on the character of modernist architecture per se. But implicit in Borletti's comparison of the pre-1930 decor to "a delicatessen's back room" was doubtless both a fear that the careless mix of textiles and colors the theater boasted flaunted chromatic rules, of which Borletti would have been well aware, and that such a mix resulted in a look that could not be further from Mussolini's "glass house" ideal. That Borletti had been so candid with Mussolini about his redecoration plans in the aforementioned letter is indicative that he had raised the matter when Mussolini received him and had every reason to believe Mussolini endorsed the plans. That the same textiles and colors did not trouble the superintendent of monuments does not mean he was immune to these chromatic pressures. Modigliani was, after all, a professional custodian of the past. All those varied textiles and colors could not offend his modern sensibilities because, in his role as superintendent of monuments, he was presumably always conscious that what stood before him was not modern in the first place. If the older decorative scheme seemed unruly, its chaos was encased within a sturdy historical frame.

Clearly, then, textiles mattered to our historical forebears; and, just as clearly, the choice of textiles for built environments was always about more than the textiles themselves. These architectural skins became a canvas onto which values were projected. Given the complex and intense feelings associated with color outlined above, it should not seem too unusual that the surfaces installed at La Scala under Borletti's watch admitted little variation. While it was not decorated in a "pure" white, the auditorium at least avoided color combinations. To some extent, textural variation substituted for chromatic interest. The wallpaper was silk, in red with "oversized" roses that were fashioned via a raised (damask) weave. The red and gold combination of the auditorium was perceived by commentators as monochrome, perhaps because gold is technically not a color but a property of luminosity and reflectivity.[34] Notably, Borletti nowhere defends his decision to render the auditorium red, nor does Modigliani take issue with the choice of red, for all his reservations about the lack of chromatic variation. No such discussion was necessary or possible, because once the decision had been made to render the auditorium in monochrome, there was no question about which monochrome it would be.

Red

Decades before this chain of letters, red had established residence in countless minds as the color that a theatrical auditorium should be. To understand why, we need to look back to the mid-nineteenth century, when red first started to dominate theatrical aesthetics. One measure of a new commitment to red can be found in the questionnaire that Charles Garnier, architect of the Paris Opéra, sent to theater directors as his theater was under construction in the 1860s. Alongside inquiries such as "How wide is the opening of the stage [at your theater]?," Garnier asked, "What is the background color of the boxes?"[35] We do not know exactly when Garnier mailed these letters or received replies, but he published the results in the volume *Le théâtre* in 1871. Given that theater auditoriums were not redecorated on an annual basis, and sometimes not for several decades, the answers he received are likely a snapshot of chromatic decisions made between the late 1840s and that date. The answers Garnier received revealed an unmistakable preference for red as the background color for boxes (table 2.1). Although Garnier asked only about the walls of the boxes, where theater directors volunteered more information, we find that whenever boxes are red, red remains the dominant hue outside boxes, such as for box curtains. Almost no respondents volunteered that their auditoriums were more than one color—at most the dominant hue tended to be complemented with some areas of white (which is achromatic) and gold.

TABLE 2.1. Summary of responses to the question "What is the background color of the boxes [at your theater]?"

Name of theater	Color
Amsterdam, Grand Théâtre	Brown with fringes of gold (painted)
Antwerp, Théâtre royal	Dark pink
Berlin, Théâtre royal	Very dark red
Bordeaux, Grand Théâtre	Velvety red; the decoration of the room matte white and gold
Cairo, Théâtre de l'Opéra	White and gold on a background of dark red
Constantinople, Théâtre Naum	Gold on a white background; the background of the boxes is red
Copenhagen, Théâtre royal	Dark red
Dublin, Théâtre royal	Dark crimson trimmed with green velvet; the general tone of the room is white and gold intensified with a cream tint
Frankfurt, Théâtre de la ville	Dark red
Florence, Théâtre de la Pergola	Until now the color of the background of the boxes has been yellow; in the autumn of 1869 it was changed and replaced with a leaden gray tone, with small gold-colored border tiles
Genoa, Théâtre Carlo Felice	Red with more or less dark lines
Geneva, Théâtre	Dark red
Hamburg, Théâtre de la ville	The balustrade of the boxes is white and gold; the background of the boxes is red
Hanover, Théâtre royal	The decoration of the room is white adorned with gold; the back of the boxes is dark red
Lisbon, Théâtre San Carlo	Dark red and garnet
London, Théâtre de Covent-Garden	Dark red
Mainz, Théâtre	Yellow and gold with red velvet
Messina, Théâtre de la Munizione	The color of the background of the boxes is red, the front of the boxes pearl white and gold
Messine, Théâtre Victor-Emmanuel	Velvety red
Milan, Théâtre de la Scala	The box owners are entirely free to decorate the boxes as they please, and according to their pleasure; but it is established that the outer curtains will be the same for all boxes and the color crimson with yellow fringe
Moscow, Grand Théâtre	Red silk
Munich, Théâtre royal de la cour	Red
New York, Académie de musique	The room is gray and gold, the background of the boxes red
Palermo, Théâtre Bellini	Red

Name of theater	Color
Paris, Théâtre de l'Opéra	Red
Philadelphia, Académie américaine de musique	The faces of the balconies and columns are white, cream, and gold in color, the backgrounds are red
Prague, Théâtre national	White
San Francisco, Théâtre California	The background of the boxes are simply covered with mortar which will soon be frescoed
Saint Petersburg, Grand Théâtre	Light yellowish
Saint-Petersburg, Théâtre Alexandra	Red
Saint Petersburg, Théâtre Michel	Light yellowish
Saint Petersburg, Théâtre Marie	Blue silk
Santiago, Théâtre municipal	Red with golden fleurs-de-lis
Stockholm, Théâtre royal de l'Opéra	Dark red
Stockholm, Théâtre royal dramatique	Dark red
Stuttgart, Théâtre royal de la cour	Cochineal striped with black
Turin, Grand Théâtre royal	Amaranth
Warsaw, Grand Théâtre	Gray
Venice, Théâtre de la Fénice	Persian white and gold checkered
Vienna, Nouvel Opéra (théâtre de la cour)	Red

Source: Charles Garnier, *Le théâtre* (Paris: Librairie Hachette, 1871), Appendix, 417–63.

Red has now become so standard that these results may seem unsurprising. They are, however, far from predictable, not least since there had been no established color aesthetic at theaters in the earlier nineteenth century. When the draftsman Paolo Toschi envisioned the decoration of the boxes at Parma's Nuovo Teatro Ducale in 1827, for instance, there would have been no argument about the brilliant cobalt blue he wanted to use.[36] In fact, whenever theaters had been redecorated, it was considered an occasion for their colorscapes to shift. La Scala's redecorations too had seen chromatic conversions. When the theater opened in 1778, luxurious fabrics lined the walls of the auditorium and the walls and furniture of the boxes; it was also used for the drapes that could be drawn across the box openings. The orchestra stalls—set aside for the lower classes—were devoid of fabric on either the floor or the seats. Box owners had a free hand when it came to the decoration within the boxes and selected a whole range of colors (with some tendencies toward a combination of reds, blues, and whites, considered fashionable neoclassical colors at the time). These colors were used in combination with textural variation to create bands, lines, and other patterns on the fabrics. The 1830 redecoration seems to have favored blues, reds, greens, and yellows, while the 1844 redecoration, putatively undertaken in reaction to "a state of filth no longer compatible with the decor of a Royal Theater," saw the Austrian authorities then in command of the theater order box holders to remove their textiles and have them dyed green.[37] This decree lasted until the Austrians were defeated in 1859; but when Garnier contacted the theater a bit more than a decade later, the response to the color question read: "The box owners are entirely free to decorate the boxes as they please, and according to their pleasure; but it is established that the outer curtains will be the same for all boxes and the color crimson with yellow fringe."[38]

If the standard red theatrical interior was an invention of the nineteenth century, and one firmly in place by 1871, it was also a choice made thousands of times around the world. Red gradually filled theatrical interiors across continents, its hegemony over an entire theatrical infrastructure so pervasive and unbending that it is now critical to ask: Whence red? How did such an unbreakable commitment to this particular color form? How, for instance, did it come to pass that when the Teatro Solís in Montevideo was constructed in the 1850s and the theater's architectural committee looked to France for advice about the interior, red was presented as the necessary choice?[39] Or that when the Teatro Municipal in Santiago was inaugurated in 1857, or when the Naum Theater in Constantinople burned down in 1870, the dominant hue in their auditoriums was also red?[40]

One could answer this by considering the values that had become attached to individual colors. We have seen how reds had been some of the most valuable colors available. Even once those associations between color and value started to be undone, red still retained residual value as a deluxe color choice. The auditoriums of teatri all'italiana were some of the most curated and rarefied built environments in use at the time and their red interiors contributed to this distinction. As the audiences at most teatri all'italiana shifted over the course of the 1800s, that essential link between these theaters and the aristocrats who used to be their most coveted patrons (and sometimes also their owners) was weakened. In this context, it is all the more significant that red had for centuries been one of the favorite colors of aristocrats and remained a favored color for the interior decoration of aristocratic residences at this time.[41] Whereas the indiscriminate use of red alarmed the wealthier classes when the lower and middle classes wore it or used it to decorate their homes, its use at teatri all'italiana affirmed connections between these theaters and an Old World order, in the same moment that democratizing political trends aimed to overturn that world order.

Since trends sometimes build momentum in a closed circuit, it is also likely that some theaters were decorated in red simply because *other* theaters had been decorated in red. These red theaters may then have aroused a sense of pleasure that intensified attachment to the decorative scheme. Relevant here is that—as we now understand—to see is, at a neuronal level, to induce a sense of touch. Since visual and tactile interaction with the world, whether literal or simulated in the mind, is linked to how we think, it could be said that to see and to touch are fundamental to the fabrication of the self.[42] Could it not then be that the rich textiles induced a sort of inner touch that stimulated the mind? And that amid the tumbling thoughts and various pleasures these surfaces afforded, audiences became attached to the architectural skin handed down to them—not because red stimulates more than other colors, but because those who entered teatri all'italiana learned, over and over, that the red silk interior would reliably stimulate such sensations? That red silk was relatively rare in interior decoration during this period, such that most audience members would not have encountered such significant amounts of it anywhere else, would in turn have intensified attachments to the decorative scheme.

But there is more to consider. In a landmark study, Michel Pastoureau made the case that the eighteenth century marked the start of "red's slow but irreparable decline, at least in modern Western societies"—a decline that saw it cede to blue as the most coveted color.[43] That decline was not equally visible in all domains of life, but it was unmistakable in the realm of cosmetics. Although cosmetic red had continued to be used in the 1700s among fashionable society, whose lead-covered, white faces with visible blue veins were never seen without rouge on the lips and cheeks, its use became muted in the 1800s, when more restrained makeup practices were the new norm. (This latter trend would last until red makeup products were made available for mass consumption after World War I).[44] But if the ascendance of red theatrical interiors tracks the decline of red on faces, could it be that the color was displaced onto theatrical textiles, perhaps to achieve similar results—to enhance and enliven faces? In addition to its association with luxury and scarcity, red silk is also a textured surface that refracts back into the auditorium certain hues and luminosities. The appeal of red, in other words, not only lay in its association with wealth and social distinction, but may also have had something to do with the color's ability to create social energy and promote aesthetic pleasure and interpersonal connections.

Sur-Face

To understand the functions of red silk as architectural skin, we must return to the moment in 1672 when Isaac Newton discovered color in a beam of light. When he held a prism between a window and a white wall, the wall was marked with a continuous stream of colors, from red to violet.[45] What was so radical about this phenomenon was that the prism did not create color but rather seemed to separate out the colors inherent in light itself, as a second experiment demonstrated. Newton seemed to have loosened color from the materials in which it had inhered, demonstrating for the first time that color could be abstracted from a visible material source. The color red could now, for instance, be invoked not as a characteristic of minerals or insects from which it was commonly extracted, but in relation to that iridescent stream of hidden colors. Although the actual material basis of color was still to be determined, Newton intuited that color derived from bundled units, which would later be named "photons." But even Newton could not banish the notion that, at an experiential level, the continuous stream of colors he had rendered visible had an eerie dimension to them. Thus, in his 1704 *Opticks* he branded his stream of colors the "spectrum."[46]

If, after Newton, color was both "out there" to be seen and also spectral, it was Goethe who did the most to detach color from the material world. The key text here is his 1810 *Zur Farbenlehre* (*Theory of Colors*), a series of observations bound into one volume and released within a few months of the author's third novel, *Die Wahlverwandtschaften* (*Elective Affinities*).[47] In *Farbenlehre*, Goethe advances the thesis that color is created in the mind. The critical realization, we are told, came to him one evening as he was directing sustained attention toward a young woman: "I had entered an inn towards evening," Goethe narrates, "and, as a well-favored girl, with a brilliantly fair complexion, black hair, and a scarlet bodice, came into the room, I looked attentively at her as she stood before me at some distance in half shadow. As she presently afterwards turned away, I saw on the white wall, which was now before me, a black face surrounded with a bright light, while the dress of the perfectly distinct figure appeared of a beautiful sea-foam green" (fig. 2.3).[48] What Goethe describes here is his mind compensating for the sudden loss of a visual stimulus. The woman moves out of his visual field, but a residual image remains on his retina. Her white face changes to black, the scarlet bodice to seafoam green. From this encounter Goethe derived two fundamental observations. First, he determined that the mind could create color even when there was no immediate visual stimulus—which meant that colors that did not exist according to the principles of physics could nevertheless be visible. Second, he showed that universal laws governed how the mind creates color. In his distinctive formulation, certain colors "demand" and "complete" one another. Each of the six fundamental colors had an opposite that made it whole, a phenomenon Goethe rendered in graphic form. Yellow demands the purple across the circle, while orange

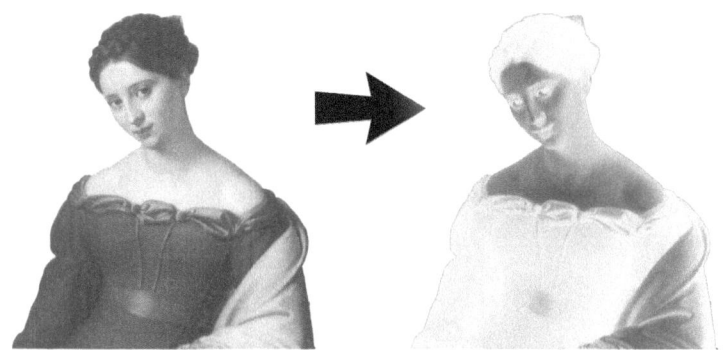

FIGURE 2.3. Scene at the inn, as described in Goethe's *Theory of Colors*. Artist: Jess Herdman.

demands blue, red demands green, and vice versa. As Riccardo Falcinelli has noted, even colors now had their "elective affinities" (fig. 2.4).[49]

This notion of complementary colors would become the conceptual basis for numerous design and decoration projects of which Chevreul and the Gobelins Manufactory were once again at the forefront. In the 1820s the tinting department at Gobelins was able to manufacture some 20,000 shades of color. When Chevreul was made head of tinting in 1824, he insisted that these colors be labeled with numbers rather than names, thereby undertaking an act of supreme classification. But for all the thousands of colors available for tinting fabrics, the chemists were unable to create an absolute black.[50] After extensive research, the color engineers at the Gobelins would conclude that what consumers experienced was not a weakness in their tints, but a phenomenon caused by a quirk of color perception: certain blacks seemed lackluster because of the room in which the color was viewed. Their solution was to work with those mental distortions. For instance, these technicians advocated weaving threads of particular hues into a blue fabric to ensure that a blue fainting couch would maintain its colors even in a red salon. They were also mindful that color perception was influenced by texture—that, for instance, for certain textiles it made a difference whether the red ran in a horizontal or vertical weave. Chevreul summarized these findings in his 1839 book, a manual on how to fashion the colorscape now that color was recognized as a function of the mind.[51]

When Chevreul arrived at the topic of theatrical decoration and color choice, however, the tenor of the manual changed. Now the concern was no longer simply the contrast between manufactured tints. Instead, he wrote *skin* into his chromatic theories, figuring the colored surfaces of the auditorium as visual filters that determined how one sees faces.

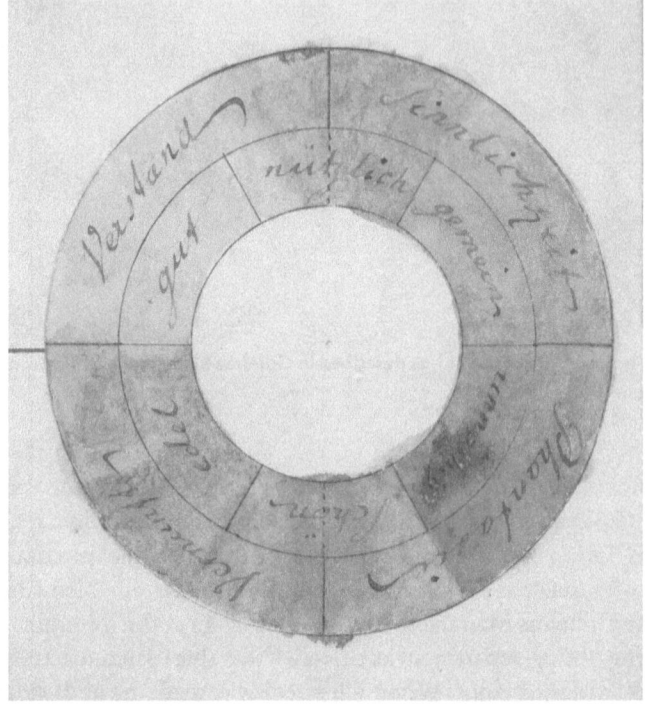

FIGURE 2.4. Color wheel demonstrating the complementarity of color according to Goethe (1809). Freies Deutsches Hochstift / Frankfurter Goethe-Museum, inv. n° III-14047, Public Domain Mark 1.0. Photo: David Hall.

His aim was to enhance the aliveness of skin, to draw attention to the fact that skin is never stable, not least because blood rushes to faces and makes skin flush. In a moment when the fashion for white lead foundations used to cover the skin's natural hue was fading, Chevreul sought to draw attention to these newly visible variations of skin tone.[52] Thus, for the auditorium, he recommended the color that "demands" or complements the rose of rose-colored cheeks—a cool and delicate green—and cautions that any other tint would detract from faces.[53]

Somewhere between the 1839 publication of Chevreul's manual and the 1871 publication of Garnier's survey, the trend for auditoriums at teatri all'italiana to all be redecorated with the same (red silk) textile took hold. That the trend did not track Chevreul's recommendations— there is little evidence that theaters were ever redecorated en masse in green—could be taken as evidence that those involved in decisions about decoration had limited interest in his work. But Chevreul had established a framework in which architectural decoration and the skin of audience members were connected, necessitating that the two be considered in tandem whenever a theater was decorated.

Indeed, when Garnier wrote *Le théâtre* some three decades later, he included an extended section on color choice. Although the trend toward the red silk interior had by then accumulated considerable momentum, Garnier advances a case for how one should conceive of theatrical walls at auditoriums. In a direct line to Chevreul, this section of the book is driven mainly by concern with how the walls can enhance the rosiness of audience members' faces. Garnier was conscious that skin varies in ways that no other surface does: it has a subtle thickness but is also transparent and tends to blush and to darken, to sweat, to reflect, to stretch, to contract. He was working with these distinctive characteristics when he advanced the idea that, as a luminous and dermal surface, skin would reflect a mix of the body's color with that of its surroundings.[54] Chevreul's recommendation here is reversed: whereas Chevreul accepted Goethe's notion that colors have their complements, Garnier concluded that theater walls should be rendered similar to the color of flushed skin. Ambient red, Garnier argued, absorbs into the dermal surface, interacts with red tones in skin—tones that would alter continuously in reaction to emotions—and, via skin's luminous, reflective characteristics, issues an even more pronounced redness back into the auditorium. Aiding this was the use of silk wallpaper: neither too matte nor too shiny, Garnier declared it the best medium to fulfill these functions.[55]

Although they reached opposite conclusions (one recommended green, the other red), what united Chevreul and Garnier was an understanding of the connection between architectural skin and audience skin. To both men, theatrical surfaces were an elusive film between the inner and the outer world. Theater walls functioned for them as *sur*-faces across which the inside is folded outward, acting as means by which the engorged and involuntary redness of embarrassment, tenderness, or shame became readable on the face. Chemists may have found a means to circumvent the extraction of color from subterranean realms—as when sourced from minerals—or the core of insects, but Chevreul and Garnier remained in pursuit of color that rose up from the depths.

While we know that as social norms shifted across the course of the nineteenth century audiences learned to be silent and still, Chevreul and Garnier remind us that in all but the darkest auditoriums faces remained landscapes in motion. What and how these faces communicated, and whose were most visible, acquired heightened relevance as other kinds of movement and communication were stilled. Indeed we cannot overlook the fact that it was one sort of face alone that concerned these men. Even as Chevreul proposes that all theaters adopt his delicate green for its ability to enhance the palest of faces, he acknowledges how unfavorable it would be to those with brown skin.[56] Garnier similarly bases all his claims on the premise that his audience would be a certain tone of white, that rosiness would enliven translucent, pale, and, above all, female faces. This motivated the use of a rich red for Garnier's own construction, the new home for the Paris Opéra, completed in 1875. That iconic building would become a reference point for what a theater should be.

The matter of how audiences at teatri all'italiana were constituted needs more research. In particular, there has been almost no research on how audience members or workers at teatri all'italiana identified in ethnic or racial terms. One result is that music histories centered on Europe in the decades under discussion read as accounts of a Europe insulated from the rest of the world, overlooking the incontestable fact that, in the words of Igiaba Scego, "European societies were and are plural, with sinuous histories and composite identities."[57] When Chevreul and Garnier were concerned with pale faces, we should not assume these were the faces of "white Europe," because no such Europe existed.[58] That the trend toward red theater decor extended across that vast theatrical infrastructure, in theaters on five continents, is another reminder that such choices were tilted toward the benefit of some over others. The teatro all'italiana is in no sense alone among built environments in creating and reinforcing notions of racial difference. But therein lies the point: architectural historians have in the past decade called for "research to write race back into architectural history."[59] To examine the numerous motivations behind the red silk interior is to address some of what has remained unwritten.

Erasure

Another way of thinking about the manners in which these textiles articulated and emphasized difference is to consider how they were sourced. As textile historians have demonstrated, for all the calm smoothness of silk, its manufacture involves tremendous violence. This begins with the slaughter of insects: hundreds of silk moths must be boiled alive to manufacture a mere swatch of the textile.[60] The human cost was also considerable: an incalculable number of people have been wounded or killed in the silk trade over the centuries.

Fundamental here is that the silk used in nineteenth-century European interiors was almost inevitably marked by the events of the Opium Wars. In the early 1800s, overseas traders secured stocks of various Chi-

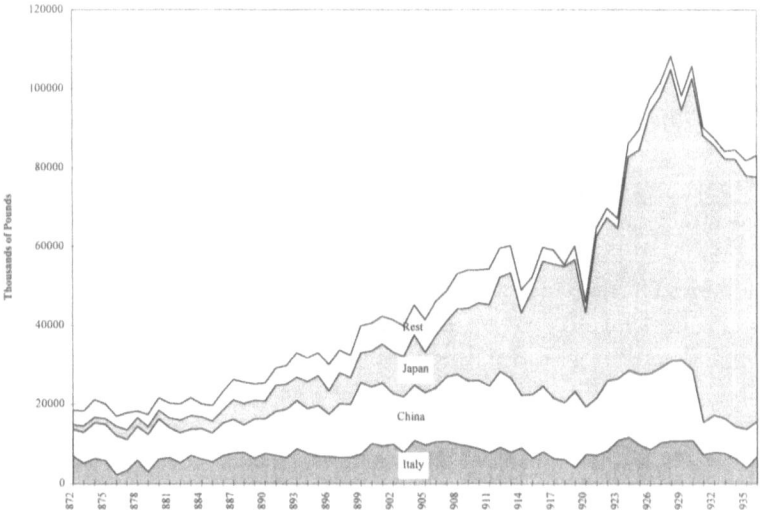

FIGURE 2.5. World production and exports of raw silk, 1872–1936. The figures for China and Japan include only export quantities. "Rest" refers to production and exports by countries other than the three countries listed. Source: Ma, "Modern Silk Road," 340. 2009 © Cambridge University Press.

nese commodities—including silk—via coercive trade that involved the deliberate circulation of this banned and addictive narcotic. Demand for opium within China soon soared to the point that traders were able to secure large quantities of tea, silk, and other commodities in return for even small amounts of the substance.[61] Alarmed at the headlong infiltration of opium into China, the Qing laid waste to a considerable stock of British opium stored in a warehouse outside the walls of Canton in 1839; famously, the British then directed force at the Chinese coast in what became known as the First Opium War. Well into the 1900s it was hard to obtain silk that had no connection with the Opium Wars and their aftermath: that first war ended with a series of "unequal treaties" which set the terms for the interaction of Europe and the United States with China for decades, even a century. Those terms ensured that countries could access Chinese commodities on terms favorable to them.

For most of the period under examination in this chapter, only three countries were able to manufacture silk on a large scale.[62] Along with China, Japan also produced silk, but the Japanese were locked into their own unequal treaties for much of this time. The third nation was none other than Italy, whose silk production constituted as much as 30 percent of its entire exports (see fig. 2.5).[63] This Italian silk was not removed from the transactions described here, however. From the later

1800s onward, the production of Italian silk would have been impossible without the collaboration of Chinese sericulturalists, from whom Italians obtained disease-free silkworm eggs.[64] At the close of the 1800s, meanwhile, Italians were part of the Eight-Nation Alliance which oversaw the beheading of Chinese men involved in the Boxer Uprising, a popular movement that aimed to roll back Euro-American encroachment on China.[65]

We cannot be certain where the fabric ordered for the 1930 redecoration of La Scala came from. In all likelihood, finished silk for La Scala was either sourced from Japan or China directly, or cocoons would have been sourced from one of these countries, nurtured to create raw silk, then turned into finished silk in one of the towns clustered around Milan.[66] Como was the most famous center of Italian silk production at the time.[67] It seems probable that Borletti used his contacts in the textile world to source the silk textiles used to line the walls of auditorium, even if his own factories did not themselves handle silk manufacture.

Raw silk also needed to be dyed. Before chemical colorants became widespread, color underwrote entire colonial economies, and as the demand for dyes increased, so did abusive labor practices and slavery.[68] Most of the red colorant that arrived in Europe from the later 1500s onward was sourced from Oaxaca, Mexico, where it was extracted from insects known as cochineals.[69] The cochineal trade underwrote Spanish imperialism until Mexican independence in 1821. Just a few decades later, the chemical revolution in color production altered all this. The rise of manufactured reds triggered a restructuring of coloration that toppled Oaxaca's dominance and devastated its economy. For all that the cochineal trade had involved the cruel and dehumanizing exploitation of locals, the collapse of that trade led to further loss of lives and livelihoods. Indeed, Oaxaca serves as a stark reminder of the vicissitudes of geopolitics.

In the end, the conversion to red silk under examination in this chapter was the last substantial conversion the sur-face of auditoriums underwent, a decisive alteration that would become sacrosanct. Having been fully embraced across the entire theatrical infrastructure, red silk is associated now with the very essence of the teatro all'italiana. The Borletti-Modigliani debate unfolded at one of the final moments in which alternatives were viable for the Teatro alla Scala: as Modigliani understood well, once introduced the decorative conversion would never be reversed. Like the auditoriums of the countless theaters modeled on it, La Scala's inner sanctum has long been a consistent, stable site of red silk, host in turn to canonical operas that themselves rearticulate the familiar rather than the new. It is a site out of time, a microcosm removed from the world. But however stable these auditoriums now seem, their sur-faces were once far more mutable. To trace their deliberate conversion to an aesthetic that is still with us is to render this architectural form visible within the fabric of time. It is in turn to understand that stability is a curated condition: even as conditions of precarious flux define much of the world, the auditoriums of teatri all'italiana remain constant in their look and feel.

THREE

Atmosphere

I start here with that same marvelous installation at the Gran Teatre del Liceu, Barcelona, in June 2020 that we examined at the outset of chapter 1. In videos of the installation, instead of an opera house auditorium filled with a human audience, we see some 2300 plants, one in each seat, assembled to hear a rendition of Puccini's "Crisantemi" String Quartet (see fig. 1.1).[1] For a moment the wondrous intrusion of the outside world indoors starts to seem natural, as if the auditorium could hold the whole world within it, as if there were no outside to this windowless world. This installation was mounted at a moment when COVID-19 lockdown restrictions were about to ease, just prior to audiences being permitted to return to auditoriums in limited numbers. The spectator shrubs were donated the next day to essential workers who had continued to labor throughout the pandemic; relocated to their homes, these houseplants became markers of the comforts and securities of a domestic realm that had eluded those who could not shelter in place.

There were moments at the start of the pandemic when an ethics of care permeated social media, when some even dared to believe that the pandemic could, in the words of Judith Butler, "function as the great leveler . . . be the occasion for imagining a more substantial equality and a more radical form of justice."[2] I tend to see the installation as an invitation to renew commitment to an ethics of care. For one, it functions as a commemoration of lives lost. It is not incidental that the music here is the "Crisantemi" Quartet. Puccini wrote it to honor the life of a deceased friend, hence the title—chrysanthemums are associated with death. Given this, those thousands of shrubs seem to be mourners, to be stand-ins for us and the collective commemorations denied us in lockdown. Commemorations do not in and of themselves mobilize an ethics of care, of course: it is easier to mourn a life lost than sustain one that is vulnerable. The sheer scale of this commemoration, however, seems to demand that COVID-related deaths be understood as an immediate social concern.

All this could have been achieved without the natural invasion of an architectural interior. What, then, does that invasion mean? In chapter 1 I drew attention to the way nature cleanses the air in the closed, windowless auditorium of accumulated toxins (CO_2) and infuses it with O_2, as if turning the auditorium into an enormous ventilator—thus artistically simulating one of the few mechanisms then available to sustain lives that would otherwise be claimed by COVID-19. Perhaps nature was also allowed to overwhelm an architectural interior to remind viewers that, throughout the lockdowns, it had filled spaces on Earth from which humans had retreated. For the artist Eugenio Ampudia and the curator Blanca de la Torre, the installation stood for a period when unbridled exploitation of the natural world had lessened, when, for a short while, humans consumed less, traveled less, and otherwise reduced their collective carbon footprint.[3] It was a moment that was about to pass as lockdown restrictions were lifted.

In this sense, nature has invaded the architectural interior as a reminder of the natural plenitude that could exist if humans were to move forward into the Biocene—a world in which human and other-than-human lifeforms interact in a circular system of give-and-take, rather than a hierarchical one in which humans preside over the ecological community. (This same aim seems to lie behind the decision to close the distance between the human and other-than-human in the installation. At least, one of the more curious dimensions of Ampudia and de la Torre's creation is that these shrubs, at once avatars for humans, are also plants that seem to *want* to listen, and to listen to music "about" chrysanthemums, no less. As the camera focuses on their glossy surfaces, we hear amplified music; the cinematography spreads the soaring soundtrack's emotional invocations onto and across their leaves. Nature here is endowed with a rich inner life, humanizing it at that critical moment. In this manner, the installation builds on recent research claiming that nature is emotionally reactive to stimuli; that some plant species "cry"—or at least emit an unusual sound—when their stems cannot draw in water.[4] As Ampudia later put it, "I don't know what the plants say, because we have not yet decoded the reverse dialogue, but I know that each of them, when they have been there attending that concert, will have undergone a change in their vital strategy in some way, by being at the concert.")[5]

What, however, of the fact that nature has invaded the interior of this particular built environment? The conventional forum for an ensemble of four instruments is not a theater that can accommodate thousands but a far more intimate venue; in its origins, the string quartet is a domestic genre. The odd imbrication of the domestic and public realms here could be understood as tracking their collapse into one another during the pandemic, as when the interiors of homes were rendered visible in conference calls. But as this book stresses, the teatro all'italiana is also one of the most rarefied environments built for music. What interests me most is how the installation's creators leaned on that. This installation presents a powerful statement about the alliance between music and the natural world. Music moves these plants but also seems to create the conditions under which nature can thrive: functioning as an alternative to the sun that does not shine in this windowless room, it nourishes them in its place. Put another way, music soothes nature and readies "her" to work. Nature in turn creates a world in which those four musicians can breathe, working to cleanse and ventilate the air. The result is that the teatro all'italiana is cast as a terrestrial paradise, in which music is an essential element for a world in balance.

Indeed, one of the most notable characteristics of this installation is the extent to which all this channels historical ideas. The notion there is an unbreakable alliance between music, clean air, and the natural world has deep roots, and it received sustained attention in nineteenth-century Europe. As James Q. Davies demonstrates in his brilliant book *Creatures of the Air: Music, Atlantic Spirits, Breath, 1817–1913*, song in the nineteenth century was on occasion described almost as a filtration mechanism, as when oratorio performances at the Birmingham Town Hall in 1846 led critics to claim that choral song swept away atmospheric evil.[6] In nineteenth-century Italy, *Il politecnico*, a scientific journal published in Milan, contained further reminders of the natural alliance between music and clean air: "While science aims to make the physical atmosphere of theaters ever healthier and more agreeable," one author asserts, "our authors [composers], for their part, should strive to make the theaters' moral atmosphere ever purer."[7]

Of course, not all musics were deemed to have such cleansing effects. But statements such as those cited above are remarkable when we find them. That such an alliance could exist must in turn be understood in relation to new ideas about music, consciousness, and air or atmosphere—issues that went hand in hand with the common trope in nineteenth century European discourse that music bettered the human and cleansed the soul. To examine the components of this alliance in turn: there was renewed attention at this time to the notion that the souls or characters of humans were themselves somehow continuous with the immediate environment around them, as the English word "atmosphere" illustrates. Deriving from the Greek *atmós* and *sphaira*, it was used from the late 1600s to denote a sphere of vapors surrounding the Earth. But around 1800 the word assumed a moral definition as well. Atmosphere was now described in relation to a series of moral attributes, as if someone's character or soul could rise into the surrounding air. This in turn can be understood as a function of new ideas about the soul itself. If, even before Descartes, for numerous thinkers bodies were considered material but minds or souls were not, this led the latter to seem aeriform—as weightless and immaterial as air or atmosphere had (incorrectly) been assumed to be.[8] Air, or atmosphere, provided the elusive coordinates for consciousness itself. Thus was the connection between music, consciousness, and air or atmosphere formed. Beautiful music—so the argument went—could not fail to cleanse its audiences' souls. And where there were clean souls, there was clean air. (It followed that the venues in which beautiful music was performed should have clean moral values and an atmosphere to match; one could scarcely allow their air to seem wretched. As we shall see, this also meant unusual attention was devoted to ventilation at these venues.)

But if the example of the Liceu is an invitation to explore some of the rich associations that have been made between music and clean air over time, this fictional Eden also beckons us to consider what it meant, more broadly, to have a world in balance in the 1800s. Attending to this question leads us back to the opera house as a site of unusual importance in historical understandings of environmental destruction.

Ransacked Earth

To begin, we can turn to the case of Antonio Stoppani—a Catholic abbot and paleontologist, who in the 1870s and '80s was also a professor of geology at Milan's Istituto Tecnico Superiore. A keen disseminator of scientific ideas to children and adults, in the 1870s Stoppani delivered a series of lectures in the city's public gardens entitled "Acqua ed aria" (Water and air).[9] Toward the close of the series, Stoppani turned to the manner in which carbonic acid accumulates in the air. In the late 1700s the chemist Joseph Black had determined that respiration releases carbon dioxide.[10] Black's research formed one of several advances in the "primal splitting of air" that occupied chemists of the time and would receive virtuosic application when, in 1798, the chemist Henry Cavendish took the composition of air and the densities of its newfound components as core data in his mission to "weigh the world."[11] One direct consequence of Black's research was the realization that when respiration occurs in the absence of ventilation, forms of carbon accumulate. In the lectures, Stoppani poses a conundrum to his audience: if we consider the atmosphere that stretches from the soil to the skies as a *gran stanza* or "large room" around the Earth, should it not be the case that this atmosphere also becomes dense with carbonic acid? In other words, when one compares a closed room in an architectural interior with the "room around the Earth," should we not see a similar accumulation of toxic carbon? How did it instead come to pass that man continues to "drink life" from the air rather than suffocate on accumulated carbonic acid?[12]

In truth, the conundrum was somewhat overstated for didactic effect, since much of this had in fact been worked out in the late 1700s, when Humphry Davy, Antoine Lavoisier, Joseph Priestley, Jan Ingenhousz, and others established the fundamental fact that humans and plants undertake equal and opposite processes: whereas humans breathe in oxygen and exhale forms of carbon, plants do the same in reverse. The air in the atmosphere does not become saturated with carbon, in other words, because nature has "her own" controls. Within a few decades this would, moreover, come to be understood as one set of transactions in a marvelous phenomenon known as carbon rotation, or the carbon cycle, that also involved the burial of carbonaceous material as sediment and release of stored carbon via volcanic eruption (fig. 3.1).[13]

But to conclude that there was no conundrum to resolve here whatsoever would be incorrect. In her 2018 monograph *Climate in Motion: Science, Empire, and the Problem of Scale*, Deborah R. Coen reveals how "essential elements of the modern understanding of climate arose [in the nineteenth century] as a means of thinking across scales of space and time."[14] Although scientists in the early 1800s had a sense that air circulated around the entire Earth, they did not have the means to relate small-scale climatic events that occurred across time and space to the atmosphere as a whole. Thus, the notion that the atmosphere was one continuous phenomenon—akin to the air in a much smaller, closed room—was only vaguely understood. It was not until the mid-twentieth century, which saw advances in data infrastructures and networks, that scientists began to model the relation between small and large atmospheric events with precision. But, as Coen relates, the 1800s nonetheless saw considerable changes in how these relations were conceived. Climate data was collected and compared across the vast territorial reach of empire; scientists, in turn, started to think in multiscalar, multicausal terms, to find evidence that a breeze that ruffled the pages of a book was related to a storm thousands of miles in the distance, or that land clearance in one location altered rainfall in another.[15] Crucially, I would add, when Stoppani drew comparisons between the *gran*

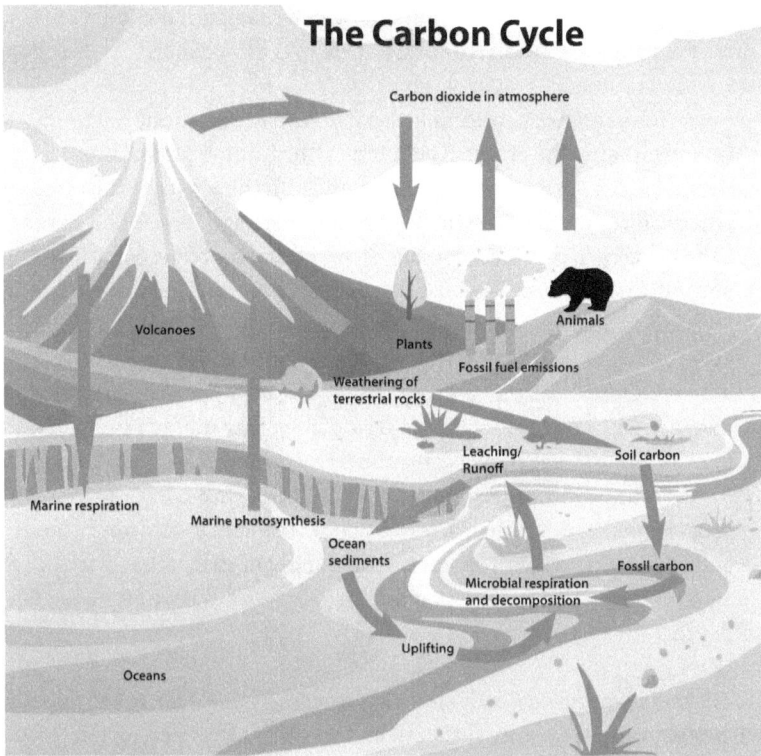

FIGURE 3.1. Illustration of the carbon cycle. Artist: Jess Herdman.

stanza and the closed room, he underscored the nascent realization that the whole atmosphere was vulnerable to actions that unfolded on the planet, much as respiration and combustion within a closed room had inescapable sequelae for that room's air. His aim, in other words, was to advance the somewhat radical idea for the time that the atmosphere was indivisible, that it was one.

With this articulated, Stoppani described the tireless rotation of carbon to his audience. For all his Catholic training, he believed in a much more ancient Earth than the world described in the Bible, one where carbon rotation had been set in motion many, many millennia earlier. Moreover, the marvel of nature was that, from the start, it was targeted to the needs of man: nature ensured there would be a constant amount of carbon in the air for the era during which man would roam the Earth; it had created one continuous, stable band of air around the Earth to sustain him. But in order to ensure balance in carbon rotation, it was essential that it be allowed to continue unhindered. In a remarkable essay from 1873 entitled "L'uomo e il suo impero sulla terra" ("Man and his dominion over the Earth"), Stoppani warned that man seemed intent on intervening in the carbon rotation nature had established:

> Pause for a moment and think about your clothes, about the foods served one after the other on your tables, the furniture in your rooms, the material from which your houses are built; think back to the place where all these things—which you call yours and which you have been using each day and depleting at your leisure—come from. Then you will find that each of you takes comfort from, and enhances your life with, the spoils of nature's three kingdoms, spoils snatched from every corner of the Earth. It was not you who ransacked the Earth, you may say. Others did this on your behalf, but it was nonetheless men who did this. They belong to the class of men who ransack and plunder the mineral, vegetable, and animal realms and collect provisions for everyone; you belong to the class of those who consume these provisions. The fact remains, however, that the human race nourishes and comforts itself with the incessant plunder of all that moves in the air or water, all that prospers on the Earth or hides in its subterranean depths.[16]

That this ransacked Earth could become out of balance is announced with even more force in the conclusion of the lectures, when Stoppani reminded readers of the forests that had once covered enormous stretches of the Earth and whose function was to eliminate carbonic acid from the air—how carbon became stored in their every fiber, and how, when floods came, these carbon-rich forests were folded into the Earth. All this carbon, he noted, was nonetheless destined to be released once more into the air when it would be exhumed by volcanic eruptions. But however tremendous the scale of this carbon rotation, Stoppani feared the steady depletion of carbon in all its forms:

> What I see today is man intent on relishing the treasures accumulated across the course of centuries. He rashly strips the Earth of its foliage; he ransacks carbon repositories that are barely full, excavates bogs ... forces himself underground like a woodworm and gnaws, exhumes forests jealously guarded and maintained over the course of centuries, since the start of protozoic times. What the future might hold, I do not know. Nature today does not cease, in its own way, to see to the needs of the universe: but who can calculate the impact of this new element [of human activity]? The impact, I mean to say, of this intelligence that imposes itself on nature with the authority of a sovereign, but does not always show wisdom in its use of force? Leaving the

impenetrable mystery of the future aside, what the past reveals ... is that, just as nature satisfied the needs of the universe, accumulating limestone, salt, iron ore, carbon, and every imaginable mineral with the use of all the coordinated forces of its three realms over the centuries, it provided for this new creature, man, with remarkable foresight, with all the fondness of a mother's devotion, with the inexhaustible resources of its infinite wisdom, with the exuberance of its limitless power. Little by little, it went about preparing for man a home packed with all that it could contain: not just that which met his needs, but which satisfied his sense of splendor; brought him pleasure; realized the wondrous concepts he dreamed up when he decided to declare himself ultimate sovereign of the Earth, across time and space.[17]

This is Stoppani at his most direct, mobilizing a concept—the Anthropocene—that would only become common coin around the year 2000. It is now commonplace to attribute the term to Stoppani himself, who used the phrase *era antropozoica* (anthropozoic era) to describe a new period in which humans had unprecedented impact on the Earth.[18] Despite this, Stoppani tends not to be closely read; critically, as I will stress later, this has contributed to an underestimation of the extent of climate change awareness in the 1800s. After all, Stoppani stands out for the candidness with which he articulated his concerns. Although we never find a direct statement in Stoppani's work to the effect that deforestation and fossil fuel combustion causes carbon dioxide to accumulate in the air and the Earth to warm (not least because this latter fact was not well established until 1896), all the fundamental mechanisms that have caused carbon imbalance are denounced in his work.[19] His voice, moreover, was not without immediate influence: as we shall see, his sentiments echo across climatic discourse at this time and can even be linked to the actions of Italian industrialists. In sum, though most nineteenth-century observers of climate change had neither the need nor the occasion to articulate far-reaching concerns about carbon rotation imbalances, this does not mean there was no awareness of these issues. Whether one invoked carbon rotation or understood matters in much looser terms, at the close of the 1800s it was clear that human-driven processes had sullied the air.

To return once more to the Liceu installation, I want to propose that one reason it induces chills—other than the fact that it memorializes one of the worst health disasters of recent times—is that it offers a powerful fiction of a microcosm in balance. The Liceu functions here as a haven within a broader world, a haven we now understand cannot, in truth, exist. There is no outside to the atmosphere, no site on Earth that is insulated from atmospheric deterioration. One could claim that all this undermines the artists' desire to raise awareness about environmental concerns. I am not sure it does. If the installation is meant to entice us to value a world in balance, the presentation of a fictional Eden is perhaps the price that must be paid to achieve that.

Pure Air

If the Liceu installation matters in the context of this book above all because it channels historical connections between music, air, and nature in a manner that makes us consider how these linkages continue to work, we should note this is not the first time that a teatro all'italiana has been fashioned as an incubator for fantasies about climate deterioration, ones that have the potential to both sensitize us to and blunt our awareness of the climate deterioration around us. We can even consider another media exhibit about the Liceu for evidence of this. As noted in chapter 1, this theater is a recent construction, built following the destruction of the Liceu's previous teatro all'italiana in a catastrophic 1994 fire. And documentation about that incident demonstrates ambivalent presentations. In one case, footage shows the older theater being devoured by flames, the air blackened with smoke, all to the sound of Wagner's *Der Ring des Nibelungen* (1876). A consummate exercise in world building, the *Ring* was at once a celebration and monumentalization of nature, and it is none other than the primordial opening sequence of this most elemental of dramas that can be heard on the soundtrack as the flames encircle the theater. Even for those unfamiliar with the *Ring*, this passage, with its awesome combination of sonic stasis and motion, can induce a sense of the extraordinary. As that music itself encircles the flames, it is not the fouled air as much as the incredible, even transcendent, power of the flame that grips the viewer. Once more, music cleanses the air (fig. 3.2).[20]

This cleansing of the air occurs mechanistically as well: elaborate devices have been introduced into teatri all'italiana to render credible that "natural" alliance between music and clean air. As Davies demonstrates, concert halls and theaters were among the spaces most likely to be ventilated in the 1800s, and some of the first to be endowed with what he describes as the "rarefied" air of the nineteenth century.[21] True, there were real health concerns that ventilation mechanisms were meant to address. These were venues where thousands of people crowded into enclosed auditoriums—locations in which air was understood to "deteriorate" quickly. They were also locations in which people frequently found themselves: the French engineer Émile Trélat estimated that in the mid-nineteenth century, Parisians who attended the theater passed

FIGURE 3.2. The Gran Teatre del Liceu destroyed by fire in 1994. Aspasios. Copyright Agencia EFE 2025. All rights reserved.

around one out of 213 hours there.[22] In an era when medical thinking was torn between environmentalist and contagionist explanations of disease, these climatic conditions were a source of considerable alarm.[23] A commentator for *The Lancet* in 1891 echoed Trélat when he wrote that "the average [of one out of 213 hours] is far short of the actual amount of suffering entailed on those who frequent theatres. The quantity of foul air breathed in theatres is so considerable as to become an important factor in the maintenance, or rather in the destruction, of the public health."[24]

But at the same time, the desire to ventilate these built environments before others is indicative of the extent to which venues such as teatri all'italiana were meant to be havens of rarefied air, and—more than this—locations where the perils of climate change were supposed to be forgotten. It was not, of course, sufficient to ventilate theaters alone, since the outdoor air was not itself immune to climate deterioration. Most theater ventilation made extensive use of vents, sometimes thousands of them, one under each seat in the orchestra stalls and several in each theater box. Ensconced within the architectural structure of the theater, auditoriums were, in other words, not dissimilar to human lungs: structures both sheltered within an interior and radically open, their millions of alveoli causing them to be in continual contact with the outside world. And so, theater ventilators started to "wash the air." One of the earliest theaters to introduce these measures was the Vienna

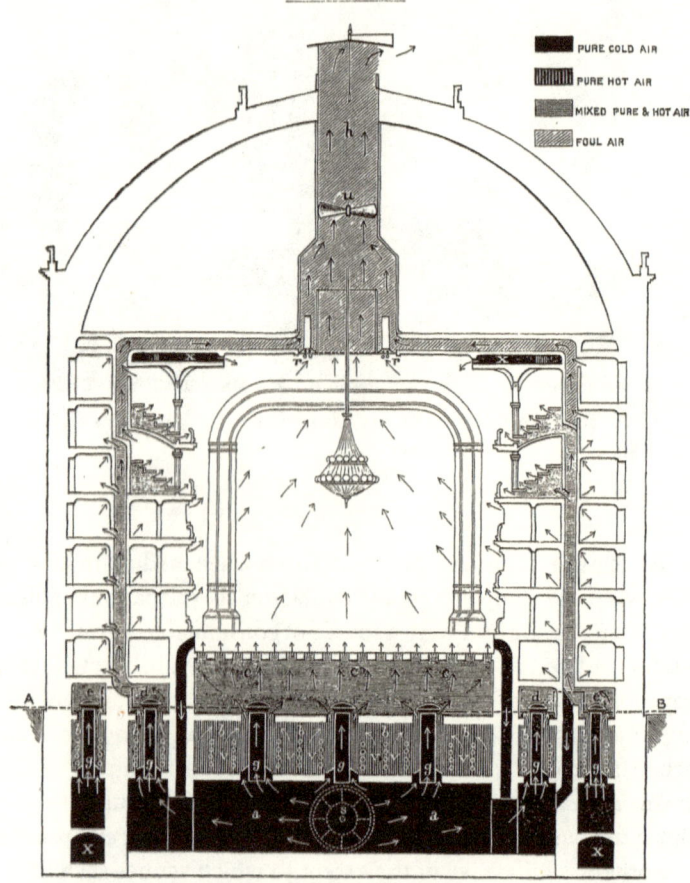

FIGURE 3.3. Ventilation at the Vienna Court Opera. Illustration in "The Report of the Sanitary Commission on the Ventilation of Theatres and Places of Public Assembly," *Lancet* (December 19, 1891).

Court Opera (now the Vienna State Opera).[25] Built over the course of the 1860s, the theater made use of three custom-built chambers beneath the auditorium to circulate over a thousand cubic feet of air per hour to each audience member (fig. 3.3). Air would first be sourced from an inner courtyard far from the street, where it had been determined to be cleanest, and then directed to the lowest chamber. One set of openings led to the second chamber immediately above, a second to shafts connected to the third chamber. The second chamber contained some sixty thousand feet of iron tubes with steam inside, used to heat the air. From this chamber air could also be released into the third, where in winter it was mixed with the cold air, filtered using fans and nets, and then released, via thousands of vents, into the auditorium in accordance with the temperature recorded at different locations within the theater; in summer the air was also washed and freshened before it was released.[26]

Although not all theaters could be retrofitted with such chambers, the Vienna Court Opera nonetheless became an important model for theaters elsewhere. Commenting on this theater in Italian trade manuals, engineers stressed that no matter how well air circulated, little would be achieved if the air was not first pure and appropriately cleansed.[27] In Milan in the 1870s, the Teatro Manzoni stood out as unusual for its lack of ventilation despite the status of the theater as a preeminent forum for spoken drama.[28] In the opinion of commentators, however, the Teatro alla Scala also remained underventilated relative to the newer opera house, the Teatro del Verme. According to one architect in the 1870s, there was no real ventilation at La Scala: rather, most air entered via vents around the stage and exited via the chimney above the main chandelier, which in turn meant that, in the winter, spectators were met with blasts of cold air as the curtains opened.[29] The search for "aria buona alla Scala" (good air at La Scala) would continue well into the 1900s.[30]

But if auditoriums are vulnerable to outside air, even nineteenth-century commentators understood that the reverse was also true: the environment is vulnerable to architecture. We now understand that architecture accounts for some 50 percent of climate change, when one considers the extraction of materials for construction, emissions when architectural structures are used, and atmospheric deterioration when these structures are demolished. It is a matter to be reckoned with, in other words, that architecture is connected with locations far removed in time and space. And it is in the nineteenth century that we start to see the first stirrings of an awareness of this—a sense that architecture, as Esther da Costa Meyer has articulated it, is "entrapped in forms of global connectivity," that every building has an impact beyond itself.[31]

This is no less true for teatri all'italiana. That these theaters contributed to climate deterioration on a massive scale was undeniable, even in the late 1800s. It was not just that commentators realized that these theaters could impact the environment just as all architectural structures could; not just, in other words, that the Earth was ransacked for materials to use in their construction, or that their carbon fumes polluted the air, or even that their rubbled remains altered its composition. All this was true; insofar as opera houses existed in their thousands in nineteenth-century Italy alone, their cumulative impact on the environment was, moreover, far from minimal. But more remarkable still is that, by the close of the 1800s, the opera house had become a critical site of fossil fuel consumption: it even paved the way for a modern, fossil fuel–intensive energy regime. If, as Dipesh Chakrabarty has written, "the mansion of [our] modern freedoms stands on an ever-expanding base of fossil-fuel use" and "most of our [modern] freedoms" are "energy-intensive," it is no exaggeration to claim that the opera house played a critical role in securing these freedoms.[32] Ultimately, I advance the thesis here that climate change denial was nurtured within the opera house even as—or perhaps precisely because—teatri all'italiana were critical instruments in the development of infrastructures that have led to mass climate deterioration.

Dirty Opera

To understand all this, we need to trace the earliest networked distribution of electrical energy, a distribution of electrons ever on the move, electrons that sometimes move as directed and sometimes—as has occurred in mass blackouts—chart their own unfathomable course.[33] The creation of this awesome infrastructure is associated with the incandescent bulb. This was the first form of electric illumination meant for domestic use, and also the first medium whose commercial potential was so vast that the financial risk associated with the construction of central stations that could direct current to consumers' homes seemed worth it. An earlier form of arc illumination was, in contrast, suited for outdoor illumination alone.[34] This fact is underscored in Émile Zola's 1883 novel *Au bonheur des dames* (*The Ladies' Paradise*) in a scene at dusk in which the department store owner Octave Mouret stares out the store's windows onto Paris's second arrondissement and marvels at the arc lights' "blinding fixity, like the reflection of some colorless star, which was killing the dusk."[35] Witnesses with much less creative inclination than Zola also insisted that arcs had tremendous control over onlookers: it was commonly said that arcs could harm those who looked at them directly.[36] In contrast, the incandescent lightbulb was effective without being paralyzing. The early 1880s saw the construction of small networks of distribution in three cities, all built to enable the sale and use of Thomas Edison's incandescent bulbs. The stations spanned several landmasses: in the United States Edison and associates built a New York–based central station, in England an overseas Edison franchise built a second station in London, and the Società Edison Italiana built a third in Milan.[37] Others soon followed.

These initial stations were experimental, given that it was far from clear that current could be delivered smoothly, and Edison exerted close control over each of them, making hard business choices about which consumers could draw current from the network and when. The Italian station is a case in point. Located beside Milan's main cathedral, the Duomo, the circuit had an ambitious reach: current could be directed down the fibrous filaments of incandescent bulbs in homes and business some six hundred meters from the station.[38] The Società Edison Italiana nonetheless decided not to send current in all directions, wherever it was demanded, but instead to direct much of it to the Teatro alla Scala, which was first connected to the network in late 1883, a few short months after a much smaller and less ambitious installation connected to the network was created at the Teatro Manzoni. The company was so invested in the seamless illumination of the Teatro alla Scala that they declined to connect new consumers to the network for the entire duration of the theater's first season in case it overtaxed the network and the opera house's illumination faltered. Committee meeting notes from 1884 relate the idea behind this earlier decision: "Prompted by caution, we proceeded with much care, as is absolutely necessary in a business as new as ours, and without haste, in the development of the Milanese installations. An error, an interruption in the illumination, above all at the Teatro alla Scala, would have had fatal consequences; perhaps would have even irreparably compromised our future. We therefore waited for the [opera] season at La Scala to finish before taking on new customers."[39]

The Società Edison Italiana, it would seem, staked all on La Scala.[40] But if the focus on the opera house at this critical moment in electrical history seems surprising, we should note that there *were* precedents for this demonstration. In the months before these three central stations were constructed, several other inventors looked to showcase their own, ultimately less marketable, incandescent bulbs. Unable to connect to a network, all installed on-site generators, and it was none other than the opera house that they selected as their chosen location: some ten opera houses were illuminated in this manner.[41] What is distinct about the case of La Scala, however, is that, connected as this was to a central station, the ultimate product on show was not so much illumination as networked power itself.

From this perspective, the demonstration at La Scala was critical to the establishment of networked power as a marketable consumer item. When the opera house "went live" on the grid in 1883, audiences saw evidence that Edison could domesticate the power he wielded. The event was seamless: thousands upon thousands of bulbs delivered clear, consistent illumination.[42] Audience members could, moreover, reach out and touch the bulbs on the walls of boxes, corridors, or lavatories and understand that electricity was not the fearsome force it was sometimes believed to be.

There is much to be said about how a successful showcase would have been unachievable elsewhere, how theaters could lure in consumers as no other venue could because the wealthiest Italians—those with the means to become electrical consumers—attended them as a matter of course in the 1800s, and did so with a visual attention that was more acute than in other more utilitarian locations, such as train stations. Edison understood where his future consumer base could be wooed: amid the luxury of the opera house. And in the months that followed this season, this base erupted as the basic structure of Italian electrical networks took form, as power lines carried electricity from countless new central stations.[43]

I am not claiming that electrical networks would have been inconceivable without the opera house. Rather, I merely observe that these opera houses and the use of electricity were briefly but utterly indivisible from one another, and that, in turn, the opera house mobilized the creation of modern energy infrastructures as we know them. With this, moreover, came an incalculable expansion in the amount of fossil fuels exhumed, burned, and shunted back into the atmosphere. The fact remains, after all, that electricity is a deferred form of power, one that needs an initial source of power to be created, and that combustion of coal has more often than not been that source.[44] In other words, from the start, the mansion of our modern freedoms rested on an ever-vaster base of fossil fuels. This was incontestable in Milan, where coal was burned at the central station, mere meters from La Scala and the Duomo, while waste fumes were channeled into the air via a fifty-two-meter chimney and promptly proceeded to cover the Duomo in fine black soot (fig. 3.4).

It should not escape our attention that, even as La Scala was wired for electrical power, those who oversaw the venture were conscious that the freedoms electricity offered were never absolute, and that even when one set aside the noxious fumes that electricity produced and the devastation these would have on certain communities—above all the urban poor—freedoms fluctuated as carbon resources were won and lost, traded and sold. If this was true on the broadest level, as fossil fuels were exhausted *overall* across the Earth, it was also true at the more divisive level of geopolitics. The main Italian collaborator who worked with Edison was Giuseppe Colombo, a mechanical engineer and founder

FIGURE 3.4. Osvaldo Lissoni, The Duomo in Milan (with the fifty-two-meter chimney of the central power station in Via Santa Radegonda visible on the right), c. 1900–1920. Gem Archive / Alamy Stock Photo.

of the Società Edison Italiana who had the office down the hall from Stoppani at the Istituto Tecnico Superiore; the two men maintained a keen interest in one another's research.[45] Colombo understood that to invest in an electrical future was to accelerate the exhaustion of fossil fuel resources on the planet, a process that, by his estimate, would lead to their complete consumption within two to three centuries. Colombo also feared that the world would hurtle unevenly toward that state of absolute exhaustion, and the closer it came, the more unstable the balance of power across the world would become. His readers would have been well aware that Italians did not have extensive fossil fuel reserves and had furthermore laid waste to their forests. If this already made them reliant on European trade to meet their fossil fuel needs, Colombo sketched out a "scarcely appealing" (*poco lieto*) future in which all the world would have to submit to China, the final frontier of fossil fuel.[46]

To secure the mansion of Italian freedoms, Colombo recommended that Italians learn to harness the force of water and use it to create electrical power and thus dominate the industrial scene. But for all his hubris, his words returned over and over to the same disquieting theme: that the venture which he himself was at the forefront of, a venture in which the opera house was accorded a central role, was precarious, and that what was at stake in this project was the potential collapse of the world as we knew it.

Escapist Fantasies

Despite these prophetic voices, we have tended to celebrate electricity and all that it can afford us. This started well before the development of an electrical infrastructure, with dreams and fantasies about an electrified future, and intensified a thousandfold in its wake. With each hurrah for the latest device that electricity has made possible, however, we have become distanced from the dirtier, messier side of electrical infrastructures, so much so that it can come as a revelation that electricity is not "clean" energy in a strict sense, that most of the time it still draws on the combustion of an initial source.

I did not arrive at these claims from a position of climate activism; I stumbled more or less blindly onto sources such as the works of Stoppani and Colombo and read them with some surprise. In part, this was because I had been primed to believe that nineteenth-century thinkers did not understand the scale and intricacies of anthropogenic climate change. Commentators on the Anthropocene are keen to remind us that it was not until 1896 that the Swedish chemist Svante Arrhenius—drawing on the work of John Tyndall—discovered that carbon dioxide (CO_2) absorbs more heat than do most gases and thus causes the Earth to warm. This has often been used as implicit evidence that the mechanisms—and even the fact—of climate change eluded most thinkers in the nineteenth century.[47] What these Milanese sources rather reveal is that, even as mechanisms such as CO_2's tendency to absorb heat mostly eluded nineteenth-century thinkers, climate was understood with laser-sharp logic; both Stoppani and Colombo were on the money with their predictions about the dangers of fossil fuels.

My surprise also stemmed from the fact that it became apparent to me, as I read Colombo, that connections between electricity and fossil fuels have been made to disappear since the late nineteenth century. From literature to dance to opera, fossil fuels have been pushed aside so successfully that they have evaded representation and now hide in plain sight/site.[48] Although the mechanisms used to achieve this concealment have been diverse, what has united them is an *aestheticization* of the electrical that distances it from its messier sources and a tendency for humanities scholars to share in electricity's aesthetic wonder.[49]

The foundation was laid in the remote past. Even before it was understood as such, electricity was first witnessed on a massive scale in the form of lightning. If, across cultures, this form induced a sense of awe, in time it also induced an association between electricity and a tear or fissure in the air. As the proverb "bolt from a clear blue sky" suggests, lightning (and thus electricity) announced itself as a force that seemed to issue from nowhere.[50]

Similar ideas were at play in the 1800s when it became common to talk about someone's "aura." Aura, as Steven Connor has described it, is a subtle emanation of character in the air about a person, an emanation that breaks out from the host but does not depart, a second skin that remains obedient to the contours of the first.[51] One could have a charismatic, calm, or choleric aura in the nineteenth century, but it also became common to be described as having an "electric" aura. Here, too, electricity was associated with that which has no clear coordinates in space, which is at once *in* the air but not *of* it.

It was no more than coincidence that the incandescent bulb, the earliest form of electrical illumination, relied on a vacuum state to function. The coincidence is nonetheless remarkable and intensified these earlier associations considerably. To set out the basics: the incandescent bulb contains a fibrous filament, selected for its heat resistance, which is housed in a vacuum. Electrical current then runs down the filament until it incandesces. From the outset it was clear that the bulb relied on distance from the world to function: shatter the bulb and the filament will cease in an instant to incandesce (as was demonstrated at the Savoy Theater in London in 1881, before a Gilbert and Sullivan performance, when the theater manager held a bulb connected to an electric battery before the audience, covered it with muslin, and rapped it with a hammer).[52] The electric current needed a non-space, a void, in order to function; it needed to be *in* the air but not *of* it.

My point here is that electricity has accumulated associations over time that make it seem to exceed the world and at the same time exist within it; and as these associations set electricity in a complex relationship with air, they also made it the ultimate competitor to rarefied air itself. If the nineteenth century was on a mission to attain pure air, electricity offered itself to the nineteenth century as a force in excess of such purity.

And so we return to where we started, to the literal and metaphorical air of the opera house. The opera house was, after all, an important site in which discourse about electricity could be controlled. Consider, for instance, the 1873 futuristic novel *Nel 2073! Sogni d'uno stravagante* (2073! Dreams of an eccentric), set two hundred years in the future. The author, Agostino Della Sala Spada, describes a scene in which the novel's hero has traveled to 2073 to attend the opera in Turin with his twenty-first-century love interest, Evangelina.[53] At first, he is underwhelmed:

> The vast hall was filled with boxes and tiers, but I did not see a great difference with the theaters of my time and, in fact, it did not seem to me all that well illuminated. I did not hesitate to tell this to Evangelina, but she replied that I should wait and I would be satisfied....
>
> While I looked around and continued to reason in this manner and make my observations ... all of a sudden the enormous hall was flooded with an incredible, brilliant, ever so slightly bluish light, which bestowed a resplendent look on everything.
>
> "See?"—Evangelina said, alluding to her earlier promise to me—"see?"
>
> "It's true"—I replied, my eyes sparkling from the reflection of the light—"I certainly could not have conceived of illumination such as this."...
>
> And immediately in that vast theater I heard a music so sweet, so soothing, that my heart seemed to skip a beat because of that sweetness. From where the music came, from which orchestra, I do not know ... ; it was like a sound wave that had diffused everywhere, a melodious atmosphere; it seemed, in short, as though the very molecules of the air, while dancing in the immensity of that hall, were conveying those blissful notes....
>
> "This music and this light is enough for me"—I replied—"and should anything more be added, I will surely faint from its sweetness."...
>
> The scene, with its marvels of optics and of electricity, made [the events] come very much alive before my eyes.[54]

Electricity is cast here on a level with music. Both seem to come from nowhere and exist nowhere; both also, nonetheless, dance in the air. In combination, these threaten to leave our hero unconscious. It is not an unwelcome unconsciousness, however, but rather a state of absolute bliss toward which he is pushed. Musical and electrical transcendence meet in this scene; both electricity and music are cast as not of this world.

This last idea is critical. Electricity is cast here as it was on countless occasions in ballets, operas, and the critical discourse that surrounded them. The more electricity was framed as somehow removed from the world, the more distance was created between electricity and the subterranean resources on which it relied, between electricity and a deteriorating climate. The entire infrastructure on which it rested could, in this manner, be set aside, from the labor to the materials needed to create the modern freedoms electricity made possible. What remained was an idea of electricity as *almost* immaterial—as a force that, at least, left no trace in the air.

And yet, it was at the opera house, the very site where modern energy infrastructures received their initial impetus and thus where the foundation for an incredible acceleration in climate change was established, where such functions were nurtured. In this sense, for all its good intentions, the Liceu installation builds on a long lineage of fantasies perpetuated within opera houses, fantasies that mask the contributions of those involved in climate change. The core distortion behind all these fantasies has been the notion that there can be a haven somehow removed from a world otherwise vulnerable to climate deterioration. Music was often held up as one such sublime escape; so too was the "pure" air of the opera house; and so too was the electrical, even as it precipitated the deterioration of the climate from which, our nineteenth-century protagonists knew, there might ultimately be no escape.

FOUR

Acoustics

In Gabriele D'Annunzio's 1894 novel *Il trionfo della morte* (*The Triumph of Death*), circumstances compel the central character to retreat to an Italian seaside town, from which he later sends for some musical scores and a piano. The arrival of the items leads Giorgio and his lover Ippolita to submit themselves to new pleasures; entire summer afternoons are lost to Schumann and Chopin. It is the score of Richard Wagner's *Tristan und Isolde* (1865), however, that causes Ippolita to lock the piano lid, fearing that this music drama will lead them to delirium. Giorgio had seen *Tristan* on his visit to the Bayreuth Festspielhaus, the state-of-the art theater built in the 1870s exclusively for the performance of Wagner's music dramas. His recollections of this theater, with a sunken orchestra concealed from view, creates a restlessness in him. The orchestral music, Giorgio recalls, had reached out to its audience as "sonorous flames" from a "furnace": with a "devouring fury" the "intoxication of the melodious flame embraced everything," while "all that was sovereign in the world vibrated passionately in the immense ravishment."[1] As if in deliberate compensation for the invisibility of the orchestra, he casts these remembered sounds in visual form.

That the orchestra was concealed from view at the Festspielhaus was, to be sure, remarkable. At the time, most orchestras at teatri all'italiana were not lowered or concealed at all; rather, they were located at the level of the auditorium floor, a meter or two from the audience in the stalls, on the auditorium (rather than the stage) side of the proscenium arch. The Festspielhaus orchestra was instead both lowered to an unusual extent and hidden from view via the use of double proscenium arches—one close to the stage and a wider one closer to the audience—from which wooden covers extended (fig. 4.1). The arches ensured that the action that unfolded seemed somewhat more distant than it would otherwise,

FIGURE 4.1. Cross-section of the Bayreuth Festspielhaus. Note the deep orchestra pit and double proscenium arches. In George C. Izenour, *Theater Design* (New York: Yale University Press, 1977), 223. © Yale University Press. Used with permission.

and thus that much more dreamlike and unreal. But more than this, the architectural modification enabled the orchestral sound to float into the area between the two arches—a zone the composer liked to term the "mystic abyss" (*mystischer Abgrund*)—and from there into the auditorium via a fairly narrow uncovered area. D'Annunzio's protagonist here conceives of the music as contained within this novel architectural structure, much as a furnace holds in heat. To reach the audience it must—in a rather literal sense—transcend its material enclosure, the wooden covers and walls that hold it in. A transformative drama unfolds before our characters, drawing them into a world of dreams.

Even now this architectural structure remains one of the most radical orchestral enclosures ever created and continues to surprise contemporary audience members. In the words of the critic Joseph Wechsberg, for instance, who attended a performance of *Das Rheingold* at the Festspielhaus in the 1950s, "There was silence, and out of the darkness came a sustained E-flat—so low that I couldn't distinguish exactly when the silence ended and sound began. Nor could I be sure where the sound came from; it might have come from the sides of the auditorium, or the rear, or the ceiling."[2] The confusion this critic describes was the result not only of the acousmatic orchestral sound, but also of the architectural acoustics of the auditorium as a whole. From the outset, the theater's auditorium was remarkable for its excessive reverberation time. As we now understand, reverberation occurs when variations in air pressure bounce off distant surfaces but reach the listener so fast that these cannot be understood as distinct echoes. Experts estimate that sound took an entire 1.55 seconds to decay at the Festspielhaus because of the especially vast distance between the floor and ceiling.[3] As noted in chapter 1, such extended reverberation fascinated the composer, who went on to score sounds in his music drama *Parsifal* that were specifically designed to reverberate. It seems Wagner realized that the odd acoustics in his theater could aid him in creating the sense of aesthetic immersion he was seeking, one also achieved through a darkened auditorium that made the spectator oblivious to his surroundings.[4] Sound, after all, exists on a continuum between silence and pain.[5] With loud, reverberant sounds listeners become conscious that the air that bounces around them also touches them; and as we also now understand, even in the absence of extreme volume, such reverberation scars the eardrum. The enormous orchestra at the Festspielhaus would have been able to operate at the far end of this dynamic continuum with ease. In Giorgio's recollection of a "melodious flame [that] embraced everything," D'Annunzio had intuitively pointed to a critical aspect of the listener's relation to reverberation at the theater: that it had the potential to *literally* mark the bodies of listeners.

But for all this, Wagner said little about architectural acoustics while the theater was under construction or indeed thereafter.[6] The unusual reverberation at the Festspielhaus could even have been an accident, or perhaps the brainchild of the theater's architect, Otto Brückwald, alone. For our purposes, the relevant detail is that the composer either had limited acoustic ambitions for the theater as a whole, including the orchestra pit, or never found the words with which to articulate them. The closest he came to an acoustic conception of the lowered orchestra was in the complete poetic texts for *Der Ring des Nibelungen*, published in 1863, in which he described a lowered and concealed orchestra as desirable in order both to hide it from view and to muffle its unwanted sounds. When heard through an acoustic sound wall, Wagner reasoned, the orchestral music would be purged of nonmusical sounds produced by the instrumentalists. He must have had in mind the uncomfortable noise created when moisture accumulates behind a reed, or in the curved bore of a brass instrument—the noise, in other words, that drew attention to the labor behind the art.[7] A decade later, in the published version of Wagner's address for the laying of the foundation stone at Bayreuth, concern with the visual comes to the fore. Now the orchestra must be concealed so that the "technical 'hearth'" of the music will be hidden from view, and in order that there be "nothing clearly perceptible between [the spectator] and the stage tableau, but merely a distance [a 'mystical abyss'], suspended as it were between the two proscenium arches by architectonic means."[8]

These were bold words. Little wonder that the Festspielhaus remains the one nineteenth-century theater where material conditions are discussed as a matter of course, their inherent interest assumed. Even now, this technical discussion retains much of its luster: the composer somehow found a formula to bind all the intricate and commonplace details of his architectural innovations into one transcendent vision. And it is no surprise that he fascinated an intellectual aesthete like D'Annunzio.[9] With its intimations of sound subsumed into a total and immersive work of art—a veritable *Gesamtkunstwerk*—the discussion of *Tristan und Isolde* in *Il trionfo della morte* underscores what mattered most about the orchestral enclosure at the Festspielhaus. The orchestra had to be concealed from view to ensure that no one element could distract the audience members from their submission to art. Indeed, in *Il trionfo della morte*, the characters are described as always on the brink of dissolving into the music drama itself.

Orchestra Chamber

It is now standard for orchestras at teatri all'italiana to be located in dedicated orchestra chambers, below the level of the auditorium floor. Our histories, however, tell us little about when this innovation took hold. Indeed, it is a marker of how much those histories are oriented around the Festspielhaus that this omission exists. Conventional wisdom reinforces this bias, with its insistence that most orchestras were lowered in reaction to the innovation at Bayreuth.

There are several reasons not to allow the Festspielhaus to dominate narratives about orchestra chambers. For a start, one of the earliest experiments with a lowered orchestra can be traced to a provincial theater in Besançon, in eastern France, where the architect Claude-Nicolas Ledoux sank the entire orchestra in the 1770s and even concealed some musicians from view.[10] Less radical orchestral enclosures were also built at numerous theaters in central Europe in the first half of the nineteenth century. It nonetheless remains true that momentum was slow to build for the trend toward lowered orchestras at teatri all'italiana, and that most orchestra chambers have been constructed since the Festspielhaus was erected. When the new theater for the Paris Opéra opened in 1875, mere months before the Festspielhaus, the orchestra was located on the same level as the auditorium floor.[11] When, in 1880, the architect Achille Sfondrini and the entrepreneur Domenico Costanzi collaborated on a new opera house in Rome, meanwhile, their decision to create an orchestra chamber was met with bemusement. In the weeks before the theater opened, it proved hard to secure a permanent conductor despite these men's ambitions to make their theater the new national opera. Writing for the broadsheet *La libertà*, one critic claimed that it was well known the lowered orchestra was the deal breaker—that several influential conductors had declined contracts with the theater because this placement broke with tradition.[12] Once resistance to the innovation lessened, however, the lowered orchestra chamber became a standard to which all teatri all'italiana would conform with time. In Italy, the innovation can for instance be dated to 1907 at Milan's Teatro alla Scala and Parma's Teatro Regio, 1909 at Busseto's Teatro Verdi, 1927 at the Teatro delle Muse in Ancona, 1930 at the Teatro Rossini in Pesaro, and 1936 at the Teatro della Fortuna in Fano.[13]

The construction of all these orchestra enclosures was overseen by an architect—often by one particular architect, Cesare Albertini, who consulted on the construction of the orchestra chamber at La Scala and on orchestra chambers at many other theaters.[14] Since most such theaters had a hollow area beneath their auditorium floors, construction did not entail alterations to their foundations. What made construction intricate were the choices involved. There were two main considerations: how large an area should be lowered, and how far. Once these choices were made, contractors built a lowered platform for the orchestra and four walls that linked the orchestra floor to that of the auditorium. As we shall see, the dimensions and conditions of these sunken enclosures were worked out with considerable care in order to create chambers in which acoustics could be customized. The result was a situation in which musicians remained somewhat visible to their audience, both because the musicians were not concealed under a cover and because the orchestra tended to rest a mere one and a half meters or so beneath the auditorium floor (fig. 4.2).

When these orchestral enclosures were built, no one seems to have had the fevered reactions of a Giorgio or Ippolita, but these innovations *were* met with some creative rhetoric. The most common term Italian critics used to describe the new enclosures was *golfo mistico* (mystic abyss).[15] Italians had used the same term decades earlier in reference to the Festspielhaus.[16] But to use the term in reference to *these* orchestra chambers was of course a misuse of the term—Wagner labeled the zone *between* his proscenium arches the *mystische Abgrund*, not the enclosure itself, and the Festspielhaus remains the only theater ever to have

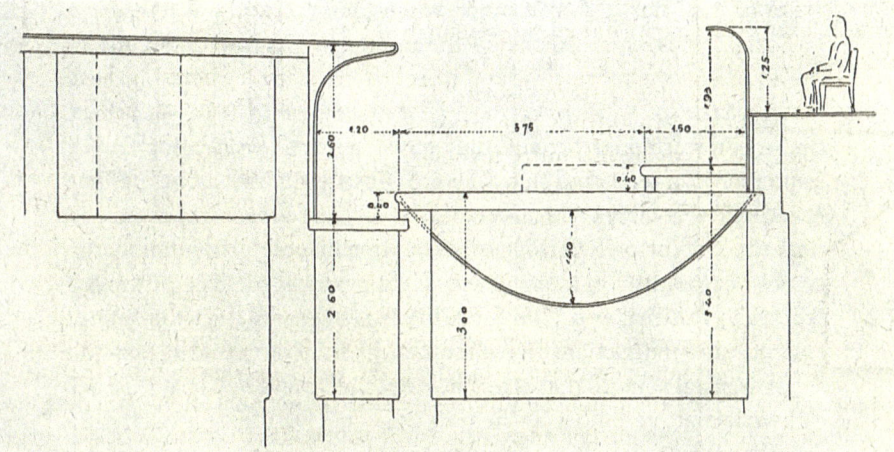

FIGURE 4.2. Architectural blueprint from 1913 showing a cross-section of the orchestra pit at the Teatro alla Scala. Albertini, "Circa la formazione del 'golfo mistico' per le orchestre dei nostri teatri," 386. Courtesy Biblioteca Nazionale Centrale di Roma.

concealed its orchestra under covers that extend from double arches. But *golfo mistico* nonetheless served critics well. At times it was used to honor the Festspielhaus as a model, even if there were minimal architectural similarities between Italian enclosures and the orchestra chamber there. At others, *golfo mistico* was used ironically, less to enshrine fascination with these new enclosures and their Teutonic model than to insist that what had been constructed in all these theaters—the Festspielhaus included—was a mere set of walls beneath an auditorium. Taken to extremes, this same attitude yielded another common term at this time, *fossa orchestrale*—an "orchestral hollow" or "trench." But this term also contained intimations that these new enclosures had condemned musicians to breathe their last within them: *fossa orchestrale* also translates as "orchestral tomb."

The *fossa* as tomb is an association to which we shall return. For now, however, I want to draw attention to one more dimension of both *golfo mistico* and *fossa orchestrale*: the fact that neither of these evocative phrases has even the most minimal technical ring to it. This is doubtless indicative of the extent to which technical discussion of these architectural novelties was limited to the inner circles of theater administrators, the intricacies involved in their construction lost on audiences, critics included. If at the time such details hardly entered the discussion, even now, such detail is hard-won. For a start, although critics made earnest efforts to describe the innovations, orchestra chambers soon became normalized, their acoustic contribution subsumed into some capacious sense of "the music." For instance, when the orchestra was lowered at La Scala, critics remarked on how the architectural innovation rendered the sound all the more clear and direct. A critic for *Il mondo musicale* described the sonorities in Wagner's *Götterdämmerung* (1876), with which the season started, as "wonderfully pure"; another, writing for *Cosmorama pittorico*, remarked that "the new position of the orchestra" had "contributed notably to the fusion of sound."[17] But before long the acoustical effect of the orchestra chamber became inaudible. In other words, critics heard music as music, rather than music as mediated by architecture. If this makes it hard for historians to reconstruct the actions and attitudes in this transitional moment, we can nonetheless turn to a set of archival sources that reveal how architects and musicians hashed out what mattered most to them in the construction of an orchestra chamber at La Scala. These documents remind us that our conventional wisdom, with its reliance on the logic of *post hoc, ergo propter hoc* (after, therefore because), leaves us clueless about the multitude of causal factors at play in the trend toward lowered orchestras. To understand orchestra chambers, in other words, we need to leave the world that D'Annunzio built for Giorgio and Ippolita far behind, to release ourselves from our fascination with the Festspielhaus and the narratives around it and understand new orchestra enclosures on their own terms. Partial concealment of musicians and instruments at theaters could well have been intended to suture the audience into a fictional world, but to understand these enclosures only within the framework that Wagner set out is to overlook what enclosure afforded its musicians, and to remain unaware of the sonic ideals realized amid all this construction.

Calibrating Acoustics

The decision to lower the orchestra at La Scala was made on the recommendation of several commissioners appointed to assess the question. Since 1898, the theater had been under the management of the aristocratic-cum-industrialist Visconti di Modrone family, when Guido, Visconti di Modrone (1838–1902), entered into a contract to run La Scala. The contract was between him, the civic authorities (who controlled both the land on which La Scala rested and the building itself), and the box holders (who had contractual claims to individual boxes at the theater).[18] That the Modrone family was involved at all was a direct result of liberal reforms: in the summer of 1897 the civic authorities had ceased all formal subvention of the theater for the first time since the Risorgimento on the basis that expenditures "for the entertainment of the rich, for luxury" should not be sustained.[19] The Visconti di Modrone, then, turned the theater into a venture they oversaw, and with this came both an infusion of capital from them and a new managerial structure: the twin roles of general/administrative director and conductor/artistic director were introduced at the theater, with Giulio Gatti-Casazza appointed the former, a young Arturo Toscanini the latter. The lowered orchestra, meanwhile, was the direct result of a new contract that Guido's son Uberto would enter into with the civic authorities and box holders for the period 1907–16. When the terms of that contract were worked out in 1906, the civic authorities recognized their "inescapable duty" as the "co-owner of one of the most important theaters in the world [to do] everything possible to ensure that it might become accessible to all classes of citizen."[20] The result was a contract that committed them to covering the construction costs involved in tearing out seats and fashioning a gallery area that would increase the capacity of the theater and enable more tickets to be sold at lower prices. The contract also noted that it would be appropriate for the civic authorities to cover the cost of a lowered orchestra, on the basis that it would likely offer good results for the theater's acoustics. Continuous formal subvention thus gave way to more occasional support.

When serious talks about the lowered orchestra first started in the spring of 1907, then, the commission that was assembled included Toscanini, the theater's new conductor; the librettist and composer Arrigo Boito as the second in line to Gatti-Casazza; the composer Giacomo Puccini; and Gatti-Casazza himself, with the Milanese architect Albertini as consultant.[21] The documentary traces of the commission's deliberations are mostly confined to dry, technical memos, but one set of papers preserved in the archives records a far more animated and reflective conversation. The commissioners' report from April 1907 reveals the illustrious quartet heatedly debating the proper level for the orchestra.[22] News of their debate soon became fodder for the press, and the magazine *Ars et labor* captured the moment in a caricature that imagined the four famous commissioners deliberating over the matter as if it carried all the weight of that most existential of questions: to be or not to be? (fig. 4.3).

The dilemma can be summarized as follows: most were in favor of removing the orchestra from the immediate visual frame so that rows of musicians in black tie did not, for instance, pull the characters of Giuseppe Verdi's *Aida* (1871) out of their fictional world and leave them poised somewhere between the banks of the Nile and the rows of seats in the stalls. Boito, on the other hand, resisted the idea that the fictional illusion was broken just because orchestral musicians were visible. But the visual implications of the decision were far less important to these

FIGURE 4.3. "To lower or not to lower. . . ." Caricature of four commissioners (*left to right*: Gatti-Casazza, Puccini, Toscanini, and Boito). In "Istantanee scaligere," *Ars et labor: Musica e musicisti* (1907): 600. Courtesy Biblioteca Nazionale Centrale di Roma.

interlocutors than the acoustical considerations, which ultimately guided their deliberations. Puccini, Toscanini, and others were intrigued by the possibilities for greater acoustical control promised by the construction of an orchestra chamber and proposed that lowering the orchestra would result in a more blended sound and better overall balance.[23] The men also noted that, with an orchestra chamber, singers' voices would be better able to project over the instruments. Boito, however, feared that lowering the orchestra would be an acoustic disaster, as the results would be far too unpredictable.[24]

Although these men almost certainly did not know it, the world was on the cusp of a small revolution in architectural acoustics. The American physicist Wallace Sabine had recently been commissioned to improve the acoustics in Harvard University's Fogg Lecture Hall, and as he moved cushions in and out of the room and repeatedly measured how the acoustics were altered, he discovered the mathematical formula for the reverberation time: that is, he calculated the amount of time it took for the sound to decay to the point that it was inaudible to him.[25] Sabine found that two quantities had the most dramatic impact on the reverberation time: room volume and total surface area of acoustic absorbers. The equation is still used now, with modifications: Sabine's focus on cushions as acoustic absorbers never fully accounted for the fact that bodies themselves are the dominant absorbers of sound in most auditoriums. (In an altogether practical—if nonetheless brutally reductionist—move, bodies have since been assigned value within reverberation calculations as units of absorptive material.)[26]

The commissioners at La Scala did reach consensus on one issue: that tests should be conducted before a final decision about the orchestra chamber was reached. Instead of relying on formulas, the commissioners took a thoroughly practical approach to the problem, listening to the hall as materials were tried out and surfaces moved, making incremental modifications until the acoustics pleased them. Albertini, at least, must have been familiar with the classic textbooks on architectural acoustics, such as Antonio Favaro's 1882 *L'acustica applicata alla costruzione delle sale per spettacoli e pubbliche adunanze* (Practical acoustics for performance venues and public assemblies).[27] Although it was written before Sabine's discoveries, Favaro's book shows a sophisticated understanding of how acoustics work. Favaro even includes a section on the orchestra chamber and the considerations operative in its construction.[28] None of the theories in Favaro's textbook could guarantee a particular acoustic result, but they would have given the commissioners reason to believe that, with time and patience, acoustics in the orchestra chamber could be fashioned to their taste. This was quite a feat when one considers that, as recently as the 1860s, acoustics had eluded even the best theater architects. Charles Garnier, architect of the Paris Opéra, himself would record in his memoirs: "it is not my fault that acoustics and I [could] never come to an understanding. I gave myself great pains to master this bizarre science . . . I conferred industriously with philosophers . . . [but] nowhere did I find a positive rule of action to guide me."[29] Perhaps it was a similar befuddlement that rendered Wagner silent on the issue of architectural acoustics.

A measure of our commissioners' faith that acoustics could be customized can be found in their meticulous attention to detail. Their calculations would have taken into account that acoustics at the theater were, in at least certain sections of the auditorium, exemplary for the time. The reverberation time would have been around 1.2 seconds, which meant that even in the most frenetic ensembles in a Mozart or Rossini opera, much of the audience would have had a chance to make out the words.[30] The same was not true in the boxes, which, despite being the most coveted areas of the theater for most of the nineteenth century, operated under their own acoustic rules. The theater had nonetheless been touted since its construction in the 1770s as one of the finest architectural structures around, in no small part because of its acoustics. As noted in chapter 1, once architects realized that its auditorium could deliver such sound even at extreme limits—it was the vastest theater of its time and could accommodate more than two thousand audience members—scaled-down versions started to be built all around it.

Working with these acoustic tendencies at La Scala, the four commissioners spent considerable time discussing how the walls should be constructed. They settled on cement walls with chambers of air inside them.[31] They also chose to position a *cassa armonica* beneath the orchestra. This was a hollow wooden structure in the form of a half dome; it had been used in other theaters to create a blended orchestral sound, and the commissioners wanted to see how it would work at La Scala.[32] To line the walls, they chose from four woods known for their absorbent nature: maple, oak, larch, and fir, each of which was tested in demonstrations in which a vocalist performed in a similar but miniaturized environment.[33] They selected fir for all the wooden components of the pit—the trusses, girders, and the *cassa armonica*—but also to line the walls, where it would have the most immediate contact with the sound the orchestra produced, on the basis that it demonstrated "buona risonanza" (good resonance).[34] If what the commissioners understood "resonance" to mean is somewhat uncertain here, it was likely intended as a synonym of "reverberant." It was not, after all, until the first decade of the 1800s that the distinction between resonance, echo, and reverberation was understood; even well into the late nineteenth century, Italians used resonance to mean reverberation.

Determining the ideal dimensions for the pit was a more involved process. Construction workers lowered the floor on which the orchestra performed in small increments, with the commissioners listening to the resulting sonic space at each step of the way. The process continued bit by bit until the floor had been notched down one and a half meters beneath the auditorium floor. At this point, even the dissenting Boito was content that the acoustics in the theater had not been compromised, and the new design would in fact allow greater control of the orchestral sound. The overall floor space of the orchestra pit was calculated by allotting one square meter of space for each musician—which meant that to accommodate 110 musicians, the orchestra platform would ultimately need to be extended backward and some musicians would have to sit beneath the stage.

It would seem that the commissioners were aiming for a sound that would be experienced directly. The wood over the walls and the air chambers inside them would have readily absorbed air waves set in motion by the instrumentalists. In other words, although some air waves would have bounced off the walls of the orchestra chamber over and over, hurtling around its interior as reverberation, far more still would have hit a wall, been absorbed into it, and ceased to circulate. That it turn meant that overall more air waves would have reached orchestral musicians as direct sound—sound that reached the listener without first becoming reverberative. But as the wood, cement, and *cassa armonica* were introduced, the acoustic results unsettled all predictions. Air bounced around within the orchestra chamber, creating problematic echoes that were particularly pronounced in the area near the podium. The commissioners reasoned that the *cassa armonica* had caused the chain of echoes. So construction workers took a saw to the chamber once more, carving substantial slits into the floor of the *cassa armonica* to release the air that the commissioners surmised had been bouncing about within its walls. The commissioners also reconfigured the layout of the orchestra, placing the strings on a central platform and moving the timpani and horns forward from the area beneath the stage, where their sound had been overly intensified. The combination of tactics resolved the problem. It could be tempting to see this trial-and-error approach as somewhat amateur, but we should resist the temptation to do so. The commissioners did what all architectural acousticians must: they worked with the complexities of the built environment in front of them to customize results.

Protected Space

If the isolation and perfection of individual data streams was a hallmark of the modern—as media scholars from Friedrich A. Kittler to Jonathan Sterne have claimed—then the orchestra chamber, built to control the instrumental sound that issued from it, was indeed of its time.[35] But control of the sound that entered the orchestral enclosure was no less vital a dimension in all this. In essence, the orchestra chamber was a container, and like all containers it structured the activities of those within it through restraint. Verdi had understood as much when, back in the 1870s and 1890s, he observed that the orchestra was vulnerable to whatever rude noise the audience wished to surround it with: "for the orchestra . . . to play in the middle of an applauding or hissing audience," he once wrote in a letter to the conductor Edoardo Mascheroni in 1893, "is the most ridiculous thing in the world."[36] The composer, in other words, recognized that an orchestra chamber could limit both sonic and visual distractions to the musicians; in short, it could create the conditions necessary for focused labor. These were matters that became even more important around this time, with the first-ever formation of orchestral unions and associated publications such as the periodical *L'orchestra*.[37] We could even think of the orchestra chamber as a studio in the nineteenth-century Italian sense of the word: an isolated location where intellectuals and artists could be alone with their work.[38] At the close of the nineteenth century, the studio was a site associated with intense ambition, not least because it was the term used to describe the lawyer's workplace, and law had been the first profession to be formally credentialed in the new nation-state.[39] Much as lawyers' studios allowed them to sit alone with their work, the orchestra chamber allowed musicians to sit alone with their sound—in their own square meter of floor space—shielded from the chaos outside.[40]

The idea that musicians were now at one remove from the auditorium—and, crucially, from the sounds of the auditorium—dominated the limited critical reactions to the orchestra chamber at La Scala. The periodical *Ars et labor*—the one that published the satirical sketch of the four commissioners—released a series of caricatures about the orchestra chamber as construction work was beginning. These sketches imagine the orchestra enclosed in a sonic world unto itself, completely removed from the noise of the auditorium. Most of the images show the orchestral musicians operating not in air but in water; indeed, in this caricature the *fossa orchestrale* is depicted as the domain of seals (*foche*) who pack the bottom of a vast tank (fig. 4.4).[41] Their conductor is so far beneath the auditorium that his baton must extend several meters to be seen by the singers. The musicians, meanwhile, press in around him; in marked contrast with the vocalist, who inhales air with abandon, their mouths are fastened shut.

There is much worked into this caricature. Sound does not travel in water as it does in air, and so the painstaking acoustical calculations and tests undertaken by the commission are shown as being all for naught. The most dramatic distinction between sound traveling through water versus sound traveling through air is that in the former case, the ear cannot trace sound to its source. Listening becomes directionless and the coordination of an ensemble impossible in such a wash of sounds. No wonder, then, that the vocalist peers down at the conductor for visual cues, or that the balconies are filled with inattentive audience members indifferent to the action on stage. Much like the use of the term *fossa orchestrale*, the substitution of water for air in these caricatures is an indictment of the orchestra chamber at La Scala. When we recall Nietzsche's famous snide remark that when one listens to Wagner one "has to swim" amid his endless, suffocating melodies, the caricature turns into an even more consummate denouncement of the innovation at La Scala, with the model of the Festspielhaus summoned as the ultimate source of the caricaturist's scorn and orchestral musicians framed as the ultimate victims of all this innovation.[42]

It is almost irresistible to read this caricature in relation to a ban on encores introduced in the 1907 season, which further distanced orchestral musicians from audience feedback. At the outset of that season audi-

FIGURE 4.4. "The hollow of the seals." In "Istantanee scaligere," *Ars et labor: Musica e musicisti* (1907): 706. Courtesy Biblioteca Nazionale Centrale di Roma.

ences had arrived at a theater covered in notices which announced that "in the interests of public order and art," the management had banned encores.[43] This encore ban can without hesitation be attributed to Toscanini, who had famously stormed out of La Scala in 1902 when audiences ignored a previous attempt to introduce the ban. We could see the dual acoustic control and isolation enabled by the orchestra chamber as a material manifestation of the broader aesthetic Toscanini promoted at La Scala, an aesthetic that put order and streamlined sound above all else, including meaningful interaction between musicians and audience.[44] But to privilege these congruences between architectural modifications and the conductor's broadly modernist mindset is perhaps to give too much weight to the case of La Scala. The auditorium was not hollowed out for Toscanini alone.[45] And, crucially, acoustics was the dominant factor at most teatri all'italiana that lowered their orchestras around this time. What, then, made acoustic control a sine qua non of musical excellence in this moment? And in the relative isolation of the orchestra chamber, what did it mean for musicians to be alone with their sound?

Acoustic Signatures

One reason acoustic control mattered was simply that now, more than ever, it was within reach. An important lesson to be learned from history of acoustics in the nineteenth century is that sound was a variable, never a constant; its essence and force were always shifting and contested.[46] Especially important in architectural acoustics was the gathering notion that sound could be divided into its component parts. From the Helmholtz resonator, which dramatized the fact that tones were divisible into an overtone series, to research that used heat to make visible the motion of sound waves, the entire idea of sound modification in architectural acoustics had received a new lease on life.[47]

Favaro, the author of the Italian textbook on acoustics, had for instance insisted on a clean division between direct and reverberant sound, a division that was new for its time. As far back as the first century BCE, Vitruvius had noted the sublime chain of echoes that sound initiated in certain rooms.[48] But for Favaro, direct sound—sound that occurs when a listener comes into contact with sound waves that have not encountered an obstacle and therefore have neither become reverberant nor formed distinct echoes—was more valuable than ever. This was the "natural" sound that architectural acousticians must cultivate and safeguard, the sound created when there is no enclosure around the sound source. Thus, we read at the start of his book:

As we set about studying the application of the laws of acoustics to planning of the layout of buildings so that the human voice—and sound more generally speaking—might propagate in them in the best possible way, we should first recall the maxim of one of the most authoritative physicists in the field of acoustics: "There is no building, no matter how carefully constructed, in which the laws of acoustics are so well respected as in the outdoors."

There, in fact, when the atmosphere is completely calm, and when there are no obstacles that might affect the propagation of sound waves, we find the most favorable conditions possible for the uniform propagation of sound.[49]

In Favaro's model, reverberation was regarded as external, a distraction or divergence from direct sound, and thus an effect that had to be moderated with care. Architectural structures modified the "normal" diffusion of sound to create "the special phenomena of reflection"; it was the work of architectural acousticians to minimize the influence that those structures had on sound.[50]

The key point here is that, within these outwardly unassuming texts about sound and architecture, a new ideal was taking shape which held that the acoustic trace of the room in which sound was produced could be minimized. Scholars such as Emily Ann Thompson have brilliantly demonstrated the commitment with which this ideal was pursued around this time in the United States, and it seems to have had no less of a hold on Italian architects such as Favaro and Albertini.[51] What our commissioners did, in the mere act of constructing a chamber around the orchestra, was control the surfaces that the instrumental sound first encountered, and so limit the acoustic trace of the auditorium walls themselves. And with all their modifications to the orchestra chamber at La Scala, our commissioners also fashioned an acoustic that had a limited ambient trace of the orchestral enclosure. The modified *cassa armonica*, air chambers inside the cement, and wood on the walls all inhibited reverberation and, in turn, lessened the acoustic signature of the chamber. Perhaps to be alone with one's sound in this dedicated workspace, then, was to connect with what was now imagined to be the "natural" sound of the orchestra, one exempt from the mediation of the room.

None of this means our commissioners and their contemporaries were somehow not interested in immersive reverberation within built enclosures at all. One need only listen to the sounds of Puccini, Giordano, and the *giovane scuola* in the late nineteenth century for evidence that this was not the case. As noted in chapter 1, their use of violinata entailed voice and instruments of the orchestra issuing the same melodic line from separate locations; in turn, this entailed a minuscule but detectable mismatch between the reverberation of both forces' melodic lines. This was to include the theater walls in calculations about orchestration—to create a small amount of immersive sonic confusion that countered the nonreverberative tendencies of La Scala and the thousands of theaters modeled on it. But *counter* remains the core term here: the trend for violinata cannot be understood outside the context of new movements in architectural acoustics.

Pure Sound?

To close, I want to venture outside the theater to consider one more dimension in all of this. At almost the exact moment that the commissioners first met to discuss the lowered orchestra, another venture was initiated in Milan that placed musicians at one remove from their audience. In 1904 several associates founded the Società Italiana di Fonotipia, a recording firm that, decades later, would be absorbed into EMI. The firm occupied a suite on the top floor of Via Dante 4, a short walk from La Scala. Its directors included Uberto, Visconti di Modrone; the composer Giordano; and Tito Ricordi, of the famed music publishing firm.[52] With Edison's invention of the phonograph in 1877, it had become possible for variations in air pressure to be transduced into a series of etched grooves that could then be converted back to sound. If the results were sometimes so faint as to be almost indiscernible, it was Emile Berliner's invention of the flat disc around 1890 that assured the commercial potential of sound recording. The etched grooves in the shellac disc created a much louder sound when reproduced, and crucially, the discs could also be copied.[53]

Fonotipia, then, was established at the outset of a new era in commercial recording. Their business model was announced in a stream of advertisements in music periodicals. The publicity displayed here accompanied the launch of its first catalog of records (fig. 4.5). It tells us that although there have been endless records made of second-rate artists, almost none are available of true musicians. Beneath the boldface, oversized "Perchè?" ("Why?") we hear that other firms lacked the artistic vision that has enabled Fonotipia to attract the best artists. Rather more bizarrely, the advertisement assures readers that each disc will bear the artist's autograph, in order to guarantee that it is in fact a performance by that artist and that the artist endorses it as a faithful reproduction of their voice and art.

SOCIETÀ ITALIANA DI FONOTIPIA

Direttore Generale: ALFREDO MICHAELIS
Direttore Artistico: UMBERTO GIORDANO

4, Via Dante - MILANO - Via Dante, 4

ESISTONO *migliaia di dischi cantati da artisti* di secondo ordine.
ESISTE *soltanto qualche disco* di grande artista.
NON ESISTE *un repertorio completo, a soli duetti, terzetti, quartetti*, di grandi opere cantate da grandi artisti.

PERCHÈ?

PERCHÈ l'interpretazione di ogni opera musicale domanda agli artisti qualità speciali di voce, di metodo e di ingegno, che devono fondersi in omogenea interpretazione.

PERCHÈ quindi la creazione del **COMPLETO REPERTORIO DI GRANDI OPERE** cantate da grandi artisti *richiede un'organizzazione* ed una *direzione veramente artistica*, che *sinora* non esistettero.

PERCHÈ *soltanto* la **SOCIETÀ ITALIANA DI FONOTIPIA** associandosi quasi tutti i più illustri artisti ha potuto ora creare tale *organizzazione che non può essere eguagliata da altri*.

PERCHÈ soltanto ora, e sotto la direzione di un illustre Maestro:

UMBERTO GIORDANO

Artisti insigni quali:

Ada Adini Millet – Maria Barrientos – Gemma Bellincioni – R. Blanchard – Irene De Bohuss – A. Bonci – F. M. Bonini – F. Bravi – G. Bréjean-Silver – Eugenia Burzio-Ravizza – V. Capoul – Emma Carelli – Rose Charron – Lina Cavalieri – P. Cornubert – F. Corradetti – Hariclée Darclée – I. David – J. F. Delmas – Emmy Destinn – G. De Luca – Maria De Marchi – Maria Escalaïs – L. Escalaïs – Teresina Ferraris – P. Gailhard – R. Garbin – Maria Giudice – Henry Jerome – G. Krismer – Fausta Labia – G. La Puma – V. Leviva – Félia Litvinne – L. Longobardi – O. Luppi – A. Magini-Coletti – V. Maurel – E. Nani – F. Navarini – G. Pacini – Regina Pacini – Armida Parsi-Pettinella – Elisa Petri – Regina Pinkert – Maria De Rezské – J. De Rezské – Giannina Russ – Rosina Storchio – M. Sammarco – E. Scaramberg – P. Schiavazzi – Febea Strakosch – Adelina Stehle – R. Stracciari – E. Van Dyck – E. Ventura – F. Vignas – G. Zenatello

dei quali noi siamo unici concessionari (come lo siamo di Kubelik, di Goll, di Thibaud, di **Sardou**, di **Rasi**, ecc., ecc.).

stanno creando il completo repertorio a soli duetti, terzetti, quartetti, ecc. **delle grandi opere.**

UN PRIMO catalogo è pronto, ed ogni mese ne pubblicheremo il supplemento.

COSÌ GLI AMATORI potranno mano a mano formarsi una **completa discoteca** di esecuzioni operistiche.

CIASCUN nostro disco porta le firme autografe degli artisti, ciò che garantisce che il disco:

I. fu eseguito dell'artista stesso.
II. che è riconosciuto da lui come fedele riproduzione della sua voce e della sua arte.

Catalogo e Supplementi mensili gratis: in **MILANO**, *presso la Società Italiana di Fonotipia, Via Dante, 4; ed in tutta Italia presso* **G. Ricordi & C.**, *e presso ogni buon negozio del genere.*

FIGURE 4.5. Fonotipia advertisement. *Ars et labor: Musica e musicisti* (1906): 361. Courtesy Biblioteca Nazionale Centrale di Roma.

It is now a cliché that when listeners first heard recorded sound, it seemed to be an acousmatic miracle; that listeners were stunned that the voice of an artist could be summoned even in the performer's absence. We might read the Fonotipia advertisement as a rather charming admission that consumers did not hear all records as acousmatic miracles, that in order to be satisfied that the voice of the tenor Jean de Reszke or the baritone Victor Maurel was truly available to them, the recorded voice first had to be authenticated. We could also read the autographs on the records as means of orienting the listener toward the sound. To believe in the Fonotipia venture, to hear a recording as faithful to the "live event," the listener had to discriminate between sounds—to hear some as the "real" music and others as mere sounds of mediation. Above all, listeners had to filter out the invasive sounds of the recording mechanism.[54] Reassurance that the real voice of someone famous was available to them facilitated this conceptual purification of the sound. Those autographs, in other words, encouraged a form of sonic discrimination that was central to modern listening practices.[55]

Besides the infamous noise of the mechanism on records, the listener also had to contend with the fact that recorded sound was more direct than most listeners would be used to. This was, after all, the era of acoustic recording. In order for the recording horn to capture sound, musicians would have had to lean into it to ensure their sound was funneled into its bore. The acoustic trace of the room in these circumstances would have been almost nonexistent, since sound would have had limited opportunity to bounce around the room. It was not until the advent of electric recording that the ambient trace of the room—its acoustic signature—was written into the record's grooves.[56]

So, the commissioners at La Scala, carefully testing to control the acoustic dimension of a live performance, and the engineers a few blocks away at the Fonotipia studios, working with new reproductive technologies, were engaged in roughly the same project: zeroing in on a sound shorn of mediation. There are further parallels between these two commercial ventures. Calls for greater access to opera across social classes had been made from various quarters since the Risorgimento, and with even more insistence at the outset of the 1900s, when articulation of liberal and socialist ideals forced institutions such as La Scala to demonstrate their commitment to a diverse audience. Gradually opera houses were modified to increase available seating, and audiences started to be crammed in; as we saw, at La Scala a 1906 contract committed the theater's directors to ripping out entire rows of seats to make space for more compact seating, to be offered at lower prices.[57] These crowded conditions must, in turn, have created demand for a sound that reached the back of a packed auditorium, one more clear and immediate than before: the sort of sound, in other words, that could be fashioned in an orchestra chamber. Our examination of the lowered orchestra in Italy thus serves as a reminder that acoustical practices are often shaped by historical contingencies, ones that are themselves based in political priorities such as access. The case of the La Scala orchestra chamber also suggests new continuities in the musical landscape. It was not just the recording studio that erected a barrier between musician and listener in order to allow music to reach a wider audience; in the teatro all'italiana too, sound became more than ever the link between musicians and their distant audience.

We cannot overlook the fact, however, that access was an intricate proposition. It was, of course, the fantasy of absolute sonic access—of the sound of the orator delivered to each member of the demos, or the reach of music to all members of the audience—that drove so much architectural modification over the centuries. What modern acoustics contributed was a detailed understanding of the actions architectural acousticians needed to take to achieve their desired sound. If direct sound was conducive to clear transmission, then direct sound, within limits, could be achieved. But sonic access was also a notion that had a fatal contradiction at its core. Pure sound that roams free and unhindered in the outdoors, the sound Favaro described, did not and never had existed. As Favaro was well aware, variations in air pressure have to meet a listener for sound to be created: at least one body must intervene in his theoretical landscape. To deliver sound to the masses, however, bodies intrude at all turns. Once more Favaro understood as much. In his words: "It is certain that, even allowing for perfect silence on the part of the audience, those closest to [the source of the sound] will themselves be a material obstacle, limiting the propagation of sound waves. The irregular surface of their heads is far from conducive to the proper transmission of sound. Finally, we must factor in that impurities in the air and differences in its temperature caused by the breathing of the crowd and the heat their bodies emit must also have an influence [on who can hear what]."[58]

Favaro here conceives of bodies in fluid connection with their environment: even when bodies do not come into contact with the vibration of air, the accumulation of their thermal waste can redirect its motion from afar. Perhaps more radical for the time is the notion that listeners cannot ever simply hear—that to listen is also to consume, to remove vibrations from circulation, to absorb these into one's flesh, and thus to diminish what remains for fellow listeners. In other words, as acoustical control and access became more attainable than ever, rivals to that control—not least bodies and their voracious appetites—came into full focus. Little wonder that the natural sound created in the open air—the sound that roams free and encounters no obstacles, the sound of a core and originary plenitude—assumed such elevated status around this time. To be alone with one's sound in the orchestra chamber, or to sit in the audience and connect with the "natural" sound of the orchestra, could never be more than an ideal. But situated as it was just out of reach, it was an ideal that now soared in value.

FIVE

Thresholds

In a famous scene from Leroux's novel *Le fantôme de l'Opéra*, a chandelier at the center of a nineteenth-century teatro all'italiana auditorium comes loose.[1] Moments earlier the harried theater directors had heard a voice—also on the loose—warn them that the vocalist that evening would "bring the chandelier down." That "impossible [mouthless] voice" had apprised the directors while they were seated in box 5.[2] Unable to locate the source of the voice, the directors turn to the center of the auditorium. There, the vast fixture accumulates tremendous force: "The chandelier, the enormous mass of the chandelier, was moving, slipping downwards.... Unhooked, it plummeted down from the very top of the house, crashing into the middle of the stalls, amidst a thousand screams. Terror struck, followed by a general stampede."[3] Once the chandelier has traversed the massive vertical dimensions of this auditorium, what can remain but debris? This is no conventional scene of destruction, however—we do not learn about discarded items or overturned seats. Instead, we read: "The chandelier . . . crashed upon the head of a poor woman who had come to the Opera that evening for the very first time in her life, and killed her instantly.... The next day, one of the headlines read 'Two hundred thousand kilos hits concierge!' That was her sole obituary!"[4] First, the chandelier eliminates a woman; next, she is all but obliterated from the historical record. Her double murder can be understood in relation to her vulnerable social status: at the time the novel was set—the 1880s—it was not unusual for lower-class female laborers to be extended limited discursive afterlives, no matter how sensational their deaths.[5] But in this context, the second blow also reads as a function of the chandelier's descent itself, as if little else could survive once it had amassed force and delivered its fatal strike.

I start here in free fall, with the descent of a chandelier, because the scene serves as a touchstone, not only for the novel, but also for the theme of this chapter. Revealing a pronounced obsession with the vertical extensions of the teatro all'italiana, this novel dramatizes the idea of boundaries within these theaters and highlights the stakes involved in movement across their thresholds. As such, the novel is a testament to new realities at actual teatri all'italiana in the later nineteenth century, when the tallest theaters were also ones that saw an extreme proliferation in the number of thresholds these contained. I introduce all this in the section that follows. With a continued focus on *Le fantôme de l'Opéra*, I examine the circumstances under which teatri all'italiana started to contain more walls, doors, and other architectural boundaries than ever before and outline how such threshold boundaries were accomplished. In the second and third sections, I leave *Le fantôme de l'Opéra* behind as I consider the networks that enabled the erection of teatri all'italiana and all those boundaries within them, and move toward a theorization of thresholds at teatri all'italiana that foregrounds their ethical dimensions. Across these three distinct sections, one architectural material will prove pivotal: structural metal.

Ethics of Boundaries

The theater in which the chandelier falls is almost the sole setting within the novel: one enormous, and markedly vertical, crime scene whose architectural details come into focus across the story. Indeed, we are introduced to the various levels and areas of the theater with each new chapter as *Le fantôme de l'Opéra* narrates the tale of a man who aims to enchant a soprano. When this fails, he abducts her, releases her, then ensures that she continues to return to his lair, using the threat that if she does not, those close to her will be harmed. The abductor, Erik, has unusual command of the area beneath the theater, where he has built a home for himself on the far side of an underground lake. His victim, Christine, fears the lower levels of the theater as well as the trap doors that could land her there. But if lower extremes are thematized, so too are their complement. For much of the novel the main characters move between these extremes with relative abandon; the theater becomes a site of wonder and enchantment. This freedom is most marked around the middle of the novel, when Christine and her childhood-friend-turned-lover Raoul spend a month at the theater, their ecstatic love articulated in relation to the restlessness with which they ascend and descend stairs, run with breathless momentum across thresholds, and in the end find themselves atop the building on a roof as limitless as their mutual love. This roof functions as the ultimate dreamlike space, the destination where Christine and Raoul feel most liberated:

> Christine clasped Raoul's hands, gripping them with intense fervor. But soon her anxiety returned. "Higher! Higher still!" was all she said as she led him onward.
> He could hardly keep up with her. They were soon under the eaves, in a maze of timber-work. They slipped through the buttresses, the rafters, the braces, the joists and the partitions; they ran from beam to beam as if from tree to tree in a fantastic forest.
> [...]
> Thus they reached the roof.
> Light and easy, Christine glided over it like a swallow. Their eyes surveyed the open view between the three domes and the triangular pediment. Christine took a long, deep breath as she stood high above the city and gazed down at the busy valleys beneath her. She looked at Raoul confidently. She called him to her side, and together they took a walk along streets made of zinc and avenues cast in iron; they watched their twin reflections in the still water of the huge tanks into which, in the summer months, a score of little boys from the ballet school jumped and learned to swim. The shadow that had followed them still clung to their heels, lying low to the roof, reaching with its black wings over the metal crossroads, stealing by the tanks, skirting silently round the domes; but the trusting young lovers suspected nothing when at last they sat down under the mighty protection of Apollo thrusting his monumental lyre against the crimson sky with bronze grandeur.
> It was a beautiful sunset ablaze with the colors of spring. Clouds, lightly clad in gold and purple by the setting sun, drifted slowly by.[6]

At this point, Christine confesses to Raoul that she had been abducted several times in recent months, and here she determines she must flee with Raoul. Their chosen destination is the North Pole. If deliverance can come in various forms, in this instance it would come through vertical movement over the Earth's surface. In her most severe crisis, Christine channels a primal dream: a dream to soar.[7]

More than the sensationalist and second-rate novel this is sometimes said to be, *Le fantôme de l'Opéra* is a subtle testament to the notion that vertical extensions can induce wonder, and that to ascend can be breathtaking.[8] The novel reminds us, moreover, that architecture is one of the most basic means to induce such sensations. Our core means of human-made ascent—architectural structures—reveal an obsession with elevation. For instance, sacred sites are often locations in which one can stand with feet planted on a stone floor and attention directed toward a vaulted—and celestially themed—ceiling, sites in which one is conscious of the terrain below and the skies above, attuned to oneself on a vertical axis. The considerable volume of air within them stimulates dreams of ascent, all the more so because to talk or otherwise make sound in such spaces sensitizes the speaker to the outer reaches of the structure: the echo of their voice containing within it information about the enormousness of the built environment. In the absence of outsized dimensions in a room, echo is, after all, rare. But that returned voice also activates a fascination with the aerial. Echo confirms the speaker's presence and almost immediately undermines that confirmation, since the returned voice becomes fainter with each successive echo. As presence dematerializes, it can almost seem that the bearer of the voice has themselves soared toward the outer reaches of the structure, become aeriform, been absorbed into them.

Such sacred architectures privilege a theology of soul over matter, of souls that soar. But most tall built environments induce a similar sense of wonder at the vertical. One fundamental claim of this chapter is that this is also true for the teatro all'italiana—indeed, it is no coincidence that a novel set at a teatro all'italiana would limn the vertical in such detail. As Eugene J. Johnson has most comprehensively demonstrated, the forerunners to the teatro all'italiana took various forms, their construction a tale of endless permutations of seating arrangements made possible by architects' exploitation of the full vertical and horizontal extensions of a theater with inclined floors, risers, steps and balconies.[9] It is also no coincidence that the two earliest theaters to feature boxes—both built in 1580 for commedia dell'arte—were the Tron and Michiel theaters in Venice.[10] Erected within an existing built environment (now obliterated and untraceable), these theaters featured multiple levels of superimposed boxes in order, one presumes, to commodify the skies: as Johnson remarks, in a location "restricted to islands surrounded by water... stacking people up in tiers of boxes fetched a greater return from a small piece of real estate, just as skyscraper office buildings did in late-nineteenth-century America."[11] With the evolution of teatri all'italiana built for opera, these structures continued to be stretched vertically and to soar within their landscapes. Even in the nineteenth century, when, as we shall see, it became easier to erect tall built environments, these remained some of the tallest structures around, and ones in which thresholds proliferated.

These theaters too were sites where dreams of ascent were nourished. True, teatri all'italiana were stretched on the vertical axis to ensure they could accommodate hundreds, sometimes thousands, of audience members. But interest in the vertical extensions of a theater was more than a means to cash in on seat sales. Whenever the skies were commodified, there was an attendant poetics involved. The vertical extensions of teatri all'italiana allowed them to become rarefied environments in which their inhabitants were sensitized to their upper reaches. As seen in chapter 1, a Mantuan theater built *ex novo* for drama in 1501 featured a turquoise cloth "starred with those signs which that very evening were appearing in [the] hemisphere" pinned across the ceiling.[12] The most common decorative scheme for ceilings at teatri all'italiana over time has, meanwhile, been a broad, painted sky—a vision of the air to counterbalance the closed architectural form of the auditorium, an opening in an otherwise windowless built environment.[13] In the nineteenth century skies sometimes ceded to fields, Arcadias in the heavens that induced similar sensations. That these decorations were meant to be noticed is evidenced from the fact that the changes to their contours over time track conventions about where the most important seats within the theater were located. In the 1600s it was the second- or third-tier boxes that were most desirable—above all the main box opposite the stage, the so-called royal box. But in the 1800s at some theaters, the orchestra stalls started to become at least as desirable. That corresponded with a shift from ceiling decoration that was best seen as a sequence of images from the rear of the theater facing forward to more circular decoration that was best viewed from below, within the orchestra stalls.[14] In fact, it was common from the nineteenth century onward for there to be a single chandelier positioned at the center of this circular decoration—a chandelier that could be lowered and raised, thus drawing attention to the vertical dimension of the theater, a chandelier that shone like a sun at the center of the cosmos inscribed around it.[15]

If *Le fantôme de l'Opéra* documents wonder at the vertical extensions of the built environment of the teatro all'italiana, it is crucial to understand that it did this at a moment when new construction methods meant teatri all'italiana had become taller and more intricate than ever before. Indeed, as the narrator tells us, the crime scene is not an unnamed opera house, but rather the Palais Garnier in Paris—the real-life new home of the Paris Opéra, built, as we have seen, between 1861 and 1875 under the architect Charles Garnier.[16] The narrator is cast as a detective, solving mysteries that occurred in the 1880s at the Palais Garnier: how Christine was abducted, who was to blame, and how this was connected to various other incidents such as the death of the chief machinist, found hanging in the third-floor cellar at the outset of the novel. The chandelier incident did, in fact, occur—or at least, an equivalent tragedy took place, in which a counterweight from the ventilation system fell and killed a working-class woman on her first visit to the Opéra.[17] Although the rest of the events are fiction, the documentary bases for the narrator's deductions of these crimes blur the boundaries between the fictional and nonfictional: among his "forensic files" are the actual architectural treatises of Garnier: *Le théâtre* and *Le nouvel Opéra de Paris*.[18] The theater in the novel is, moreover, modeled on the real theater, a fact the narrator is keen to emphasize. The vast structure of the actual Palais Garnier stretched over an unprecedented seventeen stories, of which five were under the theater, and was built above a subterranean section of the Seine—discovered when builders started work—that needed to be contained within a double encasement to allow construction to continue.[19] However insulated the eventual theater was from this reservoir, it became lore that a lake nonetheless beat at its foundation. In this sense, the Palais Garnier was said to extend into a much deeper unknown, one that Leroux did not fail to feature.

It was structural metal that enabled the Palais Garnier to exceed the vertical stretch of all the theaters that preceded it.[20] Structural iron had been used in limited scenarios as a construction material even in the 1700s, but cost and constructional conservatism had contained its uses. Around the mid-nineteenth century advances in manufacture combined with more permissive legislative environments made its constructional use more common, including its more routine use in teatri all'italiana.[21] Its most important use, at theaters as elsewhere, was to enable frame construction, an alternative to foundational and structural support derived from timber, or from blocks bound with mortar, such as marble, brick, or limestone. In these older construction methods, walls had been essential, and as a result, they had both to extend in a line from the foundations to the roof (so that the foundations could bear the entire structural load) and to be thickest closest to the foundations. When walls were compromised—as occurred whenever there were windows or doors—they became vulnerable to collapse; thus, as more stories were amassed above the foundation, more vulnerabilities were introduced. These built environments could still soar into the skies, but as the airiness of the cathedral demonstrates, the tallest tended to reach their height in the absence of numerous load-bearing stories. Even now, houses and commercial buildings erected with these construction methods tend to be limited to ten to twelve load-bearing stories. What such construction methods cannot sustain are structures that stretch into the skies with endless habitable stories, like modern towers of Babel.[22]

In contrast, frame construction boasted some notable affordances. For one, metal frames could bear so much load that far more stories were viable than with older construction methods. This would lead to the construction, starting in the late nineteenth century, of "skyscrapers," structures that had been previously inconceivable. The new proliferation of tall, multistory structures within the landscape also induced wonder; indeed, when Leroux made the roof the ultimate dreamlike zone in *Le fantôme de l'Opéra*, he inserted it into a nexus of novels that had celebrated roofs as sites of liberation and construed the freedom they allowed as a direct function of their vertical separation from the world below.[23] That freedom was also a function of the structural metal that lined them; this made them more secure underfoot and enabled them to function as a second terrain beneath the clouds. Such ideas were prominent tropes in the novels of Émile Zola, for instance, as in *Au bonheur des dames*, the 1883 novel set in a department store, which I discussed in chapter 3. It is on the metal-lined roof of this cathedral of commerce that the heroine, Denise, meets her friend Deloche. Writes Zola: "Below them, beneath the colossal iron framework, there was the roar of the buying and selling in the silk department, the reverberation of the machine at work, the whole shop vibrating with the trampling of the crowd, the bustle of salesmen, the life of the thirty thousand people patched together there; but, carried away by their dreams, they felt this deep, muffled roar with which the roofs were resounding, and thought they were listening to the wind from the sea blowing over the pastures, shaking the tall trees as it went."[24] The oxidation of the metal sheets must have contributed to the characters' visions of green pastures in Zola. But for both Leroux and Zola, these metal sheets also offered a terra firma on which characters could reinvent themselves; or as Peter Sealy has put it, a "clearing—a large void both in the city and in the novel where a dream [could] materialize."[25]

If structural metals enabled tall structures to be built that bore more load and housed more stories than ever before, they also allowed a much more flexible distribution of walls, windows, doors, and other partitions. Once metal frames could bear the entire structural load, walls could be removed, cut into, or otherwise "compromised" without risk to the structure. Internal walls could therefore be used to divide space on one floor but not another, and external walls could contain vast windows. At teatri all'italiana built with structural metals, what this all amounted to was a new freedom in the location, nature, and number of thresholds.

To state one of the main claims of this section: although on the surface *Le fantôme de l'Opéra* may appear obsessed with the vertical extensions of the Palais Garnier, the novel can be understood more fully as a critical reaction to the new abundance of thresholds at the teatro all'italiana. Thresholds in the novel abound, are thematized at each narrative turn. The reader is repeatedly reminded that walls, doors, and other thresholds control the movement of bodies and create unevenness in what can be heard, seen, or otherwise felt. In this sense, and to make a bolder claim, *Le fantôme de l'Opéra* can be read as a novel invested in an ethics of the threshold at the teatro all'italiana.[26]

Much of this unevenness is familiar to all who have entered a teatro all'italiana, an architectural form structured around the invisible but inviolable fourth wall. The SS. Giovanni e Paolo, the first theater built *ex novo* for operatic performance, did not fail to include this division: a proscenium arch divided the main room into an auditorium on one side and a stage on the other. It therefore demarcated zones where experiences were meant to differ, zones exclusive to either audience or performer. And that other characteristic feature of teatri all'italiana, their tiers of stacked boxes, has also been used variously to create hierarchies of experience. At the Teatro di Baldracca in Florence, completed in 1576—the forerunner to the teatro all'italiana discussed in chapter 1—individuals in the Medici circles had keys to the boxlike stanzini that could be accessed via a secret corridor to ensure that those individuals did not have to encounter the wider, and less aristocratic, audience.[27] Six decades later, boxes at the SS. Giovanni e Paolo would also have been accessible via individual doors, albeit without a secret corridor. These boxes too functioned as intimate, domestic spaces within an otherwise public realm. This remains their function even if the domestic dimension has been eroded: nowadays individual ticket holders at teatri all'italiana are seated in sometimes awkward proximity to strangers.

Such unevenness in what can be heard, seen, or otherwise felt reaches extreme levels in *Le fantôme de l'Opéra*. Architecture creates the conditions under which secrets are held, crimes are committed, and freedoms are eroded. The initial momentum in the novel comes from the fact that senses seem to fail some characters: they hear a voice but are unable to see its owners; they see a tin has moved but are unable to see the moment at which it moved. Although the novel starts with the words "The Phantom of the Opera did exist.... Yes, he did exist in flesh and blood, although he assumed in every respect the appearance of a ghost," the reader is induced to believe that the paranormal is at work.[28] But as the author describes the sheer intricateness of the theater, the thousands of locked doors, the endless thresholds, it starts to make intuitive sense that in a structure this complex it would be possible to move around undetected. That the narrator's files are dense with architectural detail is the first clue that the theater is instrumental in the crimes described. The clearest indication that architecture holds the truth to the tale, however, is that Christine's abductor is a stonemason who built the theater with his own hands. He knows the built environment in practice, the details of its structure that are not even provided on its blueprints, the hollows and thicknesses—or what architects would call *pochés*—that characterize its walls.[29] Although most stonemasons are evicted the moment their work is done, ours has remained in a structure over which he has no formal claim but ultimate knowledge.

Architecture, moreover, colludes with the abductor. As we have seen, the theater shelters him, conceals his crimes. What is more, for months before Christine is abducted, a voice enchants her from behind a mirror as it coaches her, demonstrating how to execute arias with absolute vocal command. As Christine stares into the mirror, her own reflection becomes fused with the voice of her mentor. Well before she is abducted, in other words, Christine is trained to understand herself as an extension of her abductor. There is an obvious Lacanian interpretation to be made here—that the mirror becomes the device across which Christine manufactures a sense of self, and that, as all humans must, she turns initial alienation at her reflection into a cohesive ideal.[30] But a more subtle reading emerges from the architecture. The mirror turns out to be a literal threshold, one side of a revolving door (a recent fashionable architectural addition in Paris).[31] And it is the threshold across which Christine will be abducted: in the tenth chapter the mirror revolves to reveal a blank architectural space, a chasm, into which she disappears.[32] Before the mirror's status as threshold ever becomes clear, however, Christine has surrendered herself to the abductor via this reflective architecture.

Thresholds, the novel insists, can be tricky. Christine is vulnerable not to some dark and substanceless force, but to the real surfaces and walls around her. Her abduction is an act of consumption: the mirrored wall reaches out and takes her. This is no small matter. As Thomas Oles has said, walls and other thresholds "work [themselves] into the fabric of life around [them]"; these naturalize rules about access.[33] If this moment in the novel dramatizes an ethics of the threshold—a situation in which architectures work more in favor of some than of others—such architectural work is missed much of the time. Should *Le fantôme de l'Opéra* be able to issue lessons to us across the distance of more than eleven decades, the lesson here is that such partitioning abounds within teatri all'italiana. And these divisions can have profound consequences.

This is the theme in what follows here. Much as an entire world rumbled beneath Denis and Deloche—a world with a distinctive industrial roar, facilitated by structural metals—a whole world rumbled within and around teatri all'italiana once structural metals were used to build them, one with its own distinctive contours. This is, however, a fact almost never examined, not least because, as we shall see, in most cases structural metals were hidden beneath stone facades and curated interior architecture. Yet the worlds those metals created had profound ramifications. In the remainder of this chapter, I focus on how thresholds and their ethics shift at teatri all'italiana with the introduction of structural metals. For one, structural metals lent untold momentum to the creation of a theatrical infrastructure, since these made the construction of teatri all'italiana faster and cheaper, not least in locations where it would otherwise have been inconceivable to build them. But as the construction of teatri all'italiana boomed and monumental external theater walls were erected in all these locations, the cost of all this building to lives and livelihoods was magnified. I unpack the role of structural metal in two parts. First, I consider the human and material realities of all this new construction; then, with a focus on Milan's Teatro alla Scala, I consider how, upon their introduction into the teatro all'italiana, these structural metals altered how one could move through the operatic space.

Colonial Metal

We need first to rewind and consider how these structural metals—first iron and then steel—came to be. For centuries, a compound had been extracted from sediment and oxidized to create iron. Inventions in the late 1700s increased both the amount that could be created and the individual masses into which it could be molded. Around the 1860s, further inventions enabled the mass manufacture of steel. Accelerating all of this was the use of steam power.[34]

Metal was soon used to reorder how one could move around the Earth—to fashion vessels that traveled the oceans and railroads that cut across the land. Those countries that dominated iron and steel manufacture would use these materials to control formal and informal colonies, to have access to, control movement within, and extract wealth from them. But if colonialism is founded on nonchalance about the Earth, the minerals, beneath us—if it allows the foundations under us to crumble in order to facilitate movement on vessels and railroads—this is all in the name of entrenchment. To channel the words of Paul Carter in *The Lie of the Land*, it is a curious contradiction that the most colonially aggressive of cultures—and thus the most nomadic, in a certain sense—were also the most obsessed with foundations, with the antithesis of movement.[35] As soon as structural iron started to be used in architectural contexts, colonizers used this same material dug out of the Earth to create built environments in those colonies.[36]

Much of this construction occurred with haste. There was considerable demand in the middle of the nineteenth century for iron homes that could be assembled within hours of arrival at their destination, homes that could traverse the oceans unassembled and be erected with relative ease. These modular homes featured individual iron sections that were combinable and recombinable with bolts alone, that could be assembled "like a bedstead," drawing on limited construction know-how. With windows that locked and doors that bolted, these quick builds allowed colonizers to establish their own familiar foundations in new lands, to have a consummate sense of home.[37] Such was, for instance, the case in 1850s Melbourne, where the iron home became a pervasive marker of new settlements.[38]

Critically, it also became faster to construct teatri all'italiana once structural metals were used to create their frames. Much as modular structures relied on combinable sections assembled into one, these theaters' frames—if not the facades built over their frames—were also formed from standardized iron beams, columns, and trusses that were mass manufactured, then assembled in short order at their destination.[39] As this theatrical infrastructure stretched outward, all these theatrical architectural skins announced a particular set of sensibilities. Relevant here is an exhibition at the 1889 Paris Exposition Universelle, "Histoire de l'habitation humaine," which was entrusted to none other than Garnier himself alongside a collaborator, Auguste Ammann. Located on the Champ de Mars, Garnier and Ammann reconstructed a series of homes from various eras and locations. The visitor was meant to walk northeast in a line from the crudest to the most modern, from the houses of cultures that "stood outside time"—mud huts in Africa, for instance, which the exhibit insisted had remained the same for centuries—to the domiciles that the "Aryan races" had themselves constructed centuries earlier, to those built by these same "races" in modern times. As the visitor walked toward this "brilliant" future, one material came to predominate over all others: stone.

This was a metaphorical embodiment of praise for the teatro all'italiana style, for most such theaters used monumental, polished blocks of stone for their facades. Although metals could be used for both frame and facade, the architects of most built environments in the nineteenth century believed that metal facades lacked the command of stone ones. Those who shared in this sentiment included Gottfried Semper, architect of the unrealized Munich Festspielhaus, for whom metals lacked a sense of the monumental and were thus unsuitable as architectural skins.[40] And while the Garnier and Ammann exhibit culminated with the ultimate monument to structural metal at the time—the Eiffel

Tower, located at the end of the Champ de Mars, and constructed for the exposition—the decorative virtues of structural metals were neglected in the exposition's commemorative books.[41] This was unsurprising, since Garnier's own architectural aesthetic minimized metal. He even wrote a verse to mock the tower in advance of its construction:

> Yes, it will be of a splendid beauty,
> This funnel planted on a great bottom,
> And when everyone sees the pyramid,
> Everyone will say: how it's full of taste!
> Because in the world
> No other has laid
> Such a mess
> Of trellised girders.[42]

The stone used for these theaters often rendered them conspicuous within their immediate environments, as at the Teatro Amazonas in Manaus, Brazil. Constructed in the 1890s, this stone-faced theater loomed over the shorter built environments around it, ones made from local materials including straw, paxiúba palm, and other native woods.[43] The stone of its facade also communicated racialized values. For Garnier and Ammann, stone was much more than a silent material that had been used over the centuries; Frantz Jourdain, author of the book issued to commemorate the exhibit, elevated the material to a substance that could articulate a truth of its own. "Architecture ha[s] written the history of humanity in indelible characters," Jourdain wrote, adding, "there is no book more endearing, in its sincere sincerity, than these poems of stone, granite and marble."[44] Alone in its abilities to narrate the beauties of the human condition, stone was a marker of elevated culture.[45]

These stone facades also commanded attention because they channeled architectural traditions associated at the time with whiteness. Most teatri all'italiana had neoclassical facades that used ratios common to the architecture of ancient Greece and Rome; Piermarini's facade for La Scala, too, was in this sense a model for construction elsewhere (fig. 5.1). These neoclassical facades were themselves laden with racialized values, all the more so when built in locations without such classical or neoclassical architectural traditions—as occurred when a teatro all'italiana was constructed in Bombay in 1912 and became another architectural marker of colonial presence there.[46] Theaters that broke with the neoclassical tradition were uncommon, but one notable example—the Palais Garnier, at which stone was made to dance outward from exterior walls in ornamental patterns—also insinuated itself

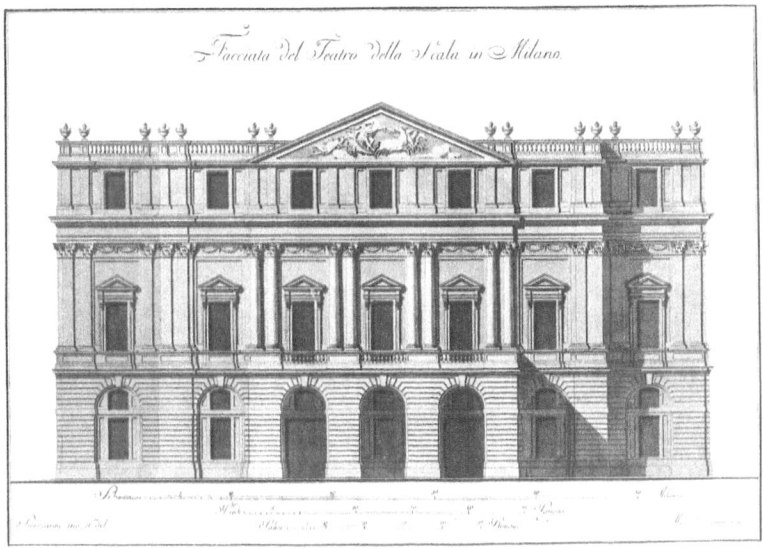

FIGURE 5.1. Drawing of the exterior architecture of the facade of the Teatro alla Scala in Milan, realized by architect Giuseppe Piermarini. The History Collection / Alamy Stock Photo.

into remote built environments, as when it became a model for Rio de Janeiro's Theatro Municipal, built in 1909 (figs. 5.2 and 5.3).[47]

To reiterate a central claim of the book: accounts that focus on the subliminal lessons encoded in opera overlook the fact that much less subtle lessons about who we are and how we relate to one another are internalized—and indeed naturalized—before a single note has sounded. To behold a teatro all'italiana even from a distance is to absorb lessons about which materials are valuable and which not, which architectural forms are valuable and which not, which cultures are valuable and which not. Such lessons can be understood from the theater's surface; no elaborate hermeneutics is called for. Moreover, they are lessons that exert a disproportionate influence on everyone.[48]

Harder to discern, when one beholds these theaters, is how their materials came to be assembled there, what chains of labor were involved. These details are nonetheless critical. Consider once more the Teatro Amazonas. Familiar to opera scholars as the theater that Jürgen Osterhammel drew attention to in *The Transformation of the World: A Global History of the Nineteenth Century*, this teatro all'italiana stands in his account as a venue where the riches of the world accumulated and, as such, where the forces of globalization can be seen in concentrated form.[49] For instance, the theater featured candlesticks from Murano, Italy; marble

FIGURE 5.2. Photograph of the Palais Garnier facade, August 15, 1867. Magite Historic / Alamy Stock Photo.

FIGURE 5.3. Photograph of the Theatro Municipal, Rio de Janeiro, c. 1909–15. In anon., *Theatro municipal do Rio de Janeiro*, 11. Public domain / Instituto Moreira Salles Collection.

from Carrara, Italy; and construction materials from Glasgow, Scotland, facts all the more remarkable because Manaus was situated some eight hundred miles inland from the Atlantic Coast, hundreds of miles into the Amazon rainforest, and was accessible only via the Amazon River. It was steel that enabled all this movement: in the 1860s, it started to be mass manufactured and to displace iron, since it cost less, weighed less, and was malleable, and yet had more tensile strength.[50] It became a crucial component in intercontinental steamboats, used for their hulls and propellers, and cut the transatlantic crossing time in half.[51] The use of iron and metal in steamboats on the Amazon River also made those waters more navigable: whereas in 1819 it took some three months to traverse the stretch from the coast to Manaus, in the 1860s the same route took, remarkably, less than a week.[52] Among the materials transported to Manaus were steel beams, trusses, and girders from Glasgow.[53] Although this theater was not the first in Manaus to host opera, it was likely the first constructed with structural metal.[54] In contrast with the Teatro Beneficente Portuguesa, built in 1875 from timber and clay, the Teatro Amazonas still stands; unable to withstand the local climate, the Beneficente Portuguesa was riddled with termites and rot within a decade.[55]

The construction of the Teatro Amazonas is one small instance in which steel was traded in the name of material dominance. So tilted was the iron and steel trade toward extraction of wealth from formal and informal colonies that in the later nineteenth century it cost less to move iron from British ports to India or Australia than on railroads to London.[56] For a time, Britain sold its steel primarily to South America, and between 1873 and 1889 Britain exported more iron and steel to South America than to China, Japan, South Africa, Australia, Canada, and India combined. Manaus even had a direct connection to Liverpool through the establishment of a shipping line between the two cities in the 1870s.[57] The riches of the world accumulated at the Teatro Amazonas, but this accumulation served as a mechanism for further riches to accumulate in remote destinations such as Europe.

The Teatro Amazonas ceased all operatic activities within a decade, resuming only in the 1990s. But the splendor of that initial decade is the theme of Werner Herzog's 1982 film *Fitzcarraldo* (albeit transposed to some time at the start of the 1900s).[58] An Irishman whose name is rebranded when he reaches South America, Fitzcarraldo is obsessed with the wealth he can accumulate from the rainforest, all because he wants to recreate the Teatro Amazonas deeper within the rainforest, in Iquitos, Peru. He tried to make his fortune with steel before the start of the film, when he invested in the failed Trans-Andean railroad. Remnants of the tracks remain in the rainforest; on one excursion Fitzcarraldo rips the tracks from the ground to repurpose them as the locals whose livelihoods depended on the railroads watch their future being torn up. In order to fuel a veritable obsession with Italian opera—above all the voice of Enrico Caruso—he needs to make his fortune by another means. The scale of the obsession becomes clear when he ascends a church tower in Iquitos, pulls on the bell ropes, and declares, "This church remains closed till this town has its opera house," then shouting "I want my opera house!" over and over.

Fitzcarraldo's new venture involves not steel but rubber. He wants to access an area of rainforest removed from the main river in order to extract natural rubber from trees. The extremes to which he will go to turn wealth from the rainforest into funds for his Teatro Amazonas become clear in an extended sequence. To extract the rubber, he takes a (steel-lined) steamboat toward an isthmus leading to a more remote branch of the river. With a mixed crew of Indigenous people and Europeans, he sails toward the mountainous isthmus with the aim of hauling the vessel over it. But this boat is not modular. It stands firm with all its ponderous heft, creaking and straining with each torturous effort to shift it. As hundreds of Indigenous people inch the boat over the mountain, they are abused in the name of this curious dream; some are even crushed between the hull and the mud in which the boat is mired.

With an eccentric main character who puts everything on the line to hear Caruso in the rainforest, this film could seem to be a testament to the strange manner opera can move individuals. But there's more to it. Fitzcarraldo drives home the colonial ethics that I emphasize here: that in order for opera to move us, we must move the Earth for opera.[59] The Teatro Amazonas featured at the start of the film did of course exist; Caruso did come to the Amazon—to the Teatro Amazonas, even; there was a Fitzcarraldo who ordered workers to disassemble a steamboat in order to access the waters across an isthmus in the name of rubber extraction. But the most notable detail here is that, much as wealth from rubber would have funded the theater in Iquitos, this same wealth was used to build the Teatro Amazonas in Manaus. With an 1839 invention that enabled natural rubber to be vulcanized, a host of new uses was created for the substance, particularly in the arenas of medicine (latex production) and transportation (tire manufacture). In the nineteenth century more rubber was sourced from the Amazon than anywhere else in the world. And with this export came both an enormous flow of wealth into cities such as Manaus and an invasive flow of Europeans.[60]

This rubber extraction involved atrocities on an incredible scale: torture, murder, and slave labor were all commonplace. When the British consul Roger Casement was sent by his government to investigate the activities of the Peruvian Amazon Company, he wrote in his diary, "The world thinks the slave trade was killed a century ago! [But] the dwindling remnant of a population once numbering millions is now perishing at the doors of an English company, under the lash, the chains, the bullet, the machete to give its shareholders a dividend."[61] It was the shameful actions of another Englishman that redirected the rubber trade and (entirely inadvertently) saved what was left of those Indigenous populations. The biothief Henry Wickham had removed rubber seeds from the Amazon in the 1870s and taken them to Kew Gardens in London. These were used to start British-run plantations in Southeast Asia and elsewhere that would have initial success in the 1890s.[62] As the Amazonian rubber trade crashed in reaction, lives and livelihoods were once more destroyed. In short order the Teatro Amazonas ceased its operatic activities.

In this sense, the film documents how much must be reordered to build a teatro all'italiana. If structural metals enabled the mass construction of teatri all'italiana, including in locations in which they otherwise never would have existed, the film demonstrates that construction cannot—and has not—occurred in the absence of movement; that foundations cannot—and have not—been laid without extraction, and that construction cannot—and has not—been undertaken without considerable destruction of nature and thus climate. Ultimately, however, as seen in my discussion of the cochineal trade in chapter 2, what in the end is eroded is life itself.

All this occurs before construction even starts. One might think that the Teatro Amazonas is a special case, but it is not. Although the stakes are perhaps especially vivid here, construction is bound into these sorts of transactions wherever it occurs. To that extent, to consider the mass construction of teatri all'italiana with structural steel is to reckon with an ineluctable ethics of the threshold.

Cellular Expansion

We have so far considered structural metals in relation to the construction of new teatri all'italiana. However, there is a more common scenario still: one in which metals are used to retrofit an older theater. It is notable that once fire ceased to be the main threat to a theater—and the introduction of electric illumination was all-important here—acoustics became their main liability. According to one account, those teatri all'italiana whose acoustics were deemed disastrous tended to be torn down within five decades; those that outlived this marker stood for considerable stretches of time.[63] In other words, opera houses are not destined to die: they are in fact less vulnerable to architectural obsolescence than most other built environments.[64] Indeed, it is this accumulation of older teatri all'italiana over time that has made the retrofit so common. Some broad claims can be made about these renovations.

First, renovations provide an occasion for us to be more aware than usual of the intricate and often harmful investments, financial or otherwise, made in walls. Oles remarks that "little has done more to degrade the nurturing capacities of walls in the modern landscape than their close association with property rights."[65] Even outside of a framework that establishes who owns which walls, emotional investments in them can be divisive, as seen in chapter 2. When renovations do proceed, these investments can cause considerable delays.

Second, the ethical outcomes of renovations are variable. When claims to walls are loosened such that renovations can be undertaken—as, for instance, when theater owners authorize the destruction of sections of a theater—new walls can be built that nurture social bonds; but this is not necessarily the case. Of course, teatri all'italiana are not transformed into social utopian architectures upon renovation. Nonetheless, as new, socialist ideals, for instance, began to take hold in Italy around 1900, it was common for renovations at teatri all'italiana to be undertaken with the intent of increasing overall audience volume and broadening audience constitution.[66]

Third, whenever the land around teatri all'italiana was unavailable for development, it became incumbent on architects to instead increase the buildings' vertical dimensions. This in turn increased the weight their foundations were made to bear, all of which would have been impossible without structural metals.

Fourth, even once structural steel was established on the construction scene, concerns about tall buildings abounded—though exceptions were made for artistic institutions. Around 1900, this made teatri all'italiana some of the tallest built environments around.[67]

Lastly, renovations of teatri all'italiana led to theaters that were more open and spacious, not least in the areas behind the stage. The result was more freedom of movement than ever before: flexible placement of internal walls, after all, was one of the main affordances of structural metal. Almost as soon as this was undertaken, however, the reverse also occurred: partitions were erected that could not be crossed. In this sense, structural metals at once facilitated unprecedented flows at teatri all'italiana and created hard-and-fast divisions as never before.

All this is evidenced in the renovations undertaken at the Teatro alla Scala in the early 1920s. Decisions about when to invest in renovations are delicate ones, and it was not until the formation of the Ente

TABLE 5.1. Ratio of surface area in the wings versus the stage of various teatri all'italiana

	Teatro alla Scala, Milan	Palais Garnier, Paris	Vienna Staatsoper	Covent Garden, London	Teatro Carlo Felice, Genoa	Teatro San Carlo, Naples	Teatro Massimo, Palermo
Ratio of the surface area of the wings to the stage	0.733	2.360	1.200	1.340	1.818	1.266	1.000

Source: Partial reproduction, in translation. Cesare Albertini, "La riforma del palcoscenico della 'Scala,'" in *Città di Milano* (April 30, 1919). The ratio is particularly low for the Teatro alla Scala.

Autonomo del Teatro alla Scala in 1920 under the direction of Milan's socialist mayor Emilio Caldara that the area behind the stage was reworked. As we saw in chapter 2, since 1778 the theater's boxes had been under the control of individual box owners. Before the advent of the Ente Autonomo, the civic authorities had a claim to the land on which La Scala rested, as well as the rest of the structure itself. This created numerous bureaucratic obstacles and reduced overall revenue. With the Ente Autonomo, however, control became centralized. The Ente managed the entire theater, boxes included; for any given performance, box seats were made available for purchase in accordance with market demand.[68] This rendered the theater lucrative for the first time in decades and emboldened investors to contribute funds to renovate the theater, including the chemical manufacturer Montecatini and the Società Edison Italiana.[69] The main architect was Cesare Albertini.

Promotional material describes the renovations as transformational, a consummate architectural achievement.[70] The "transformational" is not an uncommon conceit where renovation is involved, of course, and Albertini frequently utilized this term. Channeling another conceit still common to us now, the authors of the promo material also described the older structure as *condannato* (condemned), as if its destruction was deserved and unavoidable, its censure called for.[71]

In fairness, for those who labored behind the scenes, the renovations did allow them freedom to move, freedom they had been denied in the older structure, cramped and claustrophobic as it had been. For a measure of that constriction, table 5.1 is illustrative. No alteration was made to the distance between the external walls during the renovations, since the Ente Autonomo was unable to extend the theater into the surrounding land. But the renovations did involve the "condemnation" of twelve old timber pillars that had borne the load of the entire

FIGURE 5.4. View of the cramped conditions between the pillars prior to the renovations. In Marangoni and Vanbianchi, *La Scala: Studi e ricerche*, 508. Servizio Archivi Storici e Attività Museali, Politecnico di Milano, ACL.

architectural structure behind the proscenium arch (fig. 5.4). The renovations also involved the "condemnation" of the roof. Freedom came as a result of broad areas now clear of the obstruction of those pillars, where the cast, other workers, and materials could circulate with ease. It came with more overall room in which to move, with four additional meters beneath ground level and six additional meters above it. And it came with the smooth motion of four new elevators that could glide between floors, with movement across new external thresholds and ease of access to air via windows onto the street in each dressing room.[72]

All this was made possible via the insertion of steel: six concrete columns with steel at their core now bound the new structure into one, while a steel roof encased in concrete covered it. But almost as soon as the areas behind the stage were made to flow, as workers could move with freedom as never before, the reverse also occurred: other areas behind the scenes were compartmentalized. This same tension between removal and insertion of architectural boundaries had also characterized the smaller renovation discussed in chapter 4, in which an area of the theater was torn out in order to create a gallery that could accommodate more seats. This initial renovation was modest in cost, so it is possible that the renovation did not involve wholescale structural alteration and insertion of metal.[73] The area that resulted nonetheless resembled the girdered and cantilevered balconies found elsewhere, such as at the London Coliseum in St. Martin's Lane, a teatro all'italiana built in 1904 that initiated a trend for massive family-oriented variety theaters and whose three deep, curved galleries were carried across the width of the auditorium by steel girders and cantilevers.[74] Both La Scala and the Coliseum's galleries were meant to enable access to their theaters, to allow more seats to be sold, and at lower cost; as commissioners at La Scala said, the renovation would "serve to popularize—and to populate (no pun intended)—the theater," to serve a middle class for whom the theater was otherwise prohibitive most of the time.[75] These popularly oriented seating areas also necessitated new access routes for the additional audience members. In the case of La Scala, that involved the construction of a new stairwell that ran from the street to the gallery, a stairwell that then as now deliberately separated this new class of ticket holder from the rest.[76] For those who ascend that staircase, the contradictions around access are nothing if not obvious.

Similar tensions characterized the Scala renovations at the outset of the 1920s in the sense that, for all the new freedoms the renovations afforded, La Scala started to resemble the Garnier, which by some estimates had 1,942 locked doors.[77] The new area behind the stage contained a multitude of dedicated spaces for the cast and laborers: offices, dressing rooms, rooms en suite, closets, service elevators, storage cabinets, and countless other cellular spaces. The ultimate threshold, however, came in the form of a *lamiera metallica*, a metal curtain that sealed the proscenium arch closed. This structure descended when the auditorium was not in use to secure the areas on either side, blocking all movement between them.[78]

As walls, doors, and metal curtains interfered with the ease with which individuals could roam around the theater, La Scala became ever more segmented into zones dedicated to discrete activities, much as the orchestra enclosure discussed in chapter 4 had created a studio for musicians that facilitated new levels of concentration and focus. But the introduction of such discrete areas was undertaken more fundamentally in the name of the most valuable freedom there was. Structural steel was inserted into walls that divided rooms, corridors, and stairwells as a firewall. The lamiera metallica, meanwhile—at least while it was closed, when the theater was not in use and between acts—even ensured that audience and cast would not share the same air. (This is what enabled it to function as such an effective fire curtain.) In short, these hardened boundaries in the form of *muri tagliafuoco* (literally, firewalls) and the lamiera metallica forestalled the ultimate confinement, one long feared in teatri all'italiana: being encircled by flames.

There is a mundane and a poetic dimension to all this. This use of metal was sensible, but it was also potent and evocative. The teatro all'italiana is an architectural form, after all, based around a performative separation, an invisible division sometimes described as a fourth wall between the audience and the fictional world. The proscenium arch demarcates but does not enforce this division. Elements of interior architecture have lent substance to it over time: since the earliest teatri all'italiana, fabric curtains and scrims have swirled to the sides or ascended at the start of acts.[79] Other conventions have made that demarcation more immediate, even in the absence of material demarcation, such as bans on encores, which foreclosed interaction between cast and audience across the invisible threshold.[80] Not until the lamiera metallica was introduced, however, was that demarcation so literal, so hard and fast, so unnegotiable. Between acts the metal curtain became the ultimate fourth wall: a hermetic seal that set audience and cast in their own worlds, with their own atmospheres.

There is a broader point to be made here. Across a series of texts, the environmental humanities scholar Stephen J. Pyne has advanced the claim that, although the era in which we live now has been named the Anthropocene, it is marked with such an obsession with combustion, such a consummate, wholesale (though hidden) incineration of the Earth, that it is more accurate to label it the Pyrocene. Nowhere is this more evident than in the modern city. As Pyne notes, "Modern cities remain fire-driven eco-systems. Fire's . . . fuels flow as liquids and gases; its combustion occurs in special chambers and machines; its power is transmitted, often over vast distances, through electrical wires."[81] As a result, "like a strange attractor of chaos theory, fire's threat haunts every room and corridor, every multistoried building and mall, the plumbing of water mains and sprinkler systems, the wiring of alarms, the design of building exits, the siting of emergency services." In short, "shut down combustion and you shut down the modern city."[82]

And yet the open flame is almost nowhere to be seen: "Like a black hole in space, fire has shaped everything around it without itself being visible."[83] Among that which fire has invisibly shaped are the fire-resistant building materials that dominate modern construction—brick, cement, and steel—materials that "have already passed through the flame, though these be the forges and kilns of industrial pyrotechnology."[84]

These words touch on the contradictions that surround structural steel at teatri all'italiana. The narrative introduced in this final section could seem destined for a blunt conclusion: structural steel within built environments, the teatro all'italiana included, marked human triumph over the raw and devastating power of the flame. The claims Pyne makes, however, derive their force from several wrinkles to this. For one, the flames that potentially surround us are ones we humans create; it is an odd obsession with combustion that makes us so vulnerable to flames in the first place. And the very mechanisms used to forestall fires, such as steel-lined walls, are themselves marked with the flame; they are, in a sense, descended from it. In other words, what those firewalls do is protect the built environment from itself; to do this, some other location on the Earth must bear witness to the destructive forces of combustion. In the broadest sense, then, structural metals are mechanisms that both limit and facilitate movement. Like the thresholds to which they give rise, these complicate existential boundaries.

* * *

Understood in this manner, structural metals in teatri all'italiana draw attention to the contradictions that abound within their built environments as a whole. While such contradictions also characterize countless other sorts of built environments, there is something distinctive about the teatro all'italiana, about a built environment conceived to enclose nested microcosms, to hold a fictional world in addition to the microcosmic haven of the auditorium. To underscore this, we can consider one final idea. In January 2023, as this manuscript was being completed, the Royal Opera House in London ceased a thirty-three-year reliance on British Petroleum's corporate sponsorship.[85] The fiction of rarefied air at the teatro all'italiana, and the sublime music that resounds within its walls, seem to have diverted attention from this remarkable association between the fossil fuel giant and the opera house well into the twenty-first century. The Società Edison Italiana, meanwhile, both furnished La Scala with fossil fuel–derived electrical energy and has been one of its

FIGURE 5.5. Video still of promotional material for "La Scala green." Courtesy Edison. Photograph: Mario Ermoli.

foremost corporate sponsors. The 1920s renovations alone were reliant on Edison wealth. This relationship too has changed with time. In 2018 Edison and the theater made moves to rebrand their association when Edison launched "La Scala green," a sustainable initiative that claims to entirely offset the theater's carbon emissions. A 2021 video announcing this initiative is shot within the microcosm of its auditorium from the perspective of a young woman with wide, unblinking eyes. As the camera soars to the ceiling, it is not Piermarini's decoration we see, however, but a digitally constructed night sky studded with stars. A female voiceover tells us: "We first illuminated La Scala in 1883. Today, we contribute to making that illumination sustainable. Because an atmosphere with less CO_2 is a spectacle we also want to preserve" (fig. 5.5).[86] So, we return full circle to that theater in 1501 which featured a turquoise cloth with the same constellation of stars that appeared that very evening.[87] Even in 2023, the most powerful fiction one can tell about a teatro all'italiana is a bromidic, but comforting tale: that, for all the evidence to the contrary, the architecture of the teatro all'italiana is not atomized and distributed, nor are its thresholds divisive; that the teatro all'italiana truly contains a whole and wholesome world within it.

ACKNOWLEDGMENTS

Countless librarians have sustained the momentum of this book, tolerating an outlandish number of requests for materials and the confusion that sometimes arose when I returned dozens of items at once to a pandemic-safe collection bin, occasionally including my own books by mistake. Administrators at the Archivio Beni Architettonici e Paesaggio, Archivio di Stato, and Cittadella degli Archivi in Milan, in particular, as well as the Archivio Storico del Comune di Bologna, facilitated access to resources that profoundly influenced the direction of my research. Graduate assistants helped ease what often felt like an extraordinary teaching load with their contributions to class discussions and administrative support. I am especially grateful to Joseph Foster Harkins for his assistance during those lockdown semesters.

Sometimes even short conversations about the material in this book continued to resonate months later and contribute to the direction of this research. A not inconsiderable number of these were with students. Seminars related to the theme of this book in the fall of 2019 influenced me well into the lockdown that soon ensued. For this, I am thankful to Emma Barnaby, Erik Broess, Allison Brooks, Chase Castle, Flannery Cunningham, Armaghan Fakhraeirad, Sean Gower, Winnie Lai, and Ben Oyler, all PhD students at the University of Pennsylvania at the time; and Collin Ziegler, then at the Peabody Institute. Other such conversations have unfolded in the interstices of the academic day, while in line for a shuttle bus, or in the moments before a talk started at a conference. Harriet Boyd-Bennett, Shane Butler, Ian Hoffmann, Eugenio Refini, Emilio Sala, Susan Forscher Weiss, Gavin Williams, Flora Willson, and colleagues across the humanities at Johns Hopkins University have all contributed to this text. Sean Curran, Katharine Ellis, Vanessa Paloma Elbaz, Nour El Rayes, Judith Frishnan, Sarah Hibberd,

Saul Olyan, Olga Panteleeva, John Rink, Susan Rutherford, Emanuele Senici, Liz Tolbert, and Ben Walton listened to me talk about this book, directed me to sources I should have known about, and shared reactions that lent the book momentum. James Q. Davies, David Gutkin, Nicholas Mathew, Roger Parker, Danni Simon, and Anicia Timberlake read and commented on sections of the book—some several times. This book is much the better for their feedback.

I have never received an invitation to present this material that did not leave me stimulated to write more and to write better. At least someone in each audience—sometimes the entire audience—reacted with comments that truly cast the material in a new frame. For these invitations to their home institutions, and all the intellectual generosity that accompanied them, I would like to thank Mauro Calcagno at the University of Pennsylvania; Abigail Fine at the University of Oregon; Emily Frey at Brandeis University; Katherine Hambridge at Durham University; Alessandra Jones, Danni Simon, and Mary Ann Smart at the University of California, Berkeley; Alessandra Leonzini and Francesca Vella at the University of Cambridge; Gaby Spiegel at Johns Hopkins University; Andrew Talle at Northwestern University; and Claudio Vellutini at the University of British Columbia.

This book was written across unusual times—at least, unusual for me. I started the core work on it in 2018–19, while on sabbatical, and wrote most of it under lockdown. I could not have known that the sabbatical would (almost) run into lockdown. I was able to take that sabbatical thanks to a Johns Hopkins Catalyst Award; the book underwent a total transformation across that time. In 2022 I held a much shorter sabbatical as a visiting fellow at St. John's College, University of Cambridge. This was a memorable route out of lockdown; a "soft" transition back into the world, where I was able to finalize the manuscript. I am indebted to both institutions, and to all those who made the latter sabbatical smoother for our family as it expanded to include Raffaella.

I owe the smooth production of this manuscript to several people. First and foremost, Mary Ann Smart has been a tireless reader of this text; her insight and encouragement have been foundational to the realization of the book. For her wisdom and insight about the subtleties of translation of Italian sources used in this book, I am extremely grateful to Federica Deigan; as I am to Jess Herdman for the many editorial suggestions that enriched this book, as well as her artwork. I am also indebted to Barbara Norton for her excellent copy edits to the manuscript. I am thrilled that the book will be rendered open access, thanks to the generous support of the Johns Hopkins Open Access Publication Subvention.

ACKNOWLEDGMENTS

The DC Writers' Salon has been a constant across the development of the book. Much of it was written in the presence of Ali Cherry and the community of writers assembled there, most of them creative writers who balanced attendance at the salon with full-time work in unrelated fields. To cowrite in their presence was to be reminded over and over what writing looks like when enjoyment is a constitutive component of the process.

Behind this book are those who may not think of themselves in relation to the book at all, but without whom it would never have materialized in the same form.

The flautist Raffaele Trevisani is an extraordinary musician and rare mentor whose influence on me cannot be overstated. He and Paola Girardi are what led me to Milan to study the flute, and to the Casa di Riposo Giuseppe Verdi, a home in the center of Milan where, at the age of eighteen, I lived with retired musicians and a small number of music students like myself. Raffaele and Paola: Thank you.

Antonia Pròtano and Colin Biggs laid the foundations for this book. It was their decision to take me to the Metropolitan Opera in New York when I was six (no matter how out of place they felt) and their decision to allow me to eat an indecent number of Maltesers in the third act to stem the excitable chatter the event elicited in me. I have never since been able to separate out the dual pleasures of opera and chocolate (and have never tried). That both are alive to read these words is more fortunate than I can say. Both almost died because of the pandemic, Antonia twenty-four hours after the book was submitted. That she waited one last day to need resuscitating was more than considerate; I continue to be thankful for this gesture of love.

Anna and Sofia Vasilyeva are masters of celebration and some of the most infectiously joyful children I know. Raffaella Vasilyeva delivered several talks on this material with me while still in the womb; now a little over two, she banishes me from our home office so that she can sit in there and write. At the moment she believes all words either read "Raffaella" or "mamma." I hope one day she will indeed find her name amid all this text.

In 2020 I ventured out and, in the most incredibly fortuitous of circumstances, met my spouse, Mitya. Nothing has been quite the same since. This book is dedicated to him.

Portions of this book first appeared as Laura Vasilyeva, "Opera and the Built Environment," *Cambridge Opera Journal* 33, no. 1–2 (2021): 180–89, © 2021 by Cambridge University Press, reproduced with permission.

APPENDIX

The two most detailed and important letters in the chain of correspondence are reproduced here.

Letter 1

Senatore Borletti to Ettore Modigliani, October 2, 1930:

Illustre Signore e gentile amico,

Lei può essere sicuro d'aver piena la mia solidarietà e intero il mio ossequio, quali sono d'altronde imposti dalla legge, per ciò che concerne l'intangibilità dell'immobile e della sala del Teatro, in essa comprese le decorazioni. Non avrei certo osato toccarli senza le superiori autorizzazioni, in primo luogo la sua.

Il mio compito s'è limitato alle stoffe (tappezzerie, velluti, tappeti) escludendo anzi quei pochi palchi che ancora hanno qualche residuo di damasco o decorazioni degni di essere conservati per il loro valore artistico e storico.

Per le poltrone di platea non ci può essere questione: si trattava di vecchi catenacci di trent'anni fa disagevoli e sgangherati che non potevano né possono godere di apprezzamento alcuno.

Per il sediame dei palchi invece, io ho avuto lo scrupolo di sostituire le orrende ed incomode panchette con sgabelli indipendenti. . . . Si tratta di un notevole miglioramento di decoro e di comfort che non potrà che riscuotere anche il suo plauso.

Quanto alla stoffa dei palchi, il suo Architetto avrà potuto constatare che non s'è trattato di sostituire damaschi o lampassi antichi con nuovi, bensì di porre un finissimo damasco di seta, appositamente fabbricato e con disegno espressamente composto sull'intonazione stilistica della sala, là dove c'era tutto un campionario raffazzonato di tappezzerie che andavano dal damasco di seta sdruscito alla cotonina e perfino alla carta. Lei non può non riconoscere che tutto ciò sarà provvido e degno. Le vecchie tappezzerie sostituite erano state in gran parte apposte dai singoli proprietari dei palchi, senza controllo né linea alcuna in questi ultimi decenni.

Non credo che si possa preferire la preesistente condizione, anche se di nota caratteristica, come Lei la qualifica, di impossibile riproduzione d'altronde, alla nuova che, se avrà fatalmente uniformità, sarà pure, come in tutti i grandi teatri rimessi a nuovo, di gusto e nobiltà impeccabili. . . .

Io sono ognora a disposizione sua e dei suoi collaboratori per fare tutto quello che esigerà il rispetto delle ragioni supreme dell'arte, e ringrazio fin d'ora per l'aiuto che mi sarà offerto. Ma come vede il suo giustissimo e doveroso allarme non aveva forse ragione di essere.

Con cordialissimi saluti,
SENATORE BORLETTI

Illustrious gentleman and dear friend,

You can rest assured of my full commitment to respect the inviolability of the furniture and, more broadly, the interior of the auditorium at the theater, including its decor. (Such commitment is, besides, demanded of me by law). I would not indeed have dared to touch the decor without authorization from above, first and foremost yours.

The work I undertook was limited to the theater's fabrics (draperies/upholstery, velvet, carpet) to the exclusion of those few boxes which still have some residual damask, or decorations worth conserving for their artistic and historic value.

Regarding the chairs in the stalls, there can be no question: we were dealing with old clunkers from thirty years ago so uncomfortable and dilapidated that not a single one could hold any value.

As to the seating in the stalls, instead, I have taken great care to substitute the horrendous and uncomfortable benches with individual stools. . . . The result is a notable improvement in decor and comfort which cannot but occasion praise.

When it comes to the fabric in the boxes: your architect [who reported on the recent changes] could have noted that we are not dealing with the simple substitution of old [*antichi*] damask fabrics or lampas weaves with whatever new fabrics we could find. Rather, we upholstered the seats with refined silk damask, whose pattern is tailor-made to blend with the stylistic intonation of the hall. We thus replaced several fabrics that had been thrown haphazardly together, ranging from threadbare silk damask to cotton and even paper. You cannot but concede that this was provident and worthwhile. The old [*vecchie*] fabrics that were substituted were above all those put in place by single box owners, without control or coordination of the color and design used across boxes.

I do not believe you can prefer the preexisting condition to the new one even if it was characteristic and impossible to reproduce. If the new decor will inevitably have a certain uniformity, it nonetheless will be of noble and impeccable taste, as can be said of the decor of all the great theaters that have been modernized. . . .

I am ever at the service of you and your colleagues to do all that must be done to abide by the laws of art, and I hereby extend my thanks for the help you have thus far offered. As you can see, your alarm—albeit just and proper—was perhaps unwarranted.

Kind regards,\
SENATORE BORLETTI

Letter 2

Ettore Modigliani to Senatore Borletti, October 4, 1930:

Illustre Senatore,

Ricevo la Sua lettera del 2 ottobre e in primo luogo La ringrazio delle gentili espressioni.

D'accordo con Lei che non vi può essere questione per le poltrone di platea; e quello che avrà fatto Lei sarà ben fatto. Le stesso dicasi delle panchette dei palchi sostituite da sgabelli. . . .

Per la stoffa del palchi voglia Ella permettermi nella Sua grande cortesia, di non essere del Suo parere. Non si tratta già di aver sostituito importanti damaschi o lampassi antichi e di avere adottato invece ora una stoffaccia moderna. Ammetto che le stoffe preesistenti potessero essere tutt'altro che pregevoli, prese in sé, e adottate senza molto criterio dai diversi proprietari dei palchi; ma sta di fatto che mantenevano alla Scala una caratteristica, unica per un grande teatro, una tradizione simpaticissima che dovevasi conservare, e che io confido di poter ancora, mercè il Suo autorevole aiuto, conservare.

La stoffa nuova è tutt'altro che spregevole, anche il colore non dà luogo a obiezioni, mentre, a dire il vero, lascia alquanto a desiderare il disegno, il quale avrebbe dovuto essere Impero ovvero neoclassico, ed è tale soltanto in alcuni elementi particolari, mentre nel complesso il disegno stesso dà l'impressione di riportarsi perfino a forme quattrocentesche e cinquecentesche che, come Lei sa benissimo, con la Scala, hanno a che fare come i cavoli a merenda.

Tuttavia io non posso certamente osare di chiederLe di gettarla via, ma quello che debbo chiedere—sicuro anche di interpretare i desideri non solo di tutti gli amanti della Scala, ma anche del Ministero della Educazione Nazionale—è di dare a parte di quella stoffa (per esempio ad una metà) un'altra destinazione, o tenerla di riserva per altre circostanze, e di adottare per la tappezzeria di metà dei palchetti—tutti mescolandoli e con senso della più accidentale varietà—altri 4 o 5 tipi di damaschi che Ella non ha nessuna necessità di far eseguire apposta, ma che può trovare, e bellissimi, sul mercato, e che valgano a interrompere quella monotona uniformità assolutamente contraria alle tradizioni—che avrebbe il teatro con una stoffa, anche stupendissima ma tutta uguale....

Io sono sicuro, Senatore, che il Suo amore per la città, e specialmente per la Scala, le cui sorti sono ora affidate a Lei, non Le faranno accogliere con rammarico queste mie osservazioni dettate—Ella, che mi conosce, ne può essere certo—non davvero dal desiderio di mettere bastoni fra le ruote, ma di collaborare con Lei—come del resto me ne fa obbligo la legge—affinché il Teatro alla Scala, riconosciuto il maggior tempio dell'arte lirica, conservi anche nelle sue decorazioni quel carattere estetico che perpetua un fascino, fatto, in molti casi, anche di elementi imponderabili....

Con amichevoli ossequi,
IL SOPRINTENDENTE

Illustrious Senatore,

I received your letter dated October 2 and want first to thank you for your kind words.

I agree there can be no question about the seats in the stalls, and that which you have done will, no doubt, have been done well. The same can be said for the benches replaced with stools....

When it comes to the fabric of the boxes I would like you, kind as you are, to allow me to hold a different opinion. It is not simply a matter of having replaced important, old damask fabrics or lampas weaves and adopted an ugly modern fabric in their place. I'll admit that the preexisting fabrics could seem far from valuable, on their own terms, and selected without much judgment by the diverse box owners. But the fact remains that these lent La Scala its character, unique among top theaters, and it was a charming tradition that should have been preserved. It is, moreover, something that, by means of your influential help, I trust can still be maintained.

The new fabric [of red silk damask, with oversized roses] is anything but contemptible, and the color raises no objections, whereas, in all honesty, the pattern, which should have been Imperial or neoclassical, and is so only in some details, leaves much to be desired. Furthermore, the pattern as a whole harks back to the aesthetics of the fifteenth and sixteenth centuries, which, as you well know, have no relevance whatsoever for La Scala.

Nevertheless, I certainly cannot dare to ask you to throw [the new] fabric out. What I must ask, however—confident in the belief that this represents the desire not only of the devotees of La Scala, but also the Ministry of National Education [which is responsible for cultural monuments]—is to set aside some of that fabric (for instance, half) for some other use, or to hold it in reserve for another time, and to use another four or five types of damask for the other half of the boxes: damask that does not need to be made to order but can instead be found—and in beautiful condition—on the marketplace, and can be mixed to create a sense of almost accidental variety that will interrupt the monotonous uniformity of a theater decorated with one fabric alone. One fabric alone, after all—however stupendous the fabric may be—would be absolutely contrary to the traditions of the theater....

I am sure, Senatore, that your love for the city, and above all La Scala—whose fortunes are entrusted to you—will not lead you to resent these observations of mine. You, who know me, must be certain that I do not in any sense have the desire to throw a wrench in the works, but to collaborate with you—as indeed I am obliged to under the law—so that the Teatro alla Scala, recognized as the most important temple of opera, might continue to emanate a spellbinding, imponderable, aesthetic quality even in its decor....

Kind regards,
THE SUPERINTENDENT

The letters in the appendix are reproduced by permission of the Ministry of Culture—Soprintendenza Archeologia, Belle Arti e Paesaggio per la città metropolitana di Milano. Further reproduction is prohibited without express permission of the Ministry of Culture.

NOTES

All translations are my own unless otherwise indicated; original-language citations are included only where the source is not easily available in published literature or online.

Chapter One

1. "Barcelona Opera House Reopens to an Audience of Plants," Associated Press, June 23, 2020, video, 8:03, https://globalnews.ca/news/7098004/barcelona-opera-house-plants/.

2. A 1994 catastrophic fire destroyed the previous Liceu theater, also a teatro all'italiana. On the Liceu, see Antonio Sàbat, *Gran Teatro del Liceo* (Barcelona: Escudo de Oro, 1979).

3. Carlotta Sorba has documented the notable proliferation of teatri all'italiana across the Italian peninsula in the nineteenth century. See Sorba, *Teatri: L'Italia del melodramma nell'età del Risorgimento* (Bologna: Il Mulino, 2001). No comprehensive list of teatri all'italiana across the world has been created, to my knowledge. The staggering figures for these decades in Italy, however, suggests the broader scale of the phenomenon.

4. Fabrizio Cruciani, in *Lo spazio del teatro* (Rome: Laterza, 1997), 13, for instance, describes the fires that ravished countless nineteenth-century teatri all'italiana and occasioned their subsequent reconstruction as a feature of these theaters' "biological rhythms." For a similar approach to these theaters, see Sorba, *Teatri*, esp. the section "La diffusione della sala all'italiana," 56–61; and Georges Banu, *Le rouge et or: Une poétique du théâtre à l'italienne* (Paris: Flammarion, 1989).

5. Eugene J. Johnson has discussed architecture at the SS. Giovanni e Paolo in detail. See Johnson, *Inventing the Opera House: Theater Architecture in Renaissance and Baroque Italy* (Cambridge: Cambridge University Press, 2018), 205–26.

6. On "interior architecture" as a category, see esp. Charles Rice, *The Emergence of the Interior: Architecture, Modernity, Domesticity* (Abingdon: Routledge, 2007); Lois Weinthal, ed., *Toward a New Interior: An Anthology of Interior Design Theory* (New York: Princeton Architectural Press, 2011); and Gregory Marinic, ed., *The Interior Architecture Theory Reader* (Abingdon: Routledge, 2018).

7. Johnson, *Inventing the Opera House*, 12.

8. The original phrase appears in a letter to Francesco Gonzaga dated February 4, 1501. Cited in Johnson, *Inventing the Opera House*, 16.

9. For two recent takes on darkness in the theater, see Noam M. Elcott, *Artificial Darkness: An Obscure History of Modern Art and Media* (Chicago: University of Chicago Press, 2016); and Gabriela Cruz, *Grand Illusion: Phantasmagoria in Nineteenth-Century Opera* (Oxford: Oxford University Press, 2020).

10. Gaston Bachelard, *The Poetics of Space*, trans. Maria Jolas (New York: Penguin, 2014), 28–29. For a related approach, see Juhani Pallasmaa, *The Eyes of the Skin: Architecture and the Senses* (Chichester: Wiley-Academy, 2012).

11. Bachelard, *The Poetics of Space*, 68.

12. Banu, *Le rouge et or*. I am indebted to Emanuele Senici for drawing my attention to Banu's book at an early stage in this project.

13. Some scholars have, of course, grappled with the relationship between architecture and music. Thurston Dart keenly noted that composers have always shaped their music according to the acoustics of rooms. See Dart, *The Interpretation of Music* (London: Hutchinson, 1984), 57. Nina Sun Eidsheim has also engaged with these ideas; see Eidsheim, *Sensing Sound: Singing and Listening as Vibrational Practice* (Durham, NC: Duke University Press, 2015). Literature about architecture as it impacts acoustics—but not music per se—is much more abundant. A classic text here is Emily Ann Thompson, *The Soundscape of Modernity: Architectural Acoustics and the Culture of Listening in America, 1900–1933* (Cambridge, MA: MIT Press, 2002). See also Peter Szendy, "Spacing and Sounding Out," *Grey Room* 60 (2015): 132–44.

14. Leo L. Beranek, *Concert Halls and Opera Houses: How They Sound* (Woodbury, NY: Acoustical Society of America, 1996), 231 and 535. These reverberation times predict the decay of medium frequency sounds in fully occupied auditoriums.

15. Joseph L. Clarke, *Echo's Chambers: Architecture and the Idea of Acoustic Space* (Pittsburgh, PA: University of Pittsburgh Press, 2021), esp. the chapter "Redeeming the Senses: The Acoustics of Total Art," 151–92.

16. Scholars from outside music studies have made particular contributions to theorization of performance spaces as media. See, e.g., Robert Albrecht, *Mediating the Muse: A Communications Approach to Music, Media, and Cultural Change* (Cresskill, NJ: Hampton Press, 2004); and Darryl Cressman, *Building Musical Culture in Nineteenth-Century Amsterdam: The Concertgebouw* (Amsterdam: Amsterdam University Press, 2016). For a musicological take, see Christopher Morris, "'Too Much Music': The Media of Opera," in *The Cambridge Companion to Opera Studies*, ed. Nicholas Till (Cambridge: Cambridge University Press, 2012), 95–116.

17. Thus, as Jonathan Sterne points out, that old philosophical quandary about a tree falling in the forest is potentially resolved. By one—albeit anthropocentric—interpretation, in the absence of someone within earshot, it makes no sound. See Sterne, *The Audible Past: Cultural Origins of Sound Reproduction* (Durham, NC: Duke University Press, 2003), 10–12.

18. For lively takes on this hermeneutic bent, see Stephen Best and Sharon Marcus, "Surface Reading: An Introduction," *Representations* 108, no. 1 (2009): 1–21; Rita Felski, "Context Stinks!," *New Literary History* 42, no. 4 (2011): 573–91; and Heather Love, "Close but Not Deep: Literary Ethics and the Descriptive Turn," *New Literary History* 41, no. 2 (2010): 371–91. I am grateful to Mary Ann Smart for drawing my attention to this cluster of texts.

19. The words are Hans Ulrich Gumbrecht's, used to summarize the core thesis of Martin Heidegger's *Sein und Zeit*. See Martin Heidegger, *Sein und Zeit* (Tübingen: Max Niemeyer, 1976). Cited in Hans Ulrich Gumbrecht, *Production of Presence: What Meaning Cannot Convey* (Stanford, CA: Stanford University Press, 2004), 66.

20. Kittler's remarks about the Festspielhaus were made across several decades and several publications. See Friedrich A. Kittler, *Discourse Networks 1800/1900*, trans. Michael Metteer (Stanford, CA: Stanford University Press, 1990); Kittler, *Gramophone, Film, Typewriter*, trans. Geoffrey Winthrop-Young and Michael Wutz (Stanford, CA: Stanford University Press, 1999), esp. 24; Kittler, *The Truth of the Technological World*, trans. Erik Butler (Stanford, CA: Stanford University Press, 2013), esp. "World-Breath: On Wagner's Media Technology," 122–37, and "Signal-to-Noise Ratio," 165–77; and Kittler, *Optical Media* (Malden, MA: Polity Press, 2010). On the relevance of Kittler to music studies, see Alexander Rehding, convenor, "Colloquy: Discrete/Continuous; Music and Media Theory After Kittler," *Journal of the American Musicological Society* 70, no. 1 (2017): 221–56, esp. Rehding, "Introduction," 221–28; and Kreuzer, "Kittler's Wagner and Beyond," 228–33.

21. Kittler, *Discourse Networks 1800/1900*.

22. As Kreuzer notes, it is ironic that in the same moment an entire industry revolved around cataloguing the composer's leitmotifs, Kittler claimed the composer's novelty lay in the dissolution of meaning. See Kreuzer, "Kittler's Wagner and Beyond," 229.

23. It is not possible to document all that abundant literature here. For one of the best-documented and focused accounts of the Festspielhaus, however, see Patrick Carnegy, *Wagner and the Art of the Theatre* (New Haven, CT: Yale University Press, 2006). For an account that moves discussion of the Festspielhaus into exciting new terrain, see Gundula Kreuzer, *Curtain, Gong, Steam: Wagnerian Technologies of Nineteenth-Century Opera* (Oakland: University of California Press, 2018).

24. Theodor Adorno would famously describe this process as "phantasmagorical," noting that "the occultation of production by means of the outward appearance of the product—that is the formal law governing the works of Richard Wagner. The product presents itself as self-producing.... In the absence of any glimpse of the underlying forces or conditions of its production, this outer appearance can lay claim to the status of being." See Adorno, *In Search of Wagner*, trans. Rodney Livingstone (London: Verso, 1981), 85.

25. These are reputedly the words of the former Tory MP Sir George Young, when he was minister of housing and planning.

26. For recent work that discusses the complexities of walls, see, e.g., Thomas Oles, *Walls: Enclosure and Ethics in the Modern Landscape* (Chicago: University of Chicago Press, 2015); and Irene Cheng, Charles L. Davis II, and Mabel O. Wilson, eds., *Race and Modern Architecture: A Critical History from the Enlightenment to the Present* (Pittsburgh, PA: University of Pittsburgh Press, 2020). As a complement to this work, see also Thomas F. Gieryn, "What Buildings Do," *Theory and Society* 31, no. 1 (2002): 35–74.

27. Rosie McMahon, "Music in the Urban Amazon: A Historical Ethnography of the Manaus Opera House" (PhD diss., Oxford University, 2019), 36.

28. For more on this, see chap. 5.

29. Johnson, *Inventing the Opera House*, 115–18.

30. Johnson, *Inventing the Opera House*, 217–22.

31. Giuliana Bruno, *Surface: Matters of Aesthetics, Materiality, and Media* (Chicago: University of Chicago Press, 2014).

32. For more on this, see chap. 2.

33. Weinthal, *Toward a New Interior*, 19.

34. Kreuzer, *Curtain, Gong, Steam*.

35. Esther da Costa Meyer, "Architectural History in the Anthropocene: Towards Methodology," *Journal of Architecture* 21, no. 8 (2016): 1204; and Daniel A. Barber, *Modern Architecture and Climate: Design Before Air Conditioning* (Princeton, NJ: Princeton University Press, 2020).

36. da Costa Meyer, "Architectural History in the Anthropocene," 1206.

37. This momentum forms part of a broader trend toward global histories. On the contours and stakes of this development, see Sebastian Conrad, *What Is Global History?* (Princeton, NJ: Princeton University Press, 2017).

38. Jürgen Osterhammel, *The Transformation of the World: A Global History of the Nineteenth Century*, trans. Patrick Camiller (Princeton, NJ: Princeton University Press, 2014), 5.

39. See esp. Benjamin Walton's forthcoming monograph, *The Invention of Global Opera*; Francesca Vella, *Networking Operatic Italy* (Chicago: University of Chicago Press, 2021); and Charlotte Bentley, *New Orleans and the Creation of Transatlantic Opera, 1815–1859* (Chicago: University of Chicago Press, 2022).

40. I borrow this conceptual apparatus from Kyle Devine. See Devine, *Decomposed: The Political Ecology of Music* (Cambridge, MA: MIT Press, 2019); and Kyle Devine and Alexandrine Boudreault-Fournier, eds., *Audible Infrastructures: Music, Sound, Media* (Oxford: Oxford University Press, 2021).

41. James H. Johnson, *Listening in Paris: A Cultural History* (Berkeley and Los Angeles: University of California Press, 1995); see also Jennifer Hall-Witt, *Fashionable Acts: Opera and Elite Culture in London, 1780-1880* (Durham, NH: University of New Hampshire Press, 2007).

42. For a broader take on silence and attention in relation to social class at the time, see John M. Picker, *Victorian Soundscapes* (Oxford: Oxford University Press, 2003); Stefano Pivato, *Il secolo del rumore: Paesaggio sonoro nel novecento* (Bologna: Il Mulino, 2011). These themes also surface across Hillel Schwartz, *Making Noise: From Babel to the Big Bang and Beyond* (New York: Zone Books, 2011).

43. On theories of infrastructure, see esp. John Durham Peters, *The Marvelous Clouds: Toward a Philosophy of Elemental Media* (Chicago: University of Chicago Press, 2015); and Brian Larkin, "The Politics and Poetics of Infrastructure," *Annual Review of Anthropology* 42 (2013): 327–43. On how standards organize our world, see Geoffrey C. Bowker and Susan Leigh Star, *Sorting Things Out: Classification and Its Consequences* (Cambridge, MA: MIT Press, 1999). A classic reference point remains Michel Foucault, *The Order of Things: An Archeology of the Human Sciences* (London: Routledge, 1992), originally published in 1966.

44. Leo L. Beranek, *Music, Acoustics and Architecture* (New York: John Wiley, 1962), 51; and Sorba, *Teatri*, 56.

45. Standardization reached a peak when individual firms oversaw the construction of chains of theaters on the same model. One architectural firm alone—the Viennese Ferdinand Fellner and Hermann Helmer—for instance oversaw the construction of dozens of theaters in central and eastern Europe. See Evan Baker, *From the Score to the Stage: An Illustrated History of Continental Opera Production and*

Staging (Chicago: University of Chicago Press, 2013), 254. So obvious was all this standardization in the 1800s that various commentators reacted with unease. One-time author Domenico Buffelli would for instance complain that "Il teatro riesce la più scipita, la più indifferente cosa del mondo" (the [modern] theater is the most tasteless, most insipid thing in the world.) Buffelli, *Elementi di mimica* (Milan: Da Placido Maria Visaj, 1829), 12. The author of the most influential treatise on architectural acoustics for its time, Pierre Patte, was himself concerned about the incursion of theatrical clones into the landscape. At times he cautions that one should avoid mindless imitation; at others he notes that once one finds a formula that works it should be repeated. See Pierre Patte, *Essai sur l'architecture théâtrale* (Paris: Chez Moutard, 1782). For the Italian translation, see Paolo Landriani, trans., "Saggio sull'architettura teatrale del Sig. Patte," in Giulio Ferrario, ed., *Storia e descrizione de'principali teatri antichi e moderni* (Bologna: Arnaldo Forni, 1977), 93–291. This translation was originally published in 1830; Landriani also summarized his reactions to Patte's treatise at the close of the volume. See "Osservazioni del Signor Paolo Landriani sul detto articolo," 315–69. Georges Banu draws attention to Patte's indecision: see Banu, *Le rouge et or*, 11.

46. The architect Giulio Ferrario would for instance describe the theater as the "più vasto e più ben architettato" (the largest and best constructed) theater ever built. See Ferrario, *Storia e descrizione de'principali teatri antichi e moderni*, v. Modern architectural acousticians continue to cite the Teatro alla Scala as the most perfect theater of its time: Beranek, for one, claims the horseshoe-shaped theater "reached its apogee" with the Teatro alla Scala. See Beranek, *Concert Halls and Opera Houses*, 11. For accounts of the Teatro alla Scala at the time of Piermarini and since, see esp. Carlo Gatti, "Preliminari storici," in *Il teatro alla Scala, nella storia e nell'arte, 1778–1963*, 2 vols. (Milan: Ricordi, 1964), 1:3–37; and Pompeo Cambiasi, *La Scala, 1778–1906: Note storiche e statistiche*, 2 vols. (Milan: G. Ricordi, 1906). See also Jutta Toelle, *Bühne der Stadt: Mailand und das Teatro alla Scala zwischen Risorgimento und Fin de Siècle* (Vienna: Oldenbourg, 2009).

47. Or, as Riccardo Falcinelli puts it, the three distinct concepts of the dirty, the old, and the ruined became interchangeable in the nineteenth century. See Falcinelli, *Cromorama: Come il colore ha cambiato il nostro sguardo* (Turin: Einaudi, 2017), 27. See also Taina Syrjämaa, "The Clash of Picturesque Decay and Modern Cleanliness in Late Nineteenth-Century Rome," in *Rome, Pollution and Propriety: Dirt, Disease and Hygiene in the Eternal City from Antiquity to Modernity*, ed. Mark Bradley and Kenneth Stow (Cambridge: Cambridge University Press, 2012), 202–22.

48. See, e.g., Archivio Storico del Comune di Bologna, Carteggio Amministrativo, Tit. X, Polizia, 1924, which contains swatches of upholstery under consideration for auditorium seats.

49. As I discuss in chap. 2, the correspondence is preserved in the Archivio Beni Architettonici e Paesaggio, Milan, Teatro alla Scala, A.V. 80, Fascicolo 1.

50. See J. Q. Davies, *Creatures of the Air: Music, Atlantic Spirits, Breath, 1817–1913* (Chicago: University of Chicago Press, 2023); Davies, "Pneumotypes: Jean de Reszke's High Pianissimos and the Occult Science of Breathing," in *Nineteenth-Century Opera and the Scientific Imagination*, ed. David Trippett and Benjamin Walton (Cambridge: Cambridge University Press, 2019), 21–43; and Davies, "Elijah's Nature," *19th-Century Music* 45, no. 1 (2021): 49–63, esp. 55–56.

51. Oles, *Walls*, 164.

Chapter Two

1. Archivio Beni Architettonici e Paesaggio di Milano, A.V. 80, Fascicolo 1. Two of the most important letters in the chain are reproduced in Appendix A.

2. Senatore Borletti to Sig. Comm. Dr. Ettore Modigliani, October 2, 1930, Archivio Beni Architettonici e Paesaggio di Milano, A.V. 80, Fascicolo 1.

3. R. Sovraintendenza all'Arte Medioevale e Moderna delle Provincie Lombarde, Reparto Monumenti, Ettore Modigliani to On. senatore S. Borletti, Presidente dell'Ente Autonomo del Teatro alla Scala, October 4, 1930, Archivio Beni Architettonici e Paesaggio di Milano, A.V. 80, Fascicolo 1.

4. "Veramente coraggiosa decisione di rinnovare il teatro senza nulla chiedere a chicchessia." Senatore Borletti to Cav. Benito Mussolini, Capo del Governo, September 28, 1930, Archivio di Stato di Milano, Fondo Prefettura di Milano, Gabinetto Prima Serie, Busta 1108. Mussolini's meeting with Borletti earlier in the summer is recorded on an unnumbered sheet, also in Busta 1108.

5. Senatore conte d'Arosio Borletti (1880–1939) was a powerful Milanese industrialist who between 1929 and 1931 also served as head of the Ente Autonomo della Scala. For an initial overview of Borletti, see *Dizionario biografico degli italiani* (Rome: Istituto della Enciclopedia Italiana, 1960–2020), s.v. "Borletti, Senatore." For a short description of SNIA Viscosa, see Virginia Postrel, *The Fabric of Civilization: How Textiles Made the World* (New York: Basic Books, 2021), 36–40. For a fascinating take on "artificial" Italian textiles, see Jeffrey T. Schnapp, "The Fabric of Modern Times," *Critical Inquiry* 24, no. 1 (1997): 191–245.

6. Unlike Borletti, Modigliani (1873–1947) was never a member of the Partito Nazionale Fascista and, with the introduction of racial laws in Italy, was dismissed in 1939 from various roles because he was a Jew. Biographical sources about Modigliani are extremely sparse, notwithstanding his multiple publications, both under his own name and—in the 1930s—under the name of his collaborator, Fernanda Wittgens.

7. Literature on the power of the surface is vast. For some recent focused takes, see esp. Bruno, *Surface*; and Mark C. Taylor, *Hiding* (Chicago: University of Chicago Press, 1997).

8. "Degne di un retrobottega da salumiere," Senatore Borletti to Signor Dottor Antonio Morassi, November 15, 1930, Archivio Beni Architettonici e Paesaggio di Milano, A.V. 80, Fascicolo 1.

9. On this phenomenon, see, e.g., the issue edited by Mark Taylor entitled "Surface Consciousness" in *Architectural Design* 73, no. 2 (2003), in which various contributors discuss a slippage between surface and skin. See also Ellen Lupton, ed., *Skin: Surface, Substance, and Design* (New York: Princeton Architectural Press, 2002), esp. Alicia Imperiale's chapter "Digital Skins: The Architecture of Surface," 55–63; Pallasmaa, *The Eyes of the Skin*; and Anne Anlin Cheng, *Second Skin: Josephine Baker and the Modern Surface* (Oxford: Oxford University Press, 2011).

10. Michel Serres, *The Five Senses: A Philosophy of Mingled Bodies*, trans. Margaret Sankey and Peter Cowley (London: Bloomsbury Academic, 2021), 148. Cited in Lupton, *Skin: Surface, Substance, and Design*, 18.

11. There is a flourishing literature on skin as cultural phenomenon. For recent contributions, see, e.g., Taylor, *Hiding*; Sara Ahmed and Jackie Stacey, eds., *Thinking Through the Skin* (London: Routledge, 2001); Lupton, *Skin: Surface, Substance, and Design*; Steven Connor, *The Book of Skin* (Ithaca, NY: Cornell University Press,

2004); Cheng, *Second Skin*; Bruno, *Surface*; and Adria L. Imada, *An Archive of Skin, An Archive of Kin: Disability and Life-Making During Medical Incarceration* (Oakland: University of California Press, 2022).

12. Connor, *The Book of Skin*, 51–53.

13. "Tutti i grandi teatri di tradizione dall'Opera di Parigi, allo Stadt Theater di Berlino all'Opera di Vienna, sono passate per la stessa crisi, ma nessuno di essi, dove pure le ragioni dell'arte sono venerate e rispettate, ha tentato quello che purtroppo è intentabile. Il vecchio e l'antico non possono sostituirsi col nuovo." Senatore Borletti to Signor Dottor Antonio Morassi, November 15, 1930, Archivio Beni Architettonici e Paesaggio di Milano, A.V. 80, Fascicolo 1.

14. For corrections from within architectural studies to these omissions, see esp. Weinthal, *Toward a New Interior*; Marinic, *The Interior Architecture Theory Reader*; and Jeremy Till, *Architecture Depends* (Cambridge, MA: MIT Press, 2013), esp. 117–34.

15. The classic text on absorbed silence remains Johnson, *Listening in Paris*. See also Hall-Witt, *Fashionable Acts*, and Cressman, *Building Musical Culture in Nineteenth-Century Amsterdam*.

16. The words are Walter Benjamin's. See Benjamin, "Paris, Capital of the Nineteenth Century," in *Reflections: Essays, Aphorisms, Autobiographical Writing*, trans. Edmund Jephcott (New York: Houghton Mifflin Harcourt, 2019), 163. Cited in Lupton, *Skin: Surface, Substance, and Design*, 19. On an aesthetics of dust, see also Bruno, *Surface*, 231–47.

17. See Taylor, *Hiding*, 13.

18. See Chiara Buss, "Il tessuto del teatro," in *Per La Scala*, ed. Giorgio Cortella, Gianfranco Colombo and Chiara Buss, vol. 2, *Creativity, Innovation, and Tradition—The Fabric of the Theater* (Milan: Amici della Scala, 1992), 121–25.

19. Giuseppe Morazzoni, *I palchi del Teatro alla Scala* (Milan: Amici del Museo Teatrale, 1930).

20. Jean-Jacques Rousseau, *The Discourses and Other Early Political Writings*, ed. Victor Gourevitch (Cambridge: Cambridge University Press, 1996), 284. Cited in David Batchelor, *Chromophobia* (London: Reaktion Books, 2000), 29–30.

21. Batchelor, *Chromophobia*.

22. On the history of color production, see esp. Falcinelli, *Cromorama*.

23. Laura Anne Kalba, *Color in the Age of Impressionism: Commerce, Technology, and Art* (University Park: Penn State University Press, 2017), 28. On the rise of synthetic dyestuffs, see also Peter J. T. Morris and Anthony S. Travis, "A History of the International Dyestuff Industry," *American Dyestuff Reporter* 81, no. 11 (1992): 59–108; and Postrel, *The Fabric of Civilization*, 136–42.

24. Kalba, *Color in the Age of Impressionism*, 29.

25. Kalba, *Color in the Age of Impressionism*, 30.

26. Michel Eugène Chevreul, *The Principles of Harmony and Contrast of Colors and their Applications to the Arts*, trans. Charles Martel (London: Henry G. Bohn, 1860).

27. Kalba, *Color in the Age of Impressionism*, esp. 15–40. For more on taste formation around this time, as it relates to textiles, see in particular Leora Auslander, *Taste and Power: Furnishing Modern France* (Berkeley and Los Angeles: University of California Press, 1996).

28. Adolf Loos, *Ornament and Crime: Thoughts on Design and Materials*, trans. Shaun Whiteside (London: Penguin Books, 2019), esp. "Ornament and Crime," 187–202.

29. Le Corbusier, "A Coat of Whitewash: The Law of Ripolin," in *The Decorative Art of Today*, trans. James I. Dunnett (London: The Architectural Press, 1987), 188–89. Le Corbusier was also known as Charles-Édouard Jeanneret.

30. Batchelor, *Chromophobia*, 41–45.

31. Mark Wigley, "Chronic Whiteness," in *e-flux Architecture* (November 2020), https://www.e-flux.com/architecture/sick-architecture/360099/chronic-whiteness/.

32. On architectural responses to these words, see, e.g., Jeffrey T. Schnapp, "The People's Glass House," *South Central Review* 25, no. 3 (2008): 45–56.

33. On this and other *case del fascio*, see Schnapp, "The People's Glass House"; and Lucy M. Maulsby, "Urban Networks: Fascist Party Headquarters, 1931–1940," in *Fascism, Architecture, and the Claiming of Modern Milan, 1922–1943* (Toronto: University of Toronto Press, 2018), 106–34. On Giuseppe Terragni more broadly, see Thomas L. Schumacher, *Surface and Symbol: Giuseppe Terragni and the Architecture of Italian Rationalism* (New York: Princeton Architectural Press, 1991); and Peter Eisenman, *Giuseppe Terragni: Transformations, Decompositions, Critiques* (New York: Monacelli Press, 2003).

34. Falcinelli, *Cromorama*, 363.

35. Charles Garnier, *Le théâtre* (Paris: Librairie Hachette, 1871), 417–63.

36. Gian Battista Niccolosi, *Il nuovo teatro di Parma: Rappresentato con tavole intagliate nello studio Paolo Toschi* (Parma: Battei, 1987).

37. Information about the redecorations of La Scala in this paragraph is drawn from Buss, "Il tessuto del teatro." Secchi has also detailed the redecorations of La Scala: Luigi Lorenzo Secchi, *1778/1978: Il Teatro alla Scala* (Milan: Electa Editrice, 1977).

38. Garnier, *Le théâtre*, 441.

39. On this see Susana Salgado, *The Teatro Solís: 150 Years of Opera, Concert, and Ballet in Montevideo* (Middletown, CT: Wesleyan University Press, 2003), 18.

40. Garnier, *Le théâtre*, 456 and 426.

41. Michel Pastoureau, *Red: The History of a Color* (Princeton, NJ: Princeton University Press, 2017), 74–79.

42. Bruno argues the case in *Surface*, esp. 18–20.

43. Pastoureau, *Red*, 143.

44. Pastoureau, *Red*, 152–62.

45. Isaac Newton, *Opticks* (Amherst, NY: Prometheus Books, 2003).

46. For a stimulating account of this, see Falcinelli, *Cromorama*, 79–86.

47. Johann Wolfgang von Goethe, *Goethe's Theory of Colours*, trans. Charles Lock Eastlake (Cambridge: Cambridge University Press, 2014).

48. Goethe, *Goethe's Theory of Colours*, 22.

49. Falcinelli once more provides an interesting account of all this. See *Cromorama*, 86–92, here 90.

50. On Chevreul's work, see esp. Kalba, *Color in the Age of Impressionism*, 15–42.

51. Chevreul, *The Principles of Harmony and Contrast of Colors*.

52. On lead foundation use, see Lynn M. Thomas, "Cosmetic Practices and Colonial Crucibles," in *Beneath the Surface: A Transnational History of Skin Lighteners* (Durham, NC: Duke University Press, 2020), 22–46.

53. Chevreul, *The Principles of Harmony and Contrast of Colors*, 241–43.

54. Garnier, *Le théâtre*, 177. Garnier reasserts this stance in *Le nouvel Opéra de Paris*, 2 vols. (Paris: Ducher, 1878). Banu also discusses Garnier's preference for the red theatrical interior and indeed stands out as one of the sole scholars to do so. See Banu, *Le rouge et or*, 111–22.

55. Garnier, *Le théâtre*, 182.

56. Chevreul, *The Principles of Harmony and Contrast of Colors*, 277.

57. Igiaba Scego, "A Harlequin Europe: Unveiling Black Histories in Venice," February 16, 2024, koozArch, https://www.koozarch.com/essays/a-harlequin-europe-unveiling-black-histories-in-venice.

58. For recent research on this, see, e.g., Olivette Otele, *African Europeans: An Untold History* (New York: Basic Books, 2023).

59. Cheng, Davis, and Wilson, *Race and Modern Architecture*, 4.

60. On sericulture, see Postrel, *The Fabric of Civilization*, 26–40.

61. For an overview of these events which considers both Chinese- and English-language sources, see Julia Lovell, *The Opium War: Drugs, Dreams and the Making of China* (New York: Overlook Press, 2014). On the trade of the Qing Dynasty within the context of the Pacific at this time, see David Igler, *The Great Ocean: Pacific Worlds from Captain Cook to the Gold Rush* (Oxford: Oxford University Press, 2013).

62. On the economics of the international silk trade around this time, see Debin Ma, "The Modern Silk Road: The Global Raw-Silk Market, 1850–1930," *Journal of Economic History* 56, no. 2 (1996): 330–55.

63. Roberto Tremelloni, *L'industria tessile italiana: Come è sorta, e come è oggi* (Turin: Einaudi, 1937), 48–49. Important information about Italian silk production is also provided in Giovanni Fanelli and Rosalia Fanelli, *Il tessuto moderno: Disegno, moda, architettura, 1890–1940* (Florence: Vallecchi, 1976).

64. On this, see esp. "Italy's Orient," ed. Rolando Minuti, special issue, *Journal of Modern Italian Studies* 26, no. 2 (2021). Of particular relevance are Stefano Turina, "Beyond the Silkworm Eggs: The Role of the Italian *semai* (Silkworm Egg Merchants) in Spreading Knowledge of Japan in Italy in the Second Half of the Nineteenth Century Between Art and Science," 141–60; Claudio Zanier, "Italy, East Asia and Silk: One Hundred Years of a Relationship (1830–1940)," 173–85; and Rolando Minuti, "China and World History in Italian Nineteenth-Century Thought: Some Remarks on Giuseppe Ferrari's Work," 208–19. Collaborations between *semai* and Chinese and Japanese sericulturalists were discussed routinely in the press and captured in various books. See, e.g., Giovanni B. Castellani, *Dell'allevamento dei bachi da seta in China: Fatto ed osservato sui luoghi* (Florence: Barbèra, 1860).

65. See James L. Hevia, *English Lessons: The Pedagogy of Imperialism in Nineteenth-Century China* (Durham, NC: Duke University Press, 2003).

66. Tremelloni, *L'industria tessile italiana*, 191.

67. See Chiara Buss, ed., *Silk: The 1900's in Como* (Milan: Silvana Editoriale, 2001).

68. Elena Phipps, "Global Colors: Dyes and the Dye Trade from the Sixteenth to the Eighteenth Century," in *The Interwoven Glove: Worldwide Textile Trade 1500–1800*, ed. Amelia Peck (New York: Metropolitan Museum of Art, 2013), 120–35; and Carlos Marichal Salinas, "Mexican Cochineal, Local Technologies and the Rise of Global Trade from the Sixteenth to the Nineteenth Centuries," in *Global History and New Polycentric Approaches: Europe, Asia and the Americas in a World Network*

System, ed. Manuel Pérez García and Lúcio de Sousa (Basingstoke: Palgrave Macmillan, 2018), 255–73.

69. On this history of red, see esp. Phipps, "Global Colors"; Amy Butler Greenfield, *A Perfect Red: Empire, Espionage, and the Quest for the Color of Desire* (New York: HarperCollins, 2005); and Salinas, "Mexican Cochineal."

Chapter Three

1. "Barcelona Opera House Reopens to an Audience of Plants," Associated Press, June 23, 2020, video, 8:03, https://globalnews.ca/news/7098004/barcelona-opera-house-plants/.

2. Judith Butler, *What World Is This? A Pandemic Phenomenology* (New York: Columbia University Press, 2022), 52.

3. "Episode 154: Eugenio Ampudia in Conversation with Paul Holdengräber," *The Quarantine Tapes*, January 28, 2021, podcast, 39:01, https://quarantine-tapes.simplecast.com/episodes.

4. Muhammad Waqas, Dominique Van Der Straeten, and Christoph-Martin Geilfus, "Plants 'Cry' for Help Through Acoustic Signals," *Trends in Plant Science* 28, no. 9 (2023): 984–86.

5. "Episode 154: Eugenio Ampudia in Conversation with Paul Holdengräber."

6. Davies, *Creatures of the Air*. See also Davies, "Elijah's Nature," esp. 55–56.

7. "Mentre la scienza intende a rendere sempre più sana e piacevole l'atmosfera fisica dei teatri, i nostri scrittori s'adoperino dal canto loro a renderne sempre più pura l'atmosfera morale." See Rinaldo Ferrini, "Dei principii a cui deve informarsi un sistema di ventilazione per un teatro," *Il politecnico: Giornale dell'ingegnere architetto civile ed industriale* 21 (Milan: Tipologia e Litografia degli Ingegneri, 1873), 467.

8. Steven Connor, *The Matter of Air: Science and Art of the Ethereal* (London: Reaktion Books, 2010), 10.

9. Antonio Stoppani, *Acqua ed aria, ossia la purezza del mare e dell'atmosfera fin dai primordi del mondo animato*, ed. Alessandro Malladra (Turin: Società Editrice Internazionale, 1898). The lectures were originally published in 1875 and then rereleased under the cited title in 1882.

10. John B. West, "Joseph Black, Carbon Dioxide, Latent Heat, and the Beginnings of the Discovery of the Respiratory Gases," *American Journal of Physiology—Lung Cellular and Molecular Physiology* 306, no. 12 (2014): 1057–63.

11. John B. West, "Henry Cavendish (1731–1810): Hydrogen, Carbon Dioxide, Water, and Weighing the World," *American Journal of Physiology—Lung Cellular and Molecular Physiology* 307, no. 1 (2014): 1–6.

12. Specifically, Stoppani asked: "Come mai questa atmosfera, dopo tanti e tanti milioni di anni, dopo tanti e tanti milioni di generazioni, mantiene ancora quella purezza la quale ci inebria così, che un soffio d'aria libera è per tanti poveri o ricchi una delle più invocate delizie che si possano godere sulla terra? Vedete come una sola persona, un solo animale basti a viziare in poche ore l'aria di una stanza.... Non dovrebbe così viziarsi la gran stanza di tutti gli animali, ove milioni di viventi, pigiati su tutta quanta la superficie del globo, respirano da milioni di anni?" (How can it be that even after millions of years, and millions of generations, the Earth's atmosphere is still so pure that it exhilarates us; that a breath of fresh air is one of the most sought-after pleasures that anyone, whether rich or poor, can enjoy on the

Earth? The presence of a single person, a single animal, is enough to make the air in a room cloying over a few short hours.... Should the animals' great room—where millions of creatures, huddled together on every inch of the globe's surface, have been breathing for millions of years—not be cloying also?"). Stoppani, *Acqua ed aria*, 396.

13. The term "carbon rotation" is generally attributed to J. J. Ebelman, who first used it in his 1840s publications. On this see Matthieu Emmanuel Galvez and Jérôme Gaillardet, "Historical Constraints on the Origins of the Carbon Cycle Concept," *Comptes rendus géoscience* 344, nos. 11–12 (2012): 549–67.

14. Deborah R. Coen, *Climate in Motion: Science, Empire, and the Problem of Scale* (Chicago: University of Chicago Press, 2018), 2.

15. Coen, *Climate in Motion*, 3.

16. "Fermatevi un momento a riflettere sui vostri abiti, sulle vivande che si succedono alla vostra mensa, sui mobili delle vostre stanze e sui materiali della vostra casa; provatevi a risalire col pensiero alle origini donde provennero tutte queste cose che dite vostre e che difatto andate consumando tutti i giorni o logorando per vostro comodo, e troverete che ognuno di voi si adagia e rallegra la vita colle spoglie rapite ai tre regni della natura in tutti gli angoli della terra. Non siete andati voi a rapirle? Ci andarono altri per voi; ma questi altri son uomini. Essi appartengono alla classe degli uomini che vanno saccheggiando il regno minerale, il vegetale e l'animale, e ne raccolgono le provvigioni per tutti; voi, alla classe di quelli che lo consumano; ma il fatto sta che il genere umano si nutre e conforta colla rapina incessante di quanto si muove nell'aria o nell'acqua, di quanto prospera sopra terra o si nasconde sott'essa." Antonio Stoppani, "L'uomo e il suo impero sulla terra," in *L'exemeron: Nuovo saggio di una esegesi della storia della creazione secondo la ragione e la fede*, vol. 2 (Turin: Unione Tipografico-Editrice, 1894), 562–66. Originally published as "L'uomo e il suo impero sulla terra," in *Le prime letture* (Milan: Agnello, 1873), 124–28.

17. "Ciò che vedo in oggi è l'uomo intento a godere dei tesori accumulati in tanto giro di secoli. Egli va spogliando, anche troppo provvidamente, della sua chioma la terra; egli già saccheggia i magazzini appena ricolmi di carbone, scavando quelle torbiere . . . egli s'inoltra sotterra come il tarlo e rode, disseppellisce le foreste gelosamente riposte e custodite pel corso di tanti secoli fin dal principio dell'era protozoica. Che sia per avvenire, non so. La natura non cessa anche in oggi di provvedere a suo modo al mantenimento dell'universo: ma chi può valutare la potenza del nuovo elemento? L'efficacia vo' dire, di quell'intelligenza che s'impone alla natura coi diritti di un sovrano, che non sempre fa mostra di saggezza nell'uso della sua forza? Lasciando l'avvenire nel suo impenetrabile mistero, ciò che il passato ci rivela . . . è questo che, mentre la natura soddisfaceva ai bisogni dell'universo, accumulando per tanti secoli e calcare, e sale, e ferro, e carbone e ogni sorta di minerali, coll'impiego di tutte le forze coordinate de'suoi tre regni; provvedeva anticipatamente, con tutte le finezze di un affetto materno, colle inesauribili risorse di una saggezza infinita, con tutta l'esuberanza di un potere senza limite, a questa creatura novissima; all'uomo, a cui andava preparando man mano un abitacolo, fornito di tutto quello che può, non soltanto sopperire al bisogno, ma soddisfare alla magnificenza, servire al piacere, rendere attuabili i maravigliosi [*sic*] concetti del suo ingegno, dichiararlo in fine, nello spazio e nel tempo, sovrano della terra." Stoppani, *Acqua ed aria*, 530–31.

18. The chemist Paul J. Crutzen and the marine biologist Eugene F. Stoermer are credited with coining the term "Anthropocene." See Paul J. Crutzen and

Eugene F. Stoermer, "The 'Anthropocene,'" *Global Change Newsletter* (International Geosphere-Biosphere Programme) 41 (May 2000): 17–18. Matteo Gilebbi makes the same point about Stoppani. See Gilebbi, "Antonio Stoppani and the Teleological Interpretation of the Anthropocene," paper presented at the American Association for Italian Studies Conference, Columbus, OH (2017), 3. Stoppani introduces the term in his 1873 *Corso di geologia*: "finalmente ecco l'uomo, la cui comparsa inaugura l'era antropozoica, l'era novissima, non per la terra soltanto, ma per Tutto il creato" (finally, man arrives, and his appearance inaugurates the Anthropozoic era, not for the Earth alone but for All of creation). See Stoppani, *Corso di geologia* (Milan: G. Bernadoni & G. Brigola, 1873), 461.

19. The Swedish chemist Svante Arrhenius (1859–1927) is usually credited with being the first to quantify how much carbon dioxide warms the planet.

20. "Gran Teatre del Liceu—Barcelona," YouTube, October 22, 2021, video, 3:33, https://www.youtube.com/watch?v=ka_kp8ddhzw.

21. See Davies, *Creatures of the Air*; Davies, "Pneumotypes," 21–43; and Davies, "Elijah's Nature." A critical figure in the earliest ventilation mechanisms was the British chemist David Boswell Reid (1805–1863), otherwise known as "the ventilator." Most famous for his work at the new English Houses of Parliament between 1840–1852, Reid set down, across several treaties, his notion that air is as essential as food in the maintenance of life, and as such should be foundational in architectural planning. Reid's ultimate goal was, moreover, to ensure the circulation of "pure air" within architectural interiors. Indeed, he used the term repeatedly in his book *Illustrations of the Theory and Practice of Ventilation*. See Reid, *Illustrations of the Theory and Practice of Ventilation: With Remarks on Warming, Exclusive Lighting, and the Communication of Sound* (London: Longman, Brown, Green & Longmans, 1844). On Reid, see Henrik Schoenefeldt, *Rebuilding the Houses of Parliament: David Boswell Reid and Disruptive Environmentalism* (Abingdon: Routledge, 2021); and the aforementioned publications by Davies.

22. Cited in "Report of The Lancet Sanitary Commission on the Ventilation of Theatres and Places of Public Assembly," *Lancet* (December 19, 1891), 1411.

23. On this, see Coen, *Climate in Motion*, 181.

24. "Report of The Lancet Sanitary Commission," 1411.

25. On ventilation at the Vienna Court Opera, see "Report of The Lancet Sanitary Commission," 1411–13; and John S. Billings, *The Principles of Ventilation and Heating and Their Practical Application* (New York: Engineering and Building Record, 1889), 130–33.

26. This last role was the job of the ventilation-regulator, who was likened to a steersman: as he received temperature information via telegraph, he was tasked with navigating the weather, as it were, keeping the auditorium's "head . . . to the wind," as though it were a vessel amid the elements. "Report of The Lancet Sanitary Commission," 1413.

27. Ferrini, "Dei principii a cui deve informarsi," 466.

28. Ferrini, "Dei principii a cui deve informarsi," 458–59.

29. Luigi Broggi, "L'edificio del Teatro alla Scala in Milano," in *Il politecnico: Giornale dell'ingegnere architetto civile ed industriale* (Milan: Tipologia e Litografia degli Ingegneri, 1878), 15.

30. On the arrival of "aria buona alla Scala" see, e.g., "Cronache scaligere," *Corriere della sera* (December 30, 1934), in which the introduction of a new ventilation

system in the theater's galleries is said to "consente l'immissione di circa 20 mila mc. all'ora d'aria buona e leggermente riscaldata e alla contemporanea espulsione di altrettanta aria viziata" ("allows the introduction of approximately 20 thousand mc. per hour of clean and gently heated air and the simultaneous expulsion of the same volume of foul air"). On the later installation of an efficacious air conditioning system, see "Aria buona alla Scala," *Corriere della sera* (28–29 August, 1948).

31. da Costa Meyer, "Architectural History in the Anthropocene," 1218.

32. Dipesh Chakrabarty, "The Climate of History: Four Theses," *Critical Inquiry* 35, no. 2 (2009): 208.

33. On this, see Jane Bennett, *Vibrant Matter: A Political Ecology of Things* (Durham, NC: Duke University Press, 2010), 24–28.

34. The arc lamp's invention is commonly attributed to inventor Pavel Jablochkoff. See Lyon Playfair, "Appendix: The Jablochkoff System of Electric Illumination," in *Report from the Select Committee on Lighting by Electricity, Together with the Proceedings of the Committee, Minutes of Evidence, and Appendix* (London, 1879), 231–33; and Robert Hodson Parsons, "The Beginnings of the Power Station Industry," in *The Early Days of the Power Station Industry* (Cambridge: Cambridge University Press, 1940), 1–20.

35. For an English translation, see Émile Zola, *The Ladies' Paradise*, trans. Brian Nelson (Oxford: Oxford University Press, 1995), 426. When decades later Walter Benjamin linked the enchantment of illumination to consumerism in *The Arcades Project*, he enlivened the belief that for nineteenth-century observers, arcs had a primal force. See Walter Benjamin, *The Arcades Project*, trans. Howard Eiland and Kevin McLaughlin (Cambridge, MA: Belknap Press of Harvard University Press, 1999).

36. On this, see Sasha Archibald, "Blinded by the Light," *Cabinet* 21 (Spring 2006): 97–100. Some contemporary reports tried to dispel fears that arcs were overpowering; see, e.g., Playfair, *Report from the Select Committee on Lighting by Electricity*, 233, where it is reported that "all colors illuminated by [the Jablochkoff light] are as pure as if in the light of the sun, and the idea of its being frightening to horses or dazzling to drivers, is altogether exploded at the very first sight of such a street as the new Avenue de l'Opéra, which is illuminated from end to end by the Jablochkoff light."

37. On this, see Stephen Inwood, "The End of Darkest London," in *City of Cities: The Birth of Modern London* (London: Macmillan, 2005), 277–94; and Thomas Parke Hughes, *Networks of Power: Electrification in Western Society, 1880–1930* (Baltimore: Johns Hopkins University Press, 1983), 47–78. On the formation of the Società Edison Italiana, see esp. Società Edison, ed., *Nel cinquantenario della Società Edison, 1884–1934*, vol. 4, *Lo sviluppo della società Edison e il progresso economico di Milano* (Milan: Società Edison, 1934), esp. the chapters "L'inizio, 1881–1883," 133–44, and "La fondazione e il primo decennio di sviluppo della società, 1884–1893," 145–62. See also Claudio Pavese, "Le origini della Società Edison e il suo sviluppo fino alla costituzione del 'gruppo' (1881–1991)," in *Energia e sviluppo: L'industria italiana e la Società Edison*, ed. Bruno Bezza (Turin: Einaudi, 1986), 23–167.

38. For details of this installation, see Giuseppe Colombo, "Station centrale d'éclairage électrique de Milan: Éclairage électrique du théâtre de la Scala," *La lumière électrique* 11, no. 2 (January 12, 1884): 116–17; R. Ferrini, "L'éclairage électrique du Théâtre de la Scala à Milan," *La lumière électrique* 12, no. 14 (April 5, 1884): 12–17;

and Colombo, "Iluminazione elettrica," in *Milano tecnica dal 1859 al 1884*, ed. Francesco Ajraghi (Milan: Hoepli, 1885), 459–73. I base all technical discussion of the La Scala installation in this paragraph on these sources. Marco Capra has published the only extensive discussion of theatrical illumination at La Scala to date; see Capra, "L'illuminazione sulla scena verdiana, ovvero L'arco voltaico non acceca la luna?," in *La realizzazione scenica dello spettacolo verdiano*, ed. Fabrizio della Seta and Pierluigi Petrobelli (Parma: Istituto di Studi Verdiani, 1996), 230–64.

39. "Ragioni di prudenza assolutamente necessarie in un'impresa così nuova come la nostra, ci consigliarono di procedere con molta cautela e lentezza nello sviluppo delle installazioni di Milano. Un errore, una interruzione dell'illuminazione, soprattutto nel Teatro alla Scala, avrebbe avuto conseguenze fatali, avrebbe forse compromesso irreparabilmente il nostro avvenire. Noi abbiamo dunque lasciato passare la stagione della Scala prima di accogliere nuovi consumatori." See Pavese, "Le origini della Società Edison," 49.

40. It would not be anachronistic to label this promotion of illumination at La Scala a form of product placement, a practice that was pursued with deliberate calculation around now. A classic example of product placement can be found in Jules Verne's 1872 novel *Le Tour du monde en quatre-vingts jours (Around the World in Eighty Days)*, in which Verne had characters Phileas Fogg and his valet Jean Passepartout take to the seas on carriers that bore noticeable resemblance to ones in real life. Their evocation was rumored to be the result of clandestine deals between Verne and the owners of the liners, who had calculated that readers' interest in the liners in the novel would lead to real-world claims to them: readers, in other words, would become consumers, and make their own demands for cabins in the liners. See Jules Verne, *Around the World in Eighty Days: The Extraordinary Journeys*, ed. William Butcher (Oxford: Oxford University Press, 1995). For a historical perspective on product placement, see Jonathan Gil Harris, "Properties of Skill: Product Placement in Early English Artisanal Drama," in *Staged Properties in Early Modern English Drama*, ed. Gil Harris and Natasha Korda (Cambridge: Cambridge University Press, 2002), 35–66.

41. Sources on incandescent theatrical illumination tend to underreport the number of installations around this time. The most comprehensive source I have found is an article in the Parisian trade journal *La lumière électrique* which lists the following installations prior to La Scala's: the Savoy Theater in London, Brünn Theater, Gran Teatro de la Habana in Cuba, Bijou Theater in Boston, Théâtre Royal du Parc in Brussels, Residenztheater in Munich, Residenztheater in Stuttgart, Princess's Theater in Manchester, Teatro Manzoni in Milan and the Budapest Theater. See Aug. Guerout, "L'éclairage électrique des théâtres par les lampes à incandescence," *La lumière électrique* 12, no. 15 (April 12, 1884): 63–72. The technical and polemical manuals about electricity published in the 1880s are invaluable sources of information about the earliest electric illumination in theaters. These tended to feature a chapter on theatrical installations. Representative is Émile Alglave and J. Boulard, *La lumière électrique, son histoire, sa production et son emploi dans l'éclairage public ou privé, les phares, les théâtres, l'industrie, les travaux publics, les opérations militaires et maritimes* (Paris: Firmin-Didot, 1882), which features the chapter "La lumière électrique au théâtre," 417–28.

42. On this installation, see "Teatro alla Scala. La sera di Santo Stefano," *Il mondo artistico* (December 19, 1883); "Corriere teatrale; Il Santo Stefano alla Scala; La luce

elettrica," *Corriere della sera* (December 27, 1883); and "Teatri di Milano," *Il teatro illustrato* (January 1884).

43. Pavese, "Le origini della Società Edison," 23–167.

44. On the electrical as deferred energy source, see esp. Astrid Kander, Paolo Malanima, and Paul Warde, *Power to the People: Energy in Europe over the Last Five Centuries* (Princeton, NJ: Princeton University Press, 2014).

45. Around the time he became involved with Edison, Colombo was a professor of Industrial Mechanics at the Istituto Tecnico Superiore di Milano—now the Politecnico di Milano—where he had held a position since the 1860s, and author of the bestseller *Manuale dell'ingegnere* (1877). He also became a *consigliere comunale* (a member of the Milanese city council) in 1881. With Stoppani's appointment to the Istituto Tecnico Superiore in the 1860s, he was particularly delighted to become a colleague of the esteemed Colombo. See Angelo Maria Cornelio, *Vita di Antonio Stoppani: Onoranze alla sua memoria* (Turin: Unione Tipografico Editrice, 1898), 211. On the shared world in which both Colombo and Stoppani worked, see Elena Zanoni, *Scienza, patria, religione: Antonio Stoppani e la cultura italiana dello Ottocento* (Milan: FrancoAngeli, 2014). For Colombo's writing on electrification and correspondence with Thomas Edison, see Giuseppe Colombo, *Il "carbone bianco": Scritti sull'elettrificazione e la corrispondenza con Thomas A. Edison* (Milan: Anthelios Edizioni, 2013). On Colombo's ideas about Italian industry, see Colombo, *Industria e politica nella storia d'Italia: Scritti scelti, 1861–1916*, ed. Carlo G. Lacaita (Milan: Cariplo, 1985).

46. Giuseppe Colombo, "La trasmissione elettrica della forza e il suo significato per l'avvenire dell'industria italiana," *La perseveranza* (April 21, 1890). Reproduced in Colombo, *Il "carbone bianco,"* 53–70.

47. On current denial of historic climate change awareness, see Fabien Locher and Jean-Baptiste Fressoz, "Modernity's Frail Climate: A Climate History of Environmental Reflexivity," *Critical Inquiry* 38, no. 3 (2012): 579–98.

48. Imre Szeman and Dominic Boyer, eds., "Introduction: On the Energy Humanities," in *Energy Humanities: An Anthology* (Baltimore: Johns Hopkins University Press, 2017), 6.

49. On this, see Michael Rubenstein and Justin Neuman, *Modernism and Its Environments* (New York: Bloomsbury Academic, 2020), 36–37.

50. See Derek M. Elsom, *Lightning: Nature and Culture* (London: Reaktion Books, 2015).

51. Connor, *The Matter of Air*, 178.

52. For the text of manager Richard D'Oyly Carte's full announcement to the public that evening, see Percy Hetherington Fitzgerald, *The Savoy Opera and the Savoyards* (London: Chatto & Windus, 1894), 95–98. The bulb-smashing incident is recounted in T. A. L. Rees, *Theatre Lighting in the Age of Gas* (London: Society for Theatre Research, 1978), 168–84.

53. Agostino Della Sala Spada, *Nel 2073! Sogni d'uno stravagante*, ed. Simonetta Satragni Petruzzi (Alessandria: Edizioni dell'Orso, 1998). Scholars tend to view Jules Verne as a pioneer in science fiction, and to trace the development of Italian science fiction as a genre to the period immediately after World War II (while also conceding that two writers prefigured this development: Emilio Salgari (1862–1911), who was christened the "Italian Verne," and Enrico de' Conti Novelli da Bertinoro (1874–1945), who used the pen name Yambo). However, Della Sala Spada and these

writers were but three Italian contemporaries of Verne who contributed to futuristic and science fiction literature. The librettist Antonio Ghislanzoni wrote the futuristic novel *Abrakadabra: storia dell'avvenire* (Lecco: Piantini, 1874); other contemporaneous works include Guglielmo Folliero, *I misteri politici della luna* (Naples: Marghieri, 1863); Ulisse Grifoni, *Dalla terra alle stelle: Viaggio meraviglioso di due italiani ed un francese* (Florence: Nicolai, 1887); and Paolo Mantegazza, *L'anno 3000* (Milan: Fratelli Treves, 1897). On this literature, see Nicoletta Pireddu, "Introduction: Paolo Mantegazza, Fabulator of the Future," in Paolo Mantegazza, *The Year 3000: A Dream*, ed. Nicoletta Pireddu, trans. David Jacobson (Lincoln: University of Nebraska Press, 2010), 1–53.

54. "L'immenso salone era a logge e a gradinate, ma io non ci trovai una gran differenza dai teatri de'miei tempi ed anzi non mi parve troppo bene illuminato e lo dissi tosto ad Evangelina, ma questa mi rispose che attendessi e sarei rimasto soddisfatto . . . ; Mentre così io guardava intorno e andava facendo i miei ragionamenti e le mie osservazioni . . . ad un tratto lo stragrande salone si riempì d'una luce straordinaria, vivissima, leggermente azzurrognola, che diede ad ogni cosa un vaghissimo aspetto. 'Vedi?'—mi disse Evangelina accennando a quanto poco prima m'avea promesso—'vedi?' 'È vero'—risposi io scintillando negli occhi pel riflesso di quella luce—è un'illuminazione di cui non poteva certo formarmene idea.' . . . E subito per quel grandissimo teatro si sentì una musica così dolce, così soave che il cuore parea mi venisse meno per la dolcezza; da che parte venisse quella musica, da quale orchestra, non so; . . . era come un'onda sonora che s'era sparsa per tutto, un'atmosfera melodiosa; parea fossero insomma le medesime molecole d'aria che mandassero quelle note di paradiso nel danzare per l'immensità di quella sala. . . . 'Mi basta questa luce e questa musica'—risposi io—'e se altro vi s'aggiunge, finisco per isvenire dalla dolcezza.' . . . La scena con prodigi d'ottica e d'elettricità, vivi vivi me li porse innanzi." See Della Sala Spada, *Nel 2073! Sogni d'uno stravagante*, 257–59.

Chapter Four

1. "Divorante furia, come un incendio all'improvviso erotto da un abisso ignorato"; "Tutte le cose abbracciava l'ebrezza della fiamma canora; tutte le cose del mondo sovrane vibravano perdutamente nell'immensa ebrezza." See Gabriele D'Annunzio, *I romanzi della rosa: Trionfo della morte* (Rome: L'Oleandro, 1933), 483. For the text in translation, see D'Annunzio, *The Triumph of Death*, trans. Arthur Hornblow (New York: G. H. Richmond, 1898). The translation provided here is Hornblow's own.

2. Beranek, *Concert Halls and Opera Houses*, 232.

3. See Beranek, *Concert Halls and Opera Houses*, 231. The reverberation time here predicts the decay of medium frequency sounds in a fully occupied house. For an introduction to the technical side of architectural acoustics, see Michael Barron, *Auditorium Acoustics and Architectural Design* (London: Spon Press, 2010).

4. Clarke, *Echo's Chambers: Architecture and the Idea of Acoustic Space*, esp. the chapter "Redeeming the Senses: The Acoustics of Total Art," 151–92.

5. Michael C. Heller, "Between Silence and Pain: Loudness and the Affective Encounter," *Sound Studies: An Interdisciplinary Journal* 1, no. 1 (2015): 40–58.

6. This point merits emphasis, since scholars have made claims to the contrary. See, e.g., Meredith C. Ward, "The 'New Listening': Richard Wagner, Nineteenth-

Century Opera Culture, and Cinema Theatres," *Nineteenth Century Theatre and Film* 43, no. 1 (2016): 88–106, in which the author claims that Wagner was "among the earliest and most highly visible proponents of architectural acoustics in mainstream opera" (93). Ward bases this claim on the composer's interest in acoustics on the one hand and architecture on the other. There is, however, little evidence that Wagner ever discussed the two in relation to one another.

7. Richard Wagner, "Vorwort Herausgabe zur der Dichtung des Bühnenfestspiels 'Der Ring des Nibelungen,'" in *Sämtliche Schriften und Dichtungen*, vol. 6 (Leipzig: Breitkopf & Härtel, 1911), 272–81. Translated by Herbert Barth, Dietrich Mack, and Egon Voss, eds., *Wagner: A Documentary Study* (Oxford: Oxford University Press, 1975), 199–200.

8. Wagner, "Das Bühnenfestspielhaus in Bayreuth, nebst einem Berichte über die Grundsteinlegung desselben," in *Sämtliche Schriften und Dichtungen*, 9: 322–44; trans. Barth, Mack, and Voss, *Wagner: A Documentary Study*, 221–22.

9. *Trionfo della morte* was written in the exact same months that D'Annunzio penned *Il caso Wagner*, an impassioned defense of the composer from Nietzsche's recent, searing attack. The defense was published as three articles: see "Il caso Wagner," *La tribuna* (July 23 and August 3 and 9, 1893). For a recent translation, see Thomas Grey and James Westby, "Gabriele D'Annunzio's 'Il caso Wagner' (The Case of Wagner): Reflections on Wagner, Nietzsche, and Wagnerismo from fin-de-siècle Italy," *Leitmotiv—The Wagnerian Quarterly* (2012): 7–26.

10. On this, see Carnegy, *Wagner and the Art of the Theatre*, 71.

11. Garnier, *Le nouvel Opéra de Paris*.

12. *La libertà* (29 October 1880).

13. See Cesare Albertini, "Circa la formazione del 'golfo mistico' per le orchestre dei nostri teatri," *Il monitore tecnico* 20 (1913): 383–88; Marco Salvarani, *Le muse: Storia del Teatro di Ancona* (Ancona: Il Lavoro Editoriale, 2002), 192; Gilberto Calcagnini, *Il teatro Rossini di Pesaro fra spettacolo e cronaca, 1898-1966: Memorie cronistoriche* (Fano: Editrice Fortuna, 1997), 203; and Franco Battistelli, Luca Ferretti, and Giuseppina Boiani Tombari, *Il teatro della Fortuna in Fano: Storia dell'edificio e cronologia degli spettacoli*, 2 vols. (Fano: Carifano, 1998), 1:201.

14. See, e.g., Salvarani, *Le muse*, 192.

15. See, e.g., Albertini, "Circa la formazione del 'golfo mistico.'"

16. See, e.g., "Wagner e il suo teatro," *Gazzetta musicale di Milano* (January 16, 1876); L. T., "Wagneriana," *Rivista musicale italiana* 4 (1897), 382–86; and "Da Oberammergau: Note di viaggio," *Gazzetta musicale di Milano* (August 24, 1890).

17. "Mirabilmente pure." See Gustavo Macchi, "L'apertura della stagione alla Scala: *Il crepuscolo degli dei*," *Il mondo artistico* (January 1, 1908) / "La nuova posizione dell'orchestra ha conferito molto alla fusione dei suoni." "Scala—Il 'Crepuscolo degli dei' di R. Wagner," *Cosmorama pittorico* (January 3, 1908). For another such statement, see also "Teatri di Milano," *L'arte melodrammatica* (January 11, 1908).

18. A detailed account of the Visconti di Modrone's involvement at La Scala can be found in Gianpiero Fumi, "Imprenditori culturali: L'impegno nella gestione del Teatro alla Scala," in *I Visconti di Modrone: Nobiltà e modernità a Milano (Secoli XIX-XX)*, ed. Gianpiero Fumi (Milan: Vita e Pensiero, 2014), 237–70. On the broader climate of commercialism and industrialism in which the Visconti

di Modrone operated, see Alberto M. Banti, "Avamposti della trasformazione industriale," in *Storia della borghesia italiana: L'età liberale* (Rome: Donzelli, 1996), 143–79.

19. "Per il divertimento dei ricchi, per una spesa di lusso." Cambiasi, *La Scala, 1778–1906*, 260. On the political landscape at the time, see Christopher Duggan, *The Force of Destiny: A History of Italy Since 1796* (Boston: Houghton Mifflin, 2008), esp. the chapter "Rival Religions: Socialism and Catholicism," 350–73.

20. "Dovere imprescindibile"; "comproprietario di uno dei maggiori teatri del mondo, di fare quanto è possible perchè esso riesca accessibile a tutte le classi della cittadinanza." Cittadella degli Archivi, Milan, Fondo Teatro alla Scala, Faldone 340, Fascicolo #14, "Relazione della Commissione pel Teatro alla Scala" (March 16, 1906). For a reproduction of parts of this document, see Guido Marangoni and Carlo Vanbianchi, eds., *La Scala: Studi e ricerche, note storiche e statistiche(1906–20)* (Bergamo: Istituto Italiano d'Arti Grafiche, 1922), 179–85.

21. For a sense of Albertini's role as a civil architect in Milan, see esp. G. Laura di Leo, ed., *Cesare Albertini urbanista: Antologia di scritti* (Rome: Gangemi, 1995).

22. Cittadella degli Archivi, Milan, Fondo Teatro alla Scala, Faldone 340, Fascicolo #14, "Relazione della commissione di studio per l'abbassamento del piano orchestra del Teatro alla Scala," (1907), n.p.

23. "Relazione della commissione di studio per l'abbassamento del piano d'orchestra del Teatro alla Scala," n.p.

24. "Relazione della commissione di studio per l'abbassamento del piano d'orchestra del Teatro alla Scala," n.p.

25. Specifically, Sabine formulated that reverberation time (seconds) = $0.16 \, V / A$, where V is the total room volume in m^3 and A is the total acoustic absorption in m^2. A is the sum of every surface area multiplied by the corresponding absorption coefficient. Literature on Sabine is extensive. See esp. Thompson, *The Soundscape of Modernity*, above all the chapter "The Origins of Modern Acoustics," 13–58.

26. Various models for calculating this have been developed; Beranek's remains one of the most accurate. See Beranek, *Concert Halls and Opera Houses*, esp. 439–50.

27. Antonio Favaro, *L'acustica applicata alla costruzione delle sale per spettacoli e pubbliche adunanze* (Bologna: Forni, 1969).

28. Favaro, *L'acustica applicata alla costruzione delle sale*, 109–38.

29. Garnier, *Le nouvel Opéra de Paris*, 181.

30. Beranek, *Concert Halls and Opera Houses*, 535.

31. Albertini, "Circa la formazione del 'golfo mistico.'" Technical information in the remainder of this section is drawn from this article, unless otherwise noted. For an overview of broader renovations at La Scala around this time, as narrated by Albertini himself, see Vittorio Ferrari, *Il Teatro della Scala nella vita e nell'arte dalle origini ad oggi*, ed. Cesare Tamburini (Milan: C. Tamburini, 1922).

32. Favaro, for instance, discusses the *cassa armonica* in his book; see *L'acustica applicata alla costruzione delle sale*, 128–33.

33. On recognition of the "resonant" properties of wood and their desirability within theaters, see "Intimate and Rational Sound: Acoustics and the Enlightenment," in Joseph L. Clarke, "The Architectural Discourse of Reverberation, 1750–1900" (PhD diss., Yale University, 2014), 55–116.

34. Albertini, "Circa la formazione del 'golfo mistico,'" 386.

35. See, e.g., Kittler, *Gramophone, Film, Typewriter*; and Sterne, *The Audible Past*.

36. See Verdi to Edoardo Mascheroni (December 8, 1893) in *Verdi, interviste e incontri*, ed. Marcello Conati (Milan: Edizioni il Formichiere, 1980), 256–57: "L'orchestra che fa parte del mondo ideale poetico etc. etc. e suona in mezzo al pubblico che applaude o fischia, è la cosa più ridicola del mondo." Verdi made a similar argument in a letter to Giulio Ricordi on July 10, 1871. See Hans Busch, ed., *Verdi's "Aida": The History of an Opera in Letters and Documents*, trans. Hans Busch (Minneapolis: University of Minnesota Press, 1979), 182–83.

37. See *L'orchestra: Organo dell'Associazione Italiana fra i Professori d'Orchestra*, published in Milan between 1901 and 1913.

38. Niccolò Tommaseo and Bernardo Bellini, *Dizionario della lingua italiana* (Turin: Unione Tipografico-Editrice, 1861–79), s.v. "studio." On the history of the term, see Michael Cole and Mary Pardo, "Origins of the Studio," in *Inventions of the Studio: Renaissance to Romanticism*, ed. Michael Cole and Mary Pardo (Chapel Hill: University of North Carolina Press, 2005), 1–35.

39. See Maria Malatesta, ed., *Society and the Professions in Italy, 1860–1914*, trans. Adrian Belton (Cambridge: Cambridge University Press, 1995), 1–23.

40. Desire for sonic insulation in the studio was continuous with broader trends toward sonic privacy in late nineteenth-century Italy. One measure of this new desire for silence is the passing of an 1889 noise abatement law, under Article 457 of the penal code. On this, see Pivato, *Il secolo del rumore*, 39.

41. A further caricature from 1908, for instance, depicts the orchestra pit as a vast swimming pool and notes its utility in the summer months, when the theater tended to get hot. See "Istantanee scaligere," *Ars et labor: Musica e musicisti* (1908): 756.

42. Friedrich Nietzsche, *The Case of Wagner; Nietzsche contra Wagner; The Twilight of the Idols; The Antichrist*, trans. Thomas Common (London: H. Henry, 1896), 69–71.

43. "Ragioni di ordine pubblico e d'arte hanno indotto la direzione ad abolire la replica dei pezzi." See Filippo Sacchi, *Toscanini* (Milan: Longanesi, 1988), 158.

44. For evidence that critics heard the sound of the orchestra under Toscanini as more precise and "streamlined" than ever, see, e.g., A.[gostino] C.[ameroni], "Domenica 26 aprile 1896—1° concerto," *Lega Lombarda* (27 April 1896); G.B. Nappi, "*Il re di Lahore* di Massenet," *La perseveranza* (26 March 1899); and "*Mefistofele* di Boito," *Gazzetta teatrale italiana* (March 16, 1901). On the political implications of this sound, see Richard Taruskin, "The Dark Side of the Moon," in *The Danger of Music and Other Anti-Utopian Essays* (Berkeley and Los Angeles: University of California Press, 2009), 202–16.

45. The literature which mentions the formation of the orchestra pit at La Scala—albeit in passing—tends to attribute the innovation to Toscanini himself. I have found no evidence, however, that Toscanini had such dominance over the process. On the contrary, the documents preserved in the archives reveal the decision was far more collaborative. For an example of literature which claims the pit was hollowed out for Toscanini himself, see, e.g., Harvey Sachs, *Arturo Toscanini from 1915 to 1946: Art in the Shadow of Politics* (Turin: EDT/Musica, 1987), 7.

46. In line with Jonathan Sterne, we could indeed think about the period 1750–1925 as an age of "ensoniment," one in which the world was "rendered . . . audible in new ways." Sterne argues that sound itself (as opposed to instances of sound, such as voice or music) became "an object and domain of thought and practice" for the first time in these years. See Sterne, *The Audible Past*, 2.

47. See Hermann von Helmholtz, *On the Sensations of Tone as a Physiological Basis for the Theory of Music* (London: Longmans, Green, 1875). For a recent take on the importance of Helmholtz to late nineteenth-century acoustic understanding, see esp. Benjamin Steege, *Helmholtz and the Modern Listener* (Cambridge: Cambridge University Press, 2012). Helmholtz's work was well known in Italy: see, e.g., Valeriano Valeriani's multipart article "Consonanze e dissonanze secondo Tartini ed Helmholtz," published in the *Gazzetta musicale di Milano* between July and December 1898; and Carlo Paladini, "Il suono degli strumenti e delle vocali, e il loro timbro secondo la teoria del professor Helmholtz di Heidelberg," *Gazzetta musicale di Milano* (November 15 and 22, 1900). John Tyndall conducted the experiments into sound and heat; see Tyndall, "On the Atmosphere as a Vehicle of Sound," *Philosophical Transactions of the Royal Society of London* 164 (1874): 183–244. His work was discussed a decade later in Favaro, *L'acustica applicata alla costruzione delle sale*, 3–22.

48. Vitruvius also showed keen awareness of the acoustic properties of fan- and arena-shaped enclosures. For a modern edition of his work, see Ingrid D. Rowland, Thomas Noble Howe, and Michael J. Dewar, eds., *Vitruvius: Ten Books on Architecture* (Cambridge and New York: Cambridge University Press, 1999). See also Robin Maconie, "Musical Acoustics in the Age of Vitruvius," *Musical Times* 146, no. 1890 (2005): 75–82.

49. "Nell'accingerci a studiare la applicazione delle leggi di acustica alle disposizioni da darsi agli edifizi, nei quali interessa che la voce umana ed i suoni in generale si diffondano nel miglior modo possibile, vogliamo anzitutto ricordare la massima stabilita da uno dei fisici più autorevoli in materia di acustica, vale a dire che: 'Non v'ha edifizio, per quanto costruito con tutte le cure, nel quale le leggi della acustica sieno così bene osservate come l'aria aperta.' Quivi infatti, con una atmosfera perfettamente tranquilla, senza ostacoli i quali influenzino la propagazione delle onde sonore, il suono si troverà nelle condizioni più favorevoli ad una uniforme diffusione." Favaro, *L'acustica applicata alla costruzione delle sale*, 33.

50. "Fenomeni speciali di riflessione." See "Degli ostacoli che si oppongono alla uniforme propagazione ed alla distinta percezione dei suoni," in Favaro, *L'acustica applicata alla costruzione delle sale*, 39. On new conceptions of reverberation in the nineteenth century, see Clarke, *Echo's Chambers*.

51. See esp. Thompson, *The Soundscape of Modernity*, in which the author argues that the origin of modern acoustics can be traced to the outset of the twentieth century, when demand for an efficient, direct sound increased.

52. On Fonotipia, see esp. Frank H. Andrews, *A Fonotipia Fragmentia: A History of the Società Italiana di Fonotipia, Milano, 1903–1948* ([England]: Historic Singers Trust, 2002); and Società Italiana di Fonotipia, ed., *The Fonotipia Ledgers* (East Barnet: Symposium Records, 2002), which contains an inventory of the company's recordings. On Ricordi's involvement with Fonotipia, see esp. Stefano Baia Curioni, *Mercanti dell'Opera: Storie di Casa Ricordi* (Milan: Il Saggiatore, 2011), 190–206. On the broader history of early sound recording in Italy, see Marco Capra, "'Il Teatro in casa': L'idea di musica riprodotta in Italia tra otto e novecento," in *Il suono riprodotto: Storia, tecnica e cultura di una rivoluzione del novecento*, ed. Alessandro Rigolli and Paolo Russo (Turin: EDT, 2007), 3–11.

53. For a historical overview of sound recording, see, esp. Susan Schmidt-Horning, *Chasing Sound: Technology, Culture, and the Art of Studio Recording from Edison to the LP* (Baltimore: Johns Hopkins University Press, 2013).

54. I place "live event" in scare quotes here because liveness did not of course exist as a category until the conditions of its reproduction were available. On this, see Sterne, *The Audible Past*, 215–86; and Philip Auslander, *Liveness: Performance in a Mediatized Culture* (London: Routledge 2008).

55. Sterne has made this argument with particular force. See Sterne, *The Audible Past*, 215–86.

56. On the sonic fingerprint of studios in the age of electronic and digital recording, see Eliot Bates, "What Studios Do," *Journal on the Art of Record Production* 7 (2012), https://www.arpjournal.com/asarpwp/what-studios-do/.

57. Cittadella degli Archivi, Milan, Fondo Teatro alla Scala, Faldone 340, Fascicolo #14, "Relazione della Commissione pel Teatro alla Scala" (March 16, 1906).

58. "è certo che, anche ammettendo un silenzio perfetto per parte dell'uditorio, le persone più vicine a chi parla costituiscono esse stesse un ostacolo materiale che restringe la sfera di azione del suono; di più, la superficie irregolare costituita dalle teste dell'uditorio è tutt'altro che opportuna alla condotta del suono; finalmente una qualche influenza sarà pure esercitata dalle impurità dell'atmosfera e dalla ineguaglianza della sua temperatura cagionate dalla respirazione della folla e dal calore che da essa emana." Favaro, *L'acustica applicata alla costruzione delle sale*, 35–36.

Chapter Five

1. The novel was first released in serial form, in the Paris daily *Le gaulois*, across 1909 and 1910. Gaston Leroux, *The Phantom of the Opera*, trans. Mireille Ribière (London: Penguin, 2012).

2. Leroux, *The Phantom of the Opera*, 92.

3. Leroux, *The Phantom of the Opera*, 92.

4. Leroux, *The Phantom of the Opera*, 92.

5. On readings of the novel that are sensitive to gender dynamics, see esp. Margaret Miner, "Phantoms of Genius: Women and the Fantastic in the Opera-House Mystery," *19th-Century Music* 18, no. 2 (1994): 121–35. For other literature on *Phantom*, see esp. Cormac Newark, "The Phantom and the Buried Voices of the Paris Opéra," in *Opera in the Novel from Balzac to Proust* (Cambridge: Cambridge University Press, 2011), 136–66.

6. Leroux, *The Phantom of the Opera*, 127–28.

7. On the poetics of ascent, see esp. Gaston Bachelard, *Air and Dreams: An Essay on the Imagination of Movement*, trans. Edith R. Farrell and C. Frederick Farrell (Dallas, TX: Dallas Institute Publications, 2011). Originally published as Bachelard, *L'air et les songes, essai sur l'imagination du mouvement* (Paris: Librairie José Corti, 1943).

8. For an account that takes both the novel and its subsequent adaptations with unprecedented seriousness, see Jerrold E. Hogle, *The Undergrounds of "The Phantom of the Opera": Sublimation and the Gothic in Leroux's Novel and Its Progeny* (New York: Palgrave, 2002).

9. Johnson, *Inventing the Opera House*.

10. For the fullest account of these theatres, see Eugene J. Johnson, "The Short, Lascivious Lives of Two Venetian Theaters, 1580–85," *Renaissance Quarterly* 55, no. 3 (2002): 936–68.

11. Johnson, *Inventing the Opera House*, 119–20.

12. Johnson, *Inventing the Opera House*, 16.

13. On ceiling decoration at teatri all'italiana, see esp. Banu, *Le rouge et or*, 212–36; and Pierre Vaisse, "Le décor peint dans les théâtres (1750–1900): Problèmes esthétiques et iconographiques," in *Victor Louis et le théâtre: scénographie, mise en scène et architecture théâtrale aux XVIIIe et XIXe siècles* (Paris: Centre National de la Recherche Scientifique, 1982), 153–67. The information in this paragraph is drawn from these sources.

14. Vaisse, "Le décor peint dans les théâtres."

15. Banu, *Le rouge et or*, 233.

16. On the Palais Garnier see esp. Christopher Curtis Mead, *Charles Garnier's Paris Opéra: Architectural Empathy and the Renaissance of French Classicism* (Cambridge, MA: MIT Press, 1991). For an example of how the Palais Garnier can be brought into dialogue with recent trends in musicology, see Benjamin Walton, "Technological Phantoms of the Opéra," in *Nineteenth-Century Opera and the Scientific Imagination*, ed. David Trippett and Benjamin Walton (Cambridge: Cambridge University Press, 2019), 199–226.

17. On the actual chandelier incident, see Leroux, *The Phantom of the Opera*, xvi. As Newark notes, the class distinctions that the incident exposed were in fact, in this case, commented on in some detail in the press. See Newark, "The Phantom and the Buried Voices of the Paris Opéra," 144.

18. The narrator tells us about these files thus: "It would be churlish on my part, on the threshold of this awe-inspiring and true story, not to thank the present management of the Paris Opera House, who so kindly helped me with my enquiries, and M. Messager in particular; I should also like to thank the present administrator, the charming M. Gabion, as well as the amiable architect entrusted with the preservation of the building, who did not hesitate to lend me the works of Charles Garnier, though he guessed that I would probably never return them to him. Finally, I must pay public tribute to my friend and former colleague, M. J.-L. Croze, who allowed me to search his splendid collection of theatre books and borrow rare editions that he greatly valued.—G. L." See Leroux, *The Phantom of the Opera*, 9. For the works alluded to here, see Garnier, *Le théâtre*, and Garnier, *Le nouvel Opéra de Paris*.

19. Mead, *Charles Garnier's Paris Opéra*, 146–147.

20. On the use of structural metal at the Palais Garnier, see esp. Mead, *Charles Garnier's Paris Opéra*. For accessible introductions to structural metal and its earliest uses, see Robert Thorne, ed. *Structural Iron and Steel, 1850–1900* (Aldershot: Ashgate/Variorum, 2000); Jonathan Clarke, *Early Structural Steel in London Buildings: A Discreet Revolution* (London: English Heritage, 2014); and Paul Dobraszczyk and Peter Sealy, eds., *Function and Fantasy: Iron Architecture in the Long Nineteenth Century* (Oxford: Routledge, 2016). For a now-classic text on structural iron, see Sigfried Giedion, *Building in France, Building in Iron, Building in Ferro-Concrete* (Santa Monica, CA: Getty Center for the History of Art and the Humanities, 1995).

21. On some of the earliest uses of structural iron at theaters, see Clarke, *Early Structural Steel in London Buildings*, 107–39.

22. J. E. Gordon has in fact claimed that the structure described in the Bible would have been viable, so long as it remained uninhabited: "elementary arithmetic shows that a tower with parallel walls could have been built to a height of 7,000 feet or 2 kilometers before the bricks at the bottom would be crushed. However, by making the walls taper towards the top [a simple tower] could well have been built to such a height that the men of Shinar would have run short of oxygen and

had difficulty in breathing before the brick walls were crushed beneath their own dead weight." See Gordon, *Structures; or, Why Things Don't Fall Down* (New York: Da Capo Press, 1981), 172.

23. See Peter Sealy, "Dreams in Iron: The Wish Image in Émile Zola's Novels," in *Function and Fantasy: Iron Architecture in the Long Nineteenth Century*, ed. Paul Dobraszczyk and Peter Sealy (Oxford: Routledge, 2016), 221–45.

24. Zola, *The Ladies' Paradise*, 345.

25. Sealy, "Dreams in Iron," 236. Sealy has also noted that Giedion identified the nineteenth-century rooftop as a site removed from the pressures of historicist representation, "where the unconscious building of engineers could engender new aesthetic, spatial and social principals for architecture." See Sealy, "The Roofscape as Locus of Modernity in Giedion and Zola," in *Proceedings of the Society of Architectural Historians, Australia and New Zealand*, ed. Alexandra Brown and Andrew Leach, 2 vols. (Gold Coast, Queensland: SAHANZ, 2013), 2:891; and Giedion, *Building in France*, 117.

26. On theories of the threshold, see esp. Georg Simmel, "Bridge and Door," *Theory, Culture and Society* 11 (1994): 5–10; Bachelard, *The Poetics of Space*; Subha Mukherji, ed. *Thinking on Thresholds: The Poetics of Transitive Spaces* (London: Anthem Press, 2011); Bernhard Siegert, "Doors: on the Materiality of the Symbolic," trans. John Durham Peters *Grey Room* 47 (Spring 2012): 6–23; Siegert, *Cultural Techniques: Grids, Filters, Doors, and Other Articulations of the Real*, trans. Geoffrey Winthrop-Young (New York: Fordham University Press, 2015); and Oles, *Walls*. For a still-classic account of walls in architecture, see Lewis Mumford, *The City in History: Its Origins, Its Transformations, and Its Prospects* (New York: Harcourt, Brace & World, 1961).

27. Johnson, *Inventing the Opera House*, 115–18.

28. Leroux, *The Phantom of the Opera*, 5.

29. On the concept of *poché*, see Wolfgang Meisenheimer, "Of the Hollow Spaces in the Skin of the Architectural Body," in *Toward a New Interior: An Anthology of Interior Design Theory*, ed. Lois Weinthal (New York: Princeton Architectural Press, 2011), 625–31.

30. Jacques Lacan, "The Mirror-Phase as Formative of the Function of the I," *New Left Review* 51 (1968): 63–77.

31. On the revolving door as new architectural device, see Laurent Stalder, "Turning Architecture Inside Out: Revolving Doors and Other Threshold Devices," *Journal of Design History* 22, no. 1 (2009): 69–77.

32. As the narrator tells us, "Christine continued moving closer to the mirror, her image tilted forwards towards her. The two Christines—the real one and her reflection—eventually touched and merged." Leroux, *The Phantom of the Opera*, 112.

33. Oles, *Walls*, 164.

34. R. J. M. Sutherland, ed., *Structural Iron, 1750–1850* (Aldershot: Ashgate/Variorum, 1997).

35. Paul Carter, *The Lie of the Land* (London: Faber, 1996), 2–3. Cited in Andrew Hassam, "Portable Iron Structures and Uncertain Colonial Spaces at the Sydenham Crystal Palace," in *Imperial Cities: Landscape, Display and Identity*, ed. Felix Driver and David Gilbert (Manchester: Manchester University Press, 1999), 174–93.

36. See, e.g., John M. MacKenzie, *The British Empire Through Buildings: Structure, Function and Meaning* (Manchester: Manchester University Press, 2020); Jonathan

Clarke, "From Rational to Structurally Ornamental: Exported English Iron Architecture of the Mid-Nineteenth Century," in Dobraszczyk and Sealy, *Function and Fantasy*, 113–40; and Lucia Juarez, "Scottish Cast Iron in Argentina: Its Role in the British Informal Imperial System," in Dobraszczyk and Sealy, *Function and Fantasy*, 141–62.

37. Charles Dickens used this analogy to describe Joseph Paxton's 1851 Great Exhibition building, itself a portable iron structure. See Dickens, "The Private History of the Palace of Glass," *Household Words: A Weekly Journal* (January 18, 1851), 386. Cited in Hassam, "Portable Iron Structures," 179.

38. Hassam, "Portable Iron Structures," 174; and MacKenzie, *The British Empire Through Buildings*, 104–5.

39. On the standardization of structural metal components in the nineteenth century, see Clarke, *Early Structural Steel in London Buildings*, esp. "Part 1: Technological Preconditions and Other Contexts," 1–105. A later chapter, "Theatres and Music Halls: Advances in Safety and Sighting," 107–39, provides an overview of structural metal components at nineteenth-century theaters.

40. On this, see Sokratis Georgiadis, "Introduction," in Giedion, *Building in France*, 1–78.

41. M. Frantz Jourdain, *Constructions élevées au Champ de Mars par M. Ch. Garnier pour servir à l'histoire de l'habitation humaine* (Paris: Librairie Centrale des Beaux-Arts, 1889); and Charles Garnier and Auguste Ammann, *L'habitation humaine* (Paris: Librairie Hachette, 1892).

42. Garnier was also a signatory to a letter protesting the construction of the tower, published on February 14, 1887 in the newspaper *Le Temps*. See Mead, *Charles Garnier's Paris Opéra*, 156–57 and 303–4. The translation is taken from Mead.

43. McMahon, "Music in the Urban Amazon," 36. On theatrical spaces within their urban ecology in the same region, see Rogério Budasz, *Opera in the Tropics: Music and Theater in Early Modern Brazil* (Oxford: Oxford University Press, 2019), 157–223.

44. Jourdain, *Constructions élevées au Champ de Mars*, 1. For recent work that draws attention to such dynamics, see, e.g., Mark Crinson, '"Compartmentalized World': Race, Architecture, and Colonial Crisis in Kenya and London," in *Race and Modern Architecture: A Critical History from the Enlightenment to the Present*, ed. Irene Cheng, Charles L. Davis II, and Mabel O. Wilson (Pittsburgh, PA: University of Pittsburgh Press, 2020), 259–76.

45. On the emergence of stone as a predominant building material in the West, see, e.g., Richard Sennett, *Flesh and Stone: The Body and the City in Western Civilization* (New York: W. W. Norton, 1994), 188–90.

46. Christopher B. Balme, *The Globalization of Theatre, 1870–1930: The Theatrical Networks of Maurice E. Bandmann* (Cambridge: Cambridge University Press, 2020), 221–30; and J. J. Sheppard, ed., *Territorials in India: A Souvenir of their Historic Arrival for Military Duty in the "Land of the Rupee"; From the Royal Opera House, Bombay; Prepared in Accordance with the Instructions of the Proprietor, J. F. Karaka* (Bombay: J. J. Sheppard, 1916).

47. On the architectural history of the Theatro Municipal, see anon., *Theatro municipal do Rio de Janeiro* (Rio de Janeiro: Photo Musso, 1913).

48. Similar lack of attention to the often oppressive dynamics of architecture has also been characteristic of scholarship about built environments more broadly. For

a recent corrective to this, see, e.g., Cheng, Davis, and Wilson, *Race and Modern Architecture*.

49. Osterhammel, *The Transformation of the World*, 5–6.

50. Thorne, *Structural Iron and Steel, 1850–1900*, xv–xvi.

51. On the switch from timber to metal hulls in the context of global travel, see Osterhammel, *The Transformation of the World*, esp. 275–83. On transatlantic crossing times, see Martin Stopford, *Maritime Economics* (London: Routledge, 1997), 48.

52. McMahon, "Music in the Urban Amazon," 31–32.

53. Osterhammel, *The Transformation of the World*, 6.

54. McMahon, "Music in the Urban Amazon," 34–40.

55. McMahon, "Music in the Urban Amazon," 37–38.

56. Juarez, "Scottish Cast Iron in Argentina," 145.

57. On the former, see Juarez, "Scottish Cast Iron in Argentina," 145. On the latter, see Ana Maria Daou, *A belle époque amazônica* (Rio de Janeiro: Jorge Zahar Editor, 2000), 13–14.

58. Literature on Herzog's *Fitzcarraldo* is abundant. For an account of the film from a musicological perspective, see esp. Holly Rogers, "Fitzcarraldo's Search for Aguirre: Music and Text in the Amazonian Films of Werner Herzog," *Journal of the Royal Musical Association* 129, no. 1 (2004): 77–99; and Richard Leppert, "Opera, Aesthetic Violence, and the Imposition of Modernity: *Fitzcarraldo*," in *Sound Judgment: Selected Essays* (Aldershot: Ashgate, 2007), 11–31.

59. Again, I borrow this conceptual apparatus from Devine. See Devine, *Decomposed*; and Devine and Boudreault-Fournier, *Audible Infrastructures*.

60. On this, see Barbara Weinstein, *The Amazon Rubber Boom, 1850–1920* (Stanford, CA: Stanford University Press, 1983); and Warren Dean, *Brazil and the Struggle for Rubber: A Study in Environmental History* (Cambridge: Cambridge University Press, 2002).

61. Roger Casement, *The Amazon Journal of Roger Casement*, ed. Angus Mitchell (London: Anaconda Editions, 1997), 248–49.

62. Dean, *Brazil and the Struggle for Rubber*.

63. "[Acoustically] good and bad halls exist in every age, and good and bad halls have probably been built in every period. It is more than likely that the old halls that are still standing are among the best that were built. Very few halls that compared badly with their contemporaries are still with us. In fact, poor halls are often destroyed or replaced before they are 50 years old, as Boston's most recent Opera House (1909 to 1958) and New York's Italian Opera House (1833 to 1839) remind us. On the other hand, heroic measures are often taken to preserve good halls." See Beranek, *Music, Acoustics and Architecture*, 11.

64. On the complex phenomenon of architectural obsolescence, see esp. Daniel M. Abramson, *Obsolescence: An Architectural History* (Chicago: University of Chicago Press, 2016).

65. Oles, *Walls*, 166.

66. For a broad introduction to this political trend, see Duggan, *The Force of Destiny*, 350–73. At Milan's Teatro alla Scala, among the reasons renovations were undertaken in the 1920s was a desire to increase the volume of works the theater could offer and thereby "interessare sempre più il pubblico agli spettacoli, sfuggendo la monotonia delle repliche eccessive" (interest the public ever more in performances, avoiding the monotony of excessive repetitions [of the same work]). See Cesare Albertini,

"L'instancabile vicenda della Scala," *Città di Milano* (December 1, 1949), 199. This was continuous with other initiatives oriented toward a broader public, such as La Scala's collaboration with Milan's Teatro del Popolo, a theater constructed in 1910 on the site of the former warehouse of an electromechanical company; La Scala mounted performances both there and at their own theater with the aim to awaken in the broader public taste for instrumental and vocal music, chamber and concert music. See Giuseppe Barigazzi and Silvia Barigazzi, *La Scala racconta* (Milan: Editore Ulrico Hoepli, 2014), 310–11; and Secchi, *1778/1978: Il Teatro alla Scala*, 179.

67. In Milan, for instance, the civic authorities imposed a rule in 1920 that disallowed construction that would result in buildings taller than twelve meters unless (a) the building was of particular artistic importance and (b) an exception to the rule was granted. An absolute height limit was imposed even for buildings that met the definition of artistic importance. See anon., "Il nuovo regolamento edilizio del Comune di Milano," in *Il monitore tecnico* (1920), 274–76. For further context, see esp. Cesare Albertini, "Questioni di urbanismo: L'altezza delle case," *Ingegneria* (May 1, 1923), 3–10.

68. On the formation of the Ente Autonomo, see, e.g., Barigazzi and Barigazzi, *La Scala racconta*, 301–33.

69. For a comprehensive list of the major donors who facilitated the renovations and the amounts they donated, see Ferrari, *Il Teatro della Scala nella vita e nell'arte*, 54.

70. Cesare Albertini, "La riforma del palcoscenico della 'Scala,'" *Città di Milano* (April 30, 1919); Albertini, "Il palcoscenico si rinnova," in *La lettura: Rivista mensile del Corriere della sera* (February 1920); Albertini, "Come si rinnova il Teatro alla Scala," *Città di Milano* (May 31, 1921); Marangoni and Vanbianchi, *La Scala: Studi e ricerche*; Albertini, "Il rinnovamento," in Ferrari, *Il Teatro della Scala nella vita e nell'arte*, 59–74; Anon., "Dietro la scena," in *La stagione della Scala MCMXXII–XXIII* (1923); Albertini, "Ancora l'allestimento scenico del 'Teatro alla Scala,'" in *Rivista musicale italiana* (1923); Albertini, "Come sarà la nuova Milano," in *Rivista mensile del Comune di Milano* (August 31, 1929); and Albertini, "L'instancabile vicenda della Scala."

71. For one example alone, see, e.g., Marangoni and Vanbianchi, *La Scala: Studi e ricerche*, 513.

72. Albertini, "Il rinnovamento," in Ferrari, *Il Teatro alla Scala nella vita e nell'arte*, 59–74; and Albertini, "Come si rinnova il Teatro alla Scala."

73. A report by the commissioners for the Teatro alla Scala estimated that the cost of the planned renovations to the gallery itself would be 5000 lire and described this as "non molto costosa" (not very expensive). Cittadella degli Archivi, Milan, Fondo Teatro alla Scala, Faldone 340, Fascicolo #14, "Relazione della Commissione pel Teatro alla Scala" (March 16, 1906). For a reproduction of parts of this document, see Marangoni and Vanbianchi, *La Scala: Studi e ricerche*, 179–85. For a description of the new gallery, see Secchi, *1778/1978: Il Teatro alla Scala*, 155.

74. Clarke, *Early Structural Steel in London Buildings*, 133–39.

75. "Popolarizzare ed a popolare (sia detto senza bisticcio) il teatro," *Relazione della Commissione pel Teatro alla Scala* (March 16, 1906).

76. On the staircase within opera house design, see Edwin O. Sachs, *Modern Opera Houses and Theatres*, 3 vols. (New York: Benjamin Blom, 1968), 3:81–89. On the staircase as architectural element across time, see John A. Templer, *The Staircase*, 2 vols. (Cambridge, MA: MIT Press, 1992).

77. Leroux, *The Phantom of the Opera*, xxv.

78. This fire curtain was reportedly the work of the Società Leonardo da Vinci, Milan. See Albertini, "Il rinnovamento," in Ferrari, *Il Teatro alla Scala nella vita e nell'arte*, 73. Little has been written on the fire curtain here or elsewhere. On the idea of the fire curtain, however, see Banu, *Le rouge et or*, 256–57.

79. For a virtuosic account of the curtain that considers it to be "an integral part of theatrical architecture from the time of opera's beginnings," see Kreuzer, *Curtain, Gong, Steam*, 55. Banu is also essential reading here; Banu, *Le rouge et or*, 237–71.

80. As described in "Acoustics," an encore ban was instated at La Scala in 1907. See Sacchi, *Toscanini*, 158.

81. Stephen J. Pyne, *Fire: A Brief History* (Seattle: University of Washington Press, 2001), 116.

82. Pyne, *Fire*, 116.

83. Pyne, *Fire*, 116.

84. Pyne, *Fire*, 115.

85. Esther Addley, "BP Sponsorship of Royal Opera House Ends After 33 Years," *Guardian*, January 25, 2023, https://www.theguardian.com/culture/2023/jan/25/bp-sponsorship-of-royal-opera-house-ends-after-33-years.

86. "Abbiamo illuminato La Scala per primi nel 1883. Oggi, contribuiamo a rendere questa illuminazione sostenibile. Perchè anche un'atmosfera con meno CO_2 è uno spettacolo che vogliamo preservare." "La Scala green," Edison, video, 00:30, https://youtu.be/qzZJr70PK7M.

87. Johnson, *Inventing the Opera House*, 16.

BIBLIOGRAPHY

Archives

Archivio Beni Architettonici e Paesaggio, Milan
Archivio di Stato di Milano, Milan
Archivio Storico Civico, Milan
Archivio Storico del Comune di Bologna, Bologna
Archivio Storico della Città di Torino, Turin
Archivio Visconti di Modrone, Milan
Biblioteca Livia Simoni, Milan
Casa della Musica di Parma, Parma
Cittadella degli Archivi, Milan
Civico Archivio Fotografico, Milan

Historical Newspapers and Journals

Ars et labor: Musica e musicisti
Corriere della sera
Cosmorama pittorico
Gazzetta musicale di Milano
Gazzetta teatrale italiana
Il mondo artistico
Il monitore tecnico
Il politecnico: Giornale dell'ingegnere architetto civile ed industriale
Il secolo
Il teatro illustrato
Ingegneria
L'arte melodrammatica
L'orchestra: Organo dell'Associazione Italiana fra i Professori d'Orchestra
La libertà
La lettura: Rivista mensile del Corriere della sera
La lumière électrique
La perseveranza
La tribuna
Lega Lombarda

Rivista mensile del Comune di Milano
Rivista musicale italiana
The Lancet

Secondary Sources

Abramson, Daniel M. *Obsolescence: An Architectural History*. Chicago: University of Chicago Press, 2016.

Addley, Esther. "BP Sponsorship of Royal Opera House Ends After 33 Years." *Guardian*. January 25, 2023. https://www.theguardian.com/culture/2023/jan/25/bp-sponsorship-of-royal-opera-house-ends-after-33-years.

Adorno, Theodor. *In Search of Wagner*. Translated by Rodney Livingstone. London: Verso, 1981.

Ahmed, Sara, and Jackie Stacey, eds. *Thinking Through the Skin*. London: Routledge, 2001.

Albertini, Cesare. "Ancora l'allestimento scenico del 'Teatro alla Scala.'" *Rivista musicale italiana* (1923).

Albertini, Cesare. "Circa la formazione del 'golfo mistico' per le orchestre dei nostri teatri." *Il monitore tecnico* 20 (1913): 383–88.

Albertini, Cesare. "Come sarà la nuova Milano." *Rivista mensile del Comune di Milano* (August 31, 1929).

Albertini, Cesare. "Come si rinnova il Teatro alla Scala." *Città di Milano* (May 31, 1921).

Albertini, Cesare. "L'instancabile vicenda della Scala." *Città di Milano* (December 1, 1949).

Albertini, Cesare. "Il palcoscenico si rinnova." *La lettura: Rivista mensile del Corriere della sera* (February 1920).

Albertini, Cesare. "Questioni di urbanismo: L'altezza delle case." *Ingegneria* (May 1, 1923).

Albertini, Cesare. "La riforma del palcoscenico della 'Scala.'" *Città di Milano* (April 30, 1919).

Albertini, Cesare. "Il rinnovamento." In Vittorio Ferrari, *Il Teatro alla Scala nella vita e nell'arte dalle origini ad oggi*, edited by Cesare Albertini, 59–74. Milan: C. Tamburini, 1922.

Albrecht, Robert. *Mediating the Muse: A Communications Approach to Music, Media, and Cultural Change*. Cresskill, NJ: Hampton Press, 2004.

Alglave, Émile, and J. Boulard. *La lumière électrique, son histoire, sa production et son emploi dans l'éclairage public ou privé, les phares, les théâtres, l'industrie, les travaux publics, les opérations militaires et maritimes*. Paris: Firmin-Didot, 1882.

Andrews, H. Frank. *A Fonotipia Fragmentia: A History of the Società Italiana di Fonotipia, Milano, 1903–1948*. [England]: Historic Singers Trust, 2002.

Anon. *Theatro municipal do Rio de Janeiro*. Rio de Janeiro: Photo Musso, 1913.

Archibald, Sasha. "Blinded by the Light." *Cabinet* 21 (Spring 2006): 97–100.

Auslander, Leora. *Taste and Power: Furnishing Modern France*. Berkeley: University of California Press, 1996.

Auslander, Philip. *Liveness: Performance in a Mediatized Culture*. London: Routledge, 2008.

Bachelard, Gaston. *Air and Dreams: An Essay on the Imagination of Movement*. Translated by Edith R. Farrell and C. Frederick Farrell. Dallas, TX: Dallas Institute Publications, 2011.

Bachelard, Gaston. *The Poetics of Space*. Translated by Maria Jolas. New York: Penguin, 2014.
Baia Curioni, Stefano. *Mercanti dell'Opera: Storie di Casa Ricordi*. Milan: Il Saggiatore, 2011.
Baker, Evan. *From the Score to the Stage: An Illustrated History of Continental Opera Production and Staging*. Chicago: University of Chicago Press, 2013.
Balme, Christopher B. *The Globalization of Theatre 1870–1930: The Theatrical Networks of Maurice E. Bandmann*. Cambridge: Cambridge University Press, 2020.
Banti, Alberto M. *Storia della borghesia italiana: L'età liberale*. Rome: Donzelli, 1996.
Banu, Georges. *Le rouge et or: Une poétique du théâtre à l'italienne*. Paris: Flammarion, 1989.
Barber, Daniel A. *Modern Architecture and Climate: Design Before Air Conditioning*. Princeton, NJ: Princeton University Press, 2020.
Barblan, Guglielmo, and Eugenio Gara. *Toscanini e La Scala*. Milan: Edizioni della Scala, 1972.
"Barcelona Opera House Reopens to an Audience of Plants." Associated Press, June 23, 2020. Video, 8:03. https://globalnews.ca/news/7098004/barcelona-opera-house-plants/.
Barigazzi, Giuseppe, and Silvia Barigazzi. *La Scala racconta*. Milan: Editore Ulrico Hoepli, 2014.
Barron, Michael. *Auditorium Acoustics and Architectural Design*. London: Spon Press, 2010.
Barth, Herbert, Dietrich Mack, and Egon Voss, eds. *Wagner: A Documentary Study*. Oxford: Oxford University Press, 1975.
Bassi, Agostino. *Memoria del dottore Agostino Bassi, in addizione alla di lui opera sul calcino, unitevi le relazioni dei vantaggi ottenuti già da molti coltivatori dei bachi da seta coll'uso degli insegnamenti dell'autore*. Milan: P. A. Molina, 1837.
Batchelor, David. *Chromophobia*. London: Reaktion Books, 2000.
Bates, Eliot. "What Studios Do." *Journal on the Art of Record Production* 7 (2012). https://www.arpjournal.com/asarpwp/what-studios-do/.
Battistelli, Franco, Luca Ferretti, and Giuseppina Boiani Tombari. *Il teatro della Fortuna in Fano: Storia dell'edificio e cronologia degli spettacoli*. 2 vols. Fano: Carifano, 1998.
Benjamin, Walter. *The Arcades Project*. Translated by Howard Eiland and Kevin McLaughlin. Cambridge, MA: Belknap Press of Harvard University Press, 1999.
Benjamin, Walter. "Paris, Capital of the Nineteenth Century." In *Reflections: Essays, Aphorisms, Autobiographical Writing*, translated by Edmund Jephcott. New York: Houghton Mifflin Harcourt, 2019.
Bennett, Jane. *Vibrant Matter: A Political Ecology of Things*. Durham, NC: Duke University Press, 2010.
Bentley, Charlotte. *New Orleans and the Creation of Transatlantic Opera, 1815–1859*. Chicago: University of Chicago Press, 2022.
Beranek, Leo L. *Concert Halls and Opera Houses: How They Sound*. Woodbury, NY: Acoustical Society of America, 1996.
Beranek, Leo L. *Music, Acoustics and Architecture*. New York: Wiley, 1962.
Best, Stephen, and Sharon Marcus. "Surface Reading: An Introduction." *Representations* 108, no. 1 (2009): 1–21.
Billings, John S. *The Principles of Ventilation and Heating and Their Practical Application*. New York: Engineering and Building Record, 1889.

Bowker, Geoffrey C., and Susan Leigh Star. *Sorting Things Out: Classification and Its Consequences.* Cambridge, MA: MIT Press, 1999.

Broggi, Luigi. "L'edificio del Teatro alla Scala in Milano." In *Il politecnico: Giornale dell'ingegnere architetto civile ed industriale.* Milan: Tipologia e Litografia degli Ingegneri, 1878.

Bruno, Giuliana. *Surface: Matters of Aesthetics, Materiality, and Media.* Chicago: University of Chicago Press, 2014.

Budasz, Rogério. *Opera in the Tropics: Music and Theater in Early Modern Brazil.* Oxford: Oxford University Press, 2019.

Buffelli, Domenico. *Elementi di mimica.* Milan: Da Placido Maria Visaj, 1829.

Busch, Hans, ed. *Verdi's Aida: The History of an Opera in Letters and Documents.* Translated by Hans Busch. Minneapolis: University of Minnesota Press, 1979.

Buss, Chiara. "Il tessuto del teatro." In *Per La Scala*, vol. 2, *Creativity, Innovation, and Tradition: The Fabric of the Theater*, edited by Giorgio Cortella, Gianfranco Colombo, and Chiara Buss, 121–25. Milan: Amici della Scala, 1992.

Buss, Chiara, ed. *Silk: The 1900's in Como.* Milan: Silvana Editoriale, 2001.

Butler, Judith. *What World Is This? A Pandemic Phenomenology.* New York: Columbia University Press, 2022.

Calcagnini, Gilberto. *Il teatro Rossini di Pesaro fra spettacolo e cronaca, 1898–1966: Memorie cronistoriche.* Fano: Editrice Fortuna, 1997.

Cambiasi, Pompeo. *La Scala, 1778–1906: Note storiche e statistiche.* 2 vols. Milan: G. Ricordi, 1906.

Capra, Marco. "L'illuminazione sulla scena verdiana, ovvero L'arco voltaico non acceca la luna?" In *La realizzazione scenica dello spettacolo verdiano*, edited by Fabrizio della Seta and Pierluigi Petrobelli, 230–64. Parma: Istituto di Studi Verdiani, 1996.

Capra, Marco. "'Il Teatro in casa': L'idea di musica riprodotta in Italia tra otto e novecento." In *Il suono riprodotto: Storia, tecnica e cultura di una rivoluzione del novecento*, edited by Alessandro Rigolli and Paolo Russo, 3–11. Turin: EDT, 2007.

Carnegy, Patrick. *Wagner and the Art of the Theatre.* New Haven, CT: Yale University Press, 2006.

Carter, Paul. *The Lie of the Land.* London: Faber, 1996.

Casement, Roger. *The Amazon Journal of Roger Casement.* Edited by Angus Mitchell. London: Anaconda Editions, 1997.

Castellani, Giovanni B. *Dell'allevamento dei bachi da seta in China: Fatto ed osservato sui luoghi.* Florence: Barbèra, 1860.

Chakrabarty, Dipesh. "The Climate of History: Four Theses." *Critical Inquiry* 35, no. 2 (2009): 197–222.

Cheng, Anne Anlin. *Second Skin: Josephine Baker and the Modern Surface.* Oxford: Oxford University Press, 2011.

Cheng, Irene, Charles L. Davis II, and Mabel O. Wilson, eds. *Race and Modern Architecture: A Critical History from the Enlightenment to the Present.* Pittsburgh, PA: University of Pittsburgh Press, 2020.

Chevreul, Michel Eugène. *De la loi du contraste simultané des couleurs.* Paris: Pitois-Levrault, 1839.

Chevreul, Michel Eugène. *The Principles of Harmony and Contrast of Colors and Their Applications to the Arts.* Translated by Charles Martel. London: Henry G. Bohn, 1860.

Clarke, Jonathan. *Early Structural Steel in London Buildings: A Discreet Revolution.* London: English Heritage, 2014.

Clarke, Jonathan. "From Rational to Structurally Ornamental: Exported English Iron Architecture of the Mid-Nineteenth Century." In *Function and Fantasy*, edited by Paul Dobraszczyk and Peter Sealy, 113–40. Oxford: Routledge, 2016.

Clarke, Joseph L. "The Architectural Discourse of Reverberation, 1750–1900." PhD diss., Yale University, 2014.

Clarke, Joseph L. *Echo's Chambers: Architecture and the Idea of Acoustic Space*. Pittsburgh, PA: University of Pittsburgh Press, 2021.

Coen, Deborah R. *Climate in Motion: Science, Empire, and the Problem of Scale*. Chicago: University of Chicago Press, 2018.

Cole, Michael, and Mary Pardo, eds. *Inventions of the Studio: Renaissance to Romanticism*. Chapel Hill: University of North Carolina Press, 2005.

Colombo, Giuseppe. *Il "carbone bianco": Scritti sull'elettrificazione e la corrispondenza con Thomas A. Edison*. Milan: Anthelios Edizioni, 2013.

Colombo, Giuseppe. "Illuminazione elettrica." In *Milano tecnica dal 1859 al 1884*, edited by Francesco Ajraghi, 459–73. Milan: Hoepli, 1885.

Colombo, Giuseppe. *Industria e politica nella storia d'Italia: Scritti scelti, 1861–1916*. Edited by Carlo G. Lacaita. Milan: Cariplo, 1985.

Colombo, Giuseppe. "Station centrale d'éclairage électrique de Milan: Éclairage électrique du théâtre de la Scala." *La lumière électrique* 11, no. 2 (January 12, 1884).

Colombo, Giuseppe. "La trasmissione elettrica della forza e il suo significato per l'avvenire dell'industria italiana." *La perseveranza* (April 21, 1890).

Conati, Marcello ed. *Verdi, interviste e incontri*. Milan: Edizioni il Formichiere, 1980.

Connor, Steven. *The Book of Skin*. Ithaca, NY: Cornell University Press, 2004.

Connor, Steven. *The Matter of Air: Science and Art of the Ethereal*. London: Reaktion Books, 2010.

Conrad, Sebastian. *What Is Global History?* Princeton, NJ: Princeton University Press, 2017.

Cornelio, Angelo Maria. *Vita di Antonio Stoppani: Onoranze alla sua memoria*. Turin: Unione Tipografico-Editrice, 1898.

Cressman, Darryl. *Building Musical Culture in Nineteenth-Century Amsterdam: The Concertgebouw*. Amsterdam: Amsterdam University Press, 2016.

Crinson, Mark. '"Compartmentalized World': Race, Architecture, and Colonial Crisis in Kenya and London." In *Race and Modern Architecture: A Critical History from the Enlightenment to the Present*, edited by Irene Cheng, Charles L. Davis II, and Mabel O. Wilson, 259–76. Pittsburgh, PA: University of Pittsburgh Press, 2020.

Cruciani, Fabrizio. *Lo spazio del teatro*. Rome: Laterza, 1997.

Crutzen, Paul J., and Eugene F. Stoermer. "The 'Anthropocene.'" *Global Change Newsletter* (International Geosphere-Biosphere Programme) 41 (May 2000): 17–18.

Cruz, Gabriela. *Grand Illusion: Phantasmagoria in Nineteenth-Century Opera*. Oxford: Oxford University Press, 2020.

da Costa Meyer, Esther. "Architectural History in the Anthropocene: Towards Methodology." *Journal of Architecture* 21, no. 8 (2016): 1203–25.

D'Annunzio, Gabriele. "Il caso Wagner." *La tribuna* (July 23 and August 3 and 9, 1893).

D'Annunzio, Gabriele. *I romanzi della rosa: Trionfo della morte*. Rome: L'Oleandro, 1933.

D'Annunzio, Gabriele. *The Triumph of Death*. Translated by Arthur Hornblow. New York: G. H. Richmond, 1898.

Daou, Ana Maria. *A belle époque amazônica*. Rio de Janeiro: Jorge Zahar Editor, 2000.

Dart, Thurston. *The Interpretation of Music*. London: Hutchinson, 1984.
Davies, J. Q. *Creatures of the Air: Music, Atlantic Spirits, Breath, 1817–1913*. Chicago: University of Chicago Press, 2023.
Davies, J. Q. "Elijah's Nature." *19th-Century Music* 45, no. 1 (2021): 49–63.
Davies, J. Q. "Pneumotypes: Jean de Reszke's High Pianissimos and the Occult Science of Breathing." In *Nineteenth-Century Opera and the Scientific Imagination*, edited by David Trippett and Benjamin Walton, 21–43. Cambridge: Cambridge University Press, 2019.
Dean, Warren. *Brazil and the Struggle for Rubber: A Study in Environmental History*. Cambridge: Cambridge University Press, 2002.
Della Sala Spada, Agostino. *Nel 2073! Sogni d'uno stravagante*. Edited by Simonetta Satragni Petruzzi. Alessandria: Edizioni dell'Orso, 1998.
Devine, Kyle. *Decomposed: The Political Ecology of Music*. Cambridge, MA: MIT Press, 2019.
Devine, Kyle, and Alexandrine Boudreault-Fournier, eds. *Audible Infrastructures: Music, Sound, Media*. Oxford: Oxford University Press, 2021.
Dickens, Charles. "The Private History of the Palace of Glass." *Household Words: A Weekly Journal* (January 18, 1851).
Dizionario biografico degli italiani. Rome: Istituto della Enciclopedia Italiana, 1960–2020.
Dobraszczyk, Paul, and Peter Sealy eds., *Function and Fantasy: Iron Architecture in the Long Nineteenth Century*. Oxford: Routledge, 2016.
Duggan, Christopher. *The Force of Destiny: A History of Italy Since 1796*. Boston: Houghton Mifflin, 2008.
Eidsheim, Nina Sun. *Sensing Sound: Singing and Listening as Vibrational Practice*. Durham, NC: Duke University Press, 2015.
Eisenman, Peter. *Giuseppe Terragni: Transformations, Decompositions, Critiques*. New York: Monacelli Press, 2003.
Elcott, Noam M. *Artificial Darkness: An Obscure History of Modern Art and Media*. Chicago: University of Chicago Press, 2016.
Elsom, Derek M. *Lightning: Nature and Culture*. London: Reaktion Books, 2015.
Falcinelli, Riccardo. *Cromorama: Come il colore ha cambiato il nostro sguardo*. Turin: Einaudi, 2017.
Fanelli, Giovanni, and Rosalia Fanelli. *Il tessuto moderno: Disegno, moda, architettura, 1890–1940*. Florence: Vallecchi, 1976.
Favaro, Antonio. *L'acustica applicata alla costruzione delle sale per spettacoli e pubbliche adunanze*. Bologna: Forni, 1969.
Felski, Rita. "Context Stinks!" *New Literary History* 42, no. 4 (2011): 573–91.
Ferrari, Vittorio. *Il Teatro della Scala nella vita e nell'arte dalle origini ad oggi*. Edited by Cesare Tamburini. Milan: C. Tamburini, 1922.
Ferrario, Giulio, ed. *Storia e descrizione de'principali teatri antichi e moderni*. Bologna: Arnaldo Forni, 1977.
Ferrini, Rinaldo. "Dei principii a cui deve informarsi un sistema di ventilazione per un teatro." *Il politecnico: Giornale dell'ingegnere architetto civile ed industriale* 21. Milan: Tipologia e Litografia degli Ingegneri, 1873.
Ferrini, Rinaldo. "L'éclairage électrique du Théâtre de la Scala à Milan." *La lumière électrique* 12, no. 14 (April 5, 1884): 12–17.
Fitzgerald, Percy Hetherington. *The Savoy Opera and the Savoyards*. London: Chatto & Windus, 1894.

Folliero, Guglielmo. *I misteri politici della luna*. Naples: Marghieri, 1863.
Foucault, Michel. *The Order of Things: An Archeology of the Human Sciences*. London: Routledge, 1992.
Fumi, Gianpiero. "Imprenditori culturali: L'impegno nella gestione del Teatro alla Scala." In *I Visconti di Modrone: Nobilià e modernità a Milano (Secoli XIX–XX)*, edited by Gianpiero Fumi, 237–70. Milan: Vita e Pensiero, 2014.
Galvez, Matthieu Emmanuel, and Jérôme Gaillardet. "Historical Constraints on the Origins of the Carbon Cycle Concept." *Comptes rendus géoscience* 344, nos. 11–12 (2012): 549–67.
Garnier, Charles. *Le nouvel Opéra de Paris*. 2 vols. Paris: Ducher, 1878.
Garnier, Charles. *Le théâtre*. Paris: Librairie Hachette, 1871.
Garnier, Charles, and Auguste Ammann. *L'habitation humaine*. Paris: Librairie Hachette, 1892.
Gatti, Carlo. *Il Teatro alla Scala, nella storia e nell'arte, 1778–1963*. 2 vols. Milan: Ricordi, 1964.
Ghislanzoni, Antonio. *Abrakadabra: Storia dell'avvenire*. Lecco: Piantini, 1874.
Giedion, Sigfried. *Building in France, Building in Iron, Building in Ferro-Concrete*. Santa Monica, CA: Getty Center for the History of Art and the Humanities, 1995.
Gieryn, Thomas F. "What Buildings Do." *Theory and Society* 31, no. 1 (2002): 35–74.
Gilebbi, Matteo. "Antonio Stoppani and the Teleological Interpretation of the Anthropocene." Paper presented at the American Association for Italian Studies Conference, Columbus, OH, 2017.
Goethe, Johann Wolfgang von. *Goethe's Theory of Colours*. Translated by Charles Lock Eastlake. Cambridge: Cambridge University Press, 2014.
Gordon, J. E. *Structures; or, Why Things Don't Fall Down*. New York: Da Capo Press, 1981.
"Gran Teatre del Liceu—Barcelona." YouTube, October 22, 2021. Video, 3:33. https://www.youtube.com/watch?v=ka_kp8ddhzw.
Greenfield, Amy Butler. *A Perfect Red: Empire, Espionage, and the Quest for the Color of Desire*. New York: HarperCollins, 2005.
Grey, Thomas, and James Westby. "Gabriele D'Annunzio's 'Il caso Wagner' (The Case of Wagner): Reflections on Wagner, Nietzsche, and Wagnerismo from fin-de-siècle Italy." *Leitmotiv—The Wagnerian Quarterly* (2012): 7–26.
Grifoni, Ulisse. *Dalla terra alle stelle: Viaggio meraviglioso di due italiani ed un francese*. Florence: Nicolai, 1887.
Guerout, Aug. "L'éclairage électrique des théâtres par les lampes à incandescence." *La lumière électrique* 12, no. 15 (April 12, 1884): 63–72.
Gumbrecht, Hans Ulrich. *Production of Presence: What Meaning Cannot Convey*. Stanford, CA: Stanford University Press, 2004.
Hall-Witt, Jennifer. *Fashionable Acts: Opera and Elite Culture in London, 1780–1880*. Durham, NH: University of New Hampshire Press, 2007.
Harris, Jonathan Gil. "Properties of Skill: Product Placement in Early English Artisanal Drama." In *Staged Properties in Early Modern English Drama*, edited by Gil Harris and Natasha Korda, 35–66. Cambridge: Cambridge University Press, 2002.
Hassam, Andrew. "Portable Iron Structures and Uncertain Colonial Spaces at the Sydenham Crystal Palace." In *Imperial Cities: Landscape, Display and Identity*, edited by Felix Driver and David Gilbert, 174–93. Manchester: Manchester University Press, 1999.

Heidegger, Martin. *Sein und Zeit*. Tübingen: Max Niemeyer, 1976.
Heller, Michael C. "Between Silence and Pain: Loudness and the Affective Encounter." *Sound Studies: An Interdisciplinary Journal* 1, no. 1 (2015): 40–58.
Helmholtz, Hermann von. *On the Sensations of Tone as a Physiological Basis for the Theory of Music*. London: Longmans, Green, 1875.
Hevia, James L. *English Lessons: The Pedagogy of Imperialism in Nineteenth-Century China*. Durham, NC: Duke University Press, 2003.
Hogle, Jerrold E. *The Undergrounds of "The Phantom of the Opera": Sublimation and the Gothic in Leroux's Novel and Its Progeny*. New York: Palgrave, 2002.
Hughes, Thomas Parke. *Networks of Power: Electrification in Western Society, 1880–1930*. Baltimore: Johns Hopkins University Press, 1993.
Igler, David. *The Great Ocean: Pacific Worlds from Captain Cook to the Gold Rush*. Oxford: Oxford University Press, 2013.
Imada, Adria L. *An Archive of Skin, An Archive of Kin: Disability and Life-Making During Medical Incarceration*. Oakland: University of California Press, 2022.
Imperiale, Alicia. "Digital Skins: The Architecture of Surface." In *Skin: Surface, Substance, and Design*, edited by Ellen Lupton, 55–63. New York: Princeton Architectural Press, 2002.
Inwood, Stephen. *City of Cities: The Birth of Modern London*. London: Macmillan, 2005.
Izenour, George C. *Theater Design*. New Haven, CT: Yale University Press, 1977.
Johnson, Eugene J. *Inventing the Opera House: Theater Architecture in Renaissance and Baroque Italy*. Cambridge: Cambridge University Press, 2018.
Johnson, Eugene J. "The Short, Lascivious Lives of Two Venetian Theaters, 1580–85." *Renaissance Quarterly* 55, no. 3 (2002): 936–68.
Johnson, James H. *Listening in Paris: A Cultural History*. Berkeley: University of California Press, 1995.
Jourdain, M. Frantz. *Constructions élevées au Champ de Mars par M. Ch. Garnier pour servir à l'histoire de l'habitation humaine*. Paris: Librairie Centrale des Beaux-Arts, 1889.
Juarez, Lucia. "Scottish Cast Iron in Argentina: Its Role in the British Informal Imperial System." In *Function and Fantasy*, edited by Paul Dobraszczyk and Peter Sealy, 141–62. Oxford: Routledge, 2016.
Kalba, Laura Anne. *Color in the Age of Impressionism: Commerce, Technology, and Art*. University Park: Penn State University Press, 2017.
Kander, Astrid, Paolo Malanima, and Paul Warde. *Power to the People: Energy in Europe over the Last Five Centuries*. Princeton, NJ: Princeton University Press, 2014.
Kittler, Friedrich A. *Discourse Networks 1800/1900*. Translated by Michael Metteer. Stanford, CA: Stanford University Press, 1990.
Kittler, Friedrich A. *Gramophone, Film, Typewriter*. Translated by Geoffrey Winthrop-Young and Michael Wutz. Stanford, CA: Stanford University Press, 1999.
Kittler, Friedrich A. *Optical Media*. Malden, MA: Polity Press, 2010.
Kittler, Friedrich A. *The Truth of the Technological World*. Translated by Erik Butler. Stanford, CA: Stanford University Press, 2013.
Kreuzer, Gundula. *Curtain, Gong, Steam: Wagnerian Technologies of Nineteenth-Century Opera*. Oakland: University of California Press, 2018.
Kreuzer, Gundula. "Kittler's Wagner and Beyond." In "Colloquy: Discrete/Continuous; Music and Media Theory After Kittler," convened by Alexander Rehding. *Journal of the American Musicological Society* 70, no. 1 (2017): 228–233.

"La Scala green." Edison. Video, 00:30. https://youtu.be/qzZJr70PK7M.
Lacan, Jacques. "The Mirror-Phase as Formative of the Function of the I." *New Left Review* 51 (1968): 63–77.
Landriani, Paolo. "Osservazioni del Signor Paolo Landriani sul detto articolo." In *Storia e descrizione de'principali teatri antichi e moderni*, edited by Giulio Ferrario, 315–69. Bologna: Arnaldo Forni, 1977.
Landriani, Paolo, trans. "Saggio sull'architettura teatrale del Sig. Patte." In *Storia e descrizione de'principali teatri antichi e moderni*, edited by Giulio Ferrario, 93–291. Bologna: Arnaldo Forni, 1977.
Larkin, Brian. "The Politics and Poetics of Infrastructure." *Annual Review of Anthropology* 42 (2013): 327–43.
Latour, Bruno. *Reassembling the Social: An Introduction to Actor-Network Theory*. Oxford: Oxford University Press, 2023.
Le Corbusier. "A Coat of Whitewash: The Law of Ripolin." In *The Decorative Art of Today*, 185–92. Translated by James I. Dunnett. London: The Architectural Press, 1987.
Leo, G. Laura di, ed. *Cesare Albertini urbanista: Antologia di scritti*. Rome: Gangemi, 1995.
Leppert, Richard. *Sound Judgment: Selected Essays*. Aldershot: Ashgate, 2007.
Leroux, Gaston. *Le fantôme de l'Opéra*. Paris: P. Lafitte, 1910.
Leroux, Gaston. *The Phantom of the Opera*. Translated by Mireille Ribière. London: Penguin, 2012.
Locher, Fabien, and Jean-Baptiste Fressoz. "Modernity's Frail Climate: A Climate History of Environmental Reflexivity." *Critical Inquiry* 38, no. 3 (2012): 579–98.
Loos, Adolf. *Ornament and Crime: Thoughts on Design and Materials*. Translated by Shaun Whiteside. London: Penguin Books, 2019.
Love, Heather. "Close but Not Deep: Literary Ethics and the Descriptive Turn." *New Literary History* 41, no. 2 (2010): 371–91.
Lovell, Julia. *The Opium War: Drugs, Dreams and the Making of China*. New York: Overlook Press, 2014.
Lupton, Ellen, ed. *Skin: Surface, Substance, and Design*. New York: Princeton Architectural Press, 2002.
Ma, Debin. "The Modern Silk Road: The Global Raw-Silk Market, 1850–1930." *Journal of Economic History* 56, no. 2 (1996): 330–55.
Macchi, Gustavo. "L'apertura della stagione alla Scala: *Il crepuscolo degli dei*." *Il mondo artistico* (January 1, 1908).
MacKenzie, John M. *The British Empire Through Buildings: Structure, Function and Meaning*. Manchester: Manchester University Press, 2020.
Maconie, Robin. "Musical Acoustics in the Age of Vitruvius." *Musical Times* 146, no. 1890 (2005): 75–82.
Malatesta, Maria, ed. *Society and the Professions in Italy, 1860–1914*. Translated by Adrian Belton. Cambridge: Cambridge University Press, 1995.
Mantegazza, Paolo. *L'anno 3000*. Milan: Fratelli Treves, 1897.
Marangoni, Guido, and Carlo Vanbianchi, eds. *La Scala: Studi e ricerche, note storiche e statistiche (1906–20)*. Bergamo: Istituto Italiano d'Arti Grafiche, 1922.
Marinic, Gregory, ed. *The Interior Architecture Theory Reader*. Abingdon: Routledge, 2018.
Maulsby, Lucy M. *Fascism, Architecture, and the Claiming of Modern Milan, 1922–1943*. Toronto: University of Toronto Press, 2018.

McMahon, Rosie. "Music in the Urban Amazon: A Historical Ethnography of the Manaus Opera House." D.Phil. diss., Oxford University, 2019.

Mead, Christopher Curtis. *Charles Garnier's Paris Opéra: Architectural Empathy and the Renaissance of French Classicism*. Cambridge, MA: MIT Press, 1991.

Meisenheimer, Wolfgang. "Of the Hollow Spaces in the Skin of the Architectural Body." In *Toward a New Interior: An Anthology of Interior Design Theory*, edited by Lois Weinthal, 625–31. New York: Princeton Architectural Press, 2011.

Miner, Margaret. "Phantoms of Genius: Women and the Fantastic in the Opera-House Mystery." *19th-Century Music* 18, no. 2 (1994): 121–35.

Minuti, Rolando. "China and World History in Italian Nineteenth-Century Thought: Some Remarks on Giuseppe Ferrari's Work." In "Italy's Orient," special issue, edited by Rolando Minuti, *Journal of Modern Italian Studies* 26, no. 2 (2021): 208–19.

Minuti, Rolando, ed. "Italy's Orient." Special issue, *Journal of Modern Italian Studies* 26, no. 2 (2021).

Morazzoni, Giuseppe. *I palchi del Teatro alla Scala*. Milan: Amici del Museo Teatrale, 1930.

Morris, Christopher. "'Too Much Music': The Media of Opera." In *The Cambridge Companion to Opera Studies*, edited by Nicholas Till, 95–116. Cambridge: Cambridge University Press, 2012.

Morris, Peter J. T., and Anthony S. Travis. "A History of the International Dyestuff Industry." *American Dyestuff Reporter* 81, no. 11 (1992): 59–108.

Mukherji, Subha, ed. *Thinking on Thresholds: The Poetics of Transitive Spaces*. London: Anthem Press, 2011.

Mumford, Lewis. *The City in History: Its Origins, Its Transformations, and Its Prospects*. New York: Harcourt, Brace & World, 1961.

Newark, Cormac. *Opera in the Novel from Balzac to Proust*. Cambridge: Cambridge University Press, 2011.

Newton, Isaac. *Opticks*. Amherst, NY: Prometheus Books, 2003.

Niccolosi, Gian Battista. *Il nuovo teatro di Parma: Rappresentato con tavole intagliate nello studio Paolo Toschi*. Parma: Battei, 1987.

Nietzsche, Friedrich. *The Case of Wagner; Nietzsche contra Wagner; The Twilight of the Idols; The Antichrist*. Translated by Thomas Common. London: H. Henry, 1896.

Oles, Thomas. *Walls: Enclosure and Ethics in the Modern Landscape*. Chicago: University of Chicago Press, 2015.

Osterhammel, Jürgen. *The Transformation of the World: A Global History of the Nineteenth Century*. Translated by Patrick Camiller. Princeton, NJ: Princeton University Press, 2014.

Otele, Olivette. *African Europeans: An Untold History*. New York: Basic Books, 2023.

Paladini, Carlo. "Il suono degli strumenti e delle vocali, e il loro timbro secondo la teoria del professore Helmholtz di Heidelberg." *Gazzetta musicale di Milano* (November 15 and 22, 1900).

Pallasmaa, Juhani. *The Eyes of the Skin: Architecture and the Senses*. Chichester: Wiley-Academy, 2012.

Parsons, Robert Hodson. *The Early Days of the Power Station Industry*. Cambridge: Cambridge University Press, 1940.

Pastoureau, Michel. *Red: The History of a Color*. Princeton, NJ: Princeton University Press, 2017.

Patte, Pierre. *Essai sur l'architecture théatrale*. Paris: Chez Moutard, 1782.

Pavese, Claudio. "Le origini della Società Edison e il suo sviluppo fino alla costituzione del 'gruppo' (1881–1919)." In *Energia e sviluppo: L'industria italiana e la Società Edison*, edited by Bruno Bezza, 23–167. Turin: Einaudi, 1986.

Peck, Amelia, ed. *The Interwoven Globe: Worldwide Textile Trade 1500–1800*. New York: Metropolitan Museum of Art, 2013.

Peters, John Durham. *The Marvelous Clouds: Toward a Philosophy of Elemental Media*. Chicago: University of Chicago Press, 2015.

Phipps, Elena. "Global Colors: Dyes and the Dye Trade from the Sixteenth to the Eighteenth Century." In *The Interwoven Globe: Worldwide Textile Trade 1500–1800*, edited by Amelia Peck, 120–35. New York: Metropolitan Museum of Art, 2013.

Picker, John M. *Victorian Soundscapes*. Oxford: Oxford University Press, 2003.

Pireddu, Nicoletta. "Introduction: Paolo Mantegazza, Fabulator of the Future." In *Paolo Mantegazza, "The Year 3000: A Dream,"* edited by Nicoletta Pireddu, translated by David Jacobson, 1–53. Lincoln: University of Nebraska Press, 2010.

Pivato, Stefano. *Il secolo del rumore: Paesaggio sonoro nel novecento*. Bologna: Il Mulino, 2011.

Playfair, Lyon. "Appendix: The Jablochkoff System of Electric Illumination." In *Report from the Select Committee on Lighting by Electricity, Together with the Proceedings of the Committee, Minutes of Evidence, and Appendix*, 231–33. London, 1879.

Postrel, Virginia. *The Fabric of Civilization: How Textiles Made the World*. New York: Basic Books, 2021.

Pyne, Stephen J. *Fire: A Brief History*. Seattle: University of Washington Press, 2001.

The Quarantine Tapes. "Episode 154: Eugenio Ampudia in Conversation with Paul Holdengräber." January 28, 2021. Podcast, 39:01. https://quarantine-tapes.simple cast.com/episodes.

Rees, T. A. L. *Theatre Lighting in the Age of Gas*. London: Society for Theatre Research, 1978.

Rehding, Alexander, convenor. "Colloquy: Discrete/Continuous; Music and Media Theory After Kittler." *Journal of the American Musicological Society* 70, no. 1 (2017): 221–56.

Rehding, Alexander. "Introduction." In "Colloquy: Discrete/Continuous; Music and Media Theory After Kittler," convened by Alexander Rehding. *Journal of the American Musicological Society* 70, no. 1 (2017): 221–28.

Reid, David Boswell. *Illustrations of the Theory and Practice of Ventilation: With Remarks on Warming, Exclusive Lighting, and the Communication of Sound*. London: Longman, Brown, Green & Longmans, 1844.

"Report of The Lancet Sanitary Commission on the Ventilation of Theatres and Places of Public Assembly." *Lancet*, December 19, 1891.

Rice, Charles. *The Emergence of the Interior: Architecture, Modernity, Domesticity*. Abingdon: Routledge, 2007.

Rogers, Holly. "Fitzcarraldo's Search for Aguirre: Music and Text in the Amazonian Films of Werner Herzog." *Journal of the Royal Musical Association* 129, no. 1 (2004): 77–99.

Rousseau, Jean-Jacques. *The Discourses and Other Early Political Writings*. Edited by Victor Gourevitch. Cambridge: Cambridge University Press, 1996.

Rowland, Ingrid D., Thomas Noble Howe, and Michael J. Dewar, eds. *Vitruvius: Ten Books on Architecture*. Cambridge: Cambridge University Press, 1999.

Rubenstein, Michael, and Justin Neuman. *Modernism and Its Environments*. New York: Bloomsbury Academic, 2020.

Sàbat, Antonio. *Gran Teatro del Liceo*. Barcelona: Escudo de Oro, 1979.

Sacchi, Filippo. *Toscanini*. Milan: Longanesi, 1988.

Sachs, Edwin O. *Modern Opera Houses and Theatres*. 3 vols. New York: Benjamin Blom, 1968.

Sachs, Harvey. *Arturo Toscanini from 1915 to 1946: Art in the Shadow of Politics*. Turin: EDT/Musica, 1987.

Salgado, Susana. *The Teatro Solís: 150 Years of Opera, Concert, and Ballet in Montevideo*. Middletown, CT: Wesleyan University Press, 2003.

Salinas, Carlos Marichal. "Mexican Cochineal, Local Technologies and the Rise of Global Trade from the Sixteenth to the Nineteenth Centuries." In *Global History and New Polycentric Approaches: Europe, Asia and the Americas in a World Network System*, edited by Manuel Pérez García and Lúcio de Sousa, 255–73. Basingstoke: Palgrave Macmillan, 2018.

Scego, Igiaba. "A Harlequin Europe: Unveiling Black Histories in Venice." February 16, 2024. koozArch. https://www.koozarch.com/essays/a-harlequin-europe-unveiling-black-histories-in-venice.

Salvarani, Marco. *Le muse: Storia del Teatro di Ancona*. Ancona: Il Lavoro Editoriale, 2002.

Sheppard, J. J., ed. *Territorials in India: A Souvenir of their Historic Arrival for Military Duty in the "Land of the Rupee"; From the Royal Opera House, Bombay; Prepared in Accordance with the Instructions of the Proprietor, J. F. Karaka*. Bombay: J. J. Sheppard, 1916.

Schmidt-Horning, Susan. *Chasing Sound: Technology, Culture, and the Art of Studio Recording from Edison to the LP*. Baltimore: Johns Hopkins University Press, 2013.

Schnapp, Jeffrey T. "The Fabric of Modern Times." *Critical Inquiry* 24, no. 1 (1997): 191–245.

Schnapp, Jeffrey T. "The People's Glass House." *South Central Review* 25, no. 3 (2008): 45–56.

Schoenefeldt, Henrik. *Rebuilding the Houses of Parliament: David Boswell Reid and Disruptive Environmentalism*. Abingdon: Routledge, 2021.

Schumacher, Thomas L. *Surface and Symbol: Giuseppe Terragni and the Architecture of Italian Rationalism*. New York: Princeton Architectural Press, 1991.

Schwartz, Hillel. *Making Noise: From Babel to the Big Bang and Beyond*. New York: Zone Books, 2011.

Sealy, Peter. "Dreams in Iron: The Wish Image in Émile Zola's Novels." In *Function and Fantasy*, edited by Paul Dobraszczyk and Peter Sealy, 221–45. Oxford: Routledge, 2016.

Sealy, Peter. "The Roofscape as Locus of Modernity in Giedion and Zola." In *Proceedings of the Society of Architectural Historians, Australia and New Zealand*, edited by Alexandra Brown and Andrew Leach, 2 vols. 2:891–902. Gold Coast, Queensland: SAHANZ, 2013.

Secchi, Luigi Lorenzo. *1778/1978: Il Teatro alla Scala*. Milan: Electa Editrice, 1977.

Sennett, Richard. *Flesh and Stone: The Body and the City in Western Civilization*. New York: W. W. Norton, 1994.

Serres, Michel. *The Five Senses: A Philosophy of Mingled Bodies*. Translated by Margaret Sankey and Peter Cowley. London: Bloomsbury Academic, 2021.

Siegert, Bernhard. *Cultural Techniques: Grids, Filters, Doors, and Other Articulations of the Real*. Translated by Geoffrey Winthrop-Young. New York: Fordham University Press, 2015.

Siegert, Bernhard. "Doors: on the Materiality of the Symbolic." Translated by John Durham Peters. *Grey Room* 47 (Spring 2012): 6–23.
Simmel, Georg. "Bridge and Door." *Theory, Culture and Society* 11 (1994): 5–10.
Società Edison, ed. *Nel cinquantenario della Società Edison, 1884–1934*. Vol. 4, *Lo sviluppo della Società Edison e il progresso economico di Milano*. Milan: Società Edison, 1934.
Società Italiana di Fonotipia, ed. *The Fonotipia Ledgers*. East Barnet: Symposium Records, 2002.
Sorba, Carlotta. *Teatri: L'Italia del melodramma nell'età del Risorgimento*. Bologna: Il Mulino, 2001.
Stalder, Laurent. "Turning Architecture Inside Out: Revolving Doors and Other Threshold Devices." *Journal of Design History* 22, no. 1 (2009): 69–77.
Steege, Benjamin. *Helmholtz and the Modern Listener*. Cambridge: Cambridge University Press, 2012.
Sterne, Jonathan. *The Audible Past: Cultural Origins of Sound Reproduction*. Durham, NC: Duke University Press, 2003.
Stopford, Martin. *Maritime Economics*. London: Routledge, 1997.
Stoppani, Antonio. *Acqua ed aria, ossia la purezza del mare e dell'atmosfera fin dai primordi del mondo animato*. Edited by Alessandro Malladra. Turin: Società Editrice Internazionale, 1898.
Stoppani, Antonio. *Corso di geologia*. Milan: G. Bernadoni & G. Brigola, 1873.
Stoppani, Antonio. *L'exemeron: Nuovo saggio di una esegesi della storia della creazione secondo la ragione e la fede*. Vol. 2. Turin: Unione Tipografico-Editrice, 1894.
Sutherland, R. J. M., ed. *Structural Iron, 1750–1850*. Aldershot: Ashgate/Variorum, 1997.
Syrjämaa, Taina. "The Clash of Picturesque Decay and Modern Cleanliness in Late Nineteenth-Century Rome." In *Rome, Pollution and Propriety: Dirt, Disease and Hygiene in the Eternal City from Antiquity to Modernity*, edited by Mark Bradley and Kenneth Stow, 202–22. Cambridge: Cambridge University Press, 2012.
Szeman, Imre, and Dominic Boyer, eds. *Energy Humanities: An Anthology*. Baltimore: Johns Hopkins University Press, 2017.
Szendy, Peter. "Spacing and Sounding Out." *Grey Room* 60 (2015): 132–44.
Taruskin, Richard. *The Danger of Music and Other Anti-Utopian Essays*. Berkeley: University of California Press, 2009.
Taylor, Mark, ed. "Surface Consciousness." Special issue, *Architectural Design* 73, no. 2 (2003).
Taylor, Mark C. *Hiding*. Chicago: University of Chicago Press, 1997.
Templer, John A. *The Staircase*. 2 vols. Cambridge, MA: MIT Press, 1992.
Thomas, Lynn M. *Beneath the Surface: A Transnational History of Skin Lighteners*. Durham, NC: Duke University Press, 2020.
Thompson, Emily Ann. *The Soundscape of Modernity: Architectural Acoustics and the Culture of Listening in America, 1900–1933*. Cambridge, MA: MIT Press, 2002.
Thorne, Robert, ed. *Structural Iron and Steel, 1850–1900*. Aldershot: Ashgate/Variorum, 2000.
Till, Jeremy. *Architecture Depends*. Cambridge, MA: MIT Press, 2013.
Toelle, Jutta. *Bühne der Stadt: Mailand und das Teatro alla Scala zwischen Risorgimento und Fin de Siècle*. Vienna: Oldenbourg, 2009.

Tommaseo, Niccolò, and Bernardo Bellini. *Dizionario della lingua italiana*. Turin: Unione Tipografico-Editrice, 1861–79.

Tremelloni, Roberto. *L'industria tessile italiana: Come è sorta, e come è oggi*. Turin: Einaudi, 1937.

Turina, Stefano. "Beyond the Silkworm Eggs: The Role of the Italian *semai* (Silkworm Egg Merchants) in Spreading Knowledge of Japan in Italy in the Second Half of the Nineteenth Century Between Art and Science." In "Italy's Orient," special issue, edited by Rolando Minuti, *Journal of Modern Italian Studies* 26, no. 2 (2021): 141–60.

Tyndall, John. "On the Atmosphere as a Vehicle for Sound." *Philosophical Transactions of the Royal Society of London* 164 (1874): 183–244.

Vaisse, Pierre. "Le décor peint dans les théâtres (1750–1900): Problèmes esthétiques et iconographiques." In *Victor Louis et le théâtre: scénographie, mise en scène et architecture théâtrale aux XVIIIe et XIXe siècles*, 153–67. Paris: Centre National de la Recherche Scientifique, 1982.

Valeriani, Valeriano. "Consonanze e dissonanze secondo Tartini ed Helmholtz." *Gazzetta musicale di Milano* (July–December 1898).

Vella, Francesca. *Networking Operatic Italy*. Chicago: University of Chicago Press, 2021.

Verne, Jules. *Around the World in Eighty Days: The Extraordinary Journeys*. Edited by William Butcher. Oxford: Oxford University Press, 1995.

Wagner, Richard. *Sämtliche Schriften und Dichtungen*. 9 vols. Leipzig: Breitkopf & Härtel, 1911.

Walton, Benjamin. *The Invention of Global Opera*. Forthcoming.

Walton, Benjamin. "Technological Phantoms of the Opéra." In *Nineteenth-Century Opera and the Scientific Imagination*, edited by David Trippett and Benjamin Walton, 199–226. Cambridge: Cambridge University Press, 2019.

Waqas, Muhammad, Dominique Van Der Straeten, and Christoph-Martin Geilfus. "Plants 'Cry' for Help Through Acoustic Signals." *Trends in Plant Science* 28, no. 9 (2023): 984–86.

Ward, Meredith C. "The 'New Listening': Richard Wagner, Nineteenth-Century Opera Culture, and Cinema Theatres." *Nineteenth Century Theatre and Film* 43, no. 1 (2016): 88–106.

Weinstein, Barbara. *The Amazon Rubber Boom, 1850–1920*. Stanford, CA: Stanford University Press, 1983.

Weinthal, Lois, ed. *Toward a New Interior: An Anthology of Interior Design Theory*. New York: Princeton Architectural Press, 2011.

Wermiel, Sara. "The Development of Fireproof Construction in Great Britain and the United States in the Nineteenth Century." In *Structural Iron and Steel, 1850–1900*, edited by Robert Thorne, 69–92. Aldershot, Hampshire: Ashgate, 2000.

West, John B. "Henry Cavendish (1731–1810): Hydrogen, Carbon Dioxide, Water, and Weighing the World." *American Journal of Physiology—Lung Cellular and Molecular Physiology* 307, no. 1 (2014): 1–6.

West, John B. "Joseph Black, Carbon Dioxide, Latent Heat, and the Beginnings of the Discovery of the Respiratory Gases." *American Journal of Physiology—Lung Cellular and Molecular Physiology* 306, no. 12 (2014): 1057–63.

Wigley, Mark. "Chronic Whiteness." *e-flux Architecture* (November 2020). https://www.e-flux.com/architecture/sick-architecture/360099/chronic-whiteness/.

Zanier, Claudio. "Italy, East Asia and Silk: One Hundred Years of a Relationship (1830–1940)." In "Italy's Orient," special issue, edited by Rolando Minuti, *Journal of Modern Italian Studies* 26, no. 2 (2021): 173–85.

Zanoni, Elena. *Scienza, patria, religione: Antonio Stoppani e la cultura italiana dello Ottocento*. Milan: FrancoAngeli, 2014.

Zola, Émile. *Au bonheur des dames*. Paris: Bibliothèque-Charpentier, 1924.

Zola, Émile. *The Ladies' Paradise*. Translated by Brian Nelson. Oxford: Oxford University Press, 1995.

INDEX

Page numbers in italics refer to musical examples, figures, and tables.

abduction, 88–89, 91, 94–95
access, 11–13, 20, 29, 43, 73, 84–85, 94–96, 106–7
acousmatic sound, 67, 83
acoustics, 136n3, 137n6, 138n25, 140nn47–48, 140n51, 145n63, 147n80; and architecture, 4, 16, 19, 103, 122n13, 125nn45–46; and isolation, 77–82; and lowered orchestras, 66–77, 136n3; and purity, 82–85. *See also* reverberation
aesthetics, 3, 5, 98, 119, 127n16, 143n25; and acoustics, 68–69, 80; and color, 37, 45; and decoration, 23, 27, 33, 35; and electricity, 19, 63. *See also* beauty
Africa, 97, 101; South Africa, 101
air, 3, 5, 10, 18–19; and acoustics, 67–68, 76–78, 81–82, 85; and atmospheres, 47–58, 60, 63–65, 130n12, 132n21, 133n30; and thresholds, 90–92, 106, 108–9
Albertini, Cesare, 70, 73, 75, 81, 105, 138n31
Amazon, 101–3. *See also* Teatro Amazonas, Manaus
Ammann, Auguste, 97–98
Ampudia, Eugenio, 47
animals, 15, 28, 52, 130n12
Anthropocene, 14, 18, 53, 62, 108, 131n18
architects, 4, 12, 15–16, 33, 91, 95, 125n46, 142n18; and acoustics, 68–75, 138n21; and metals, 97–98, 104–5; and surfaces, 24, 30–31, 116. *See also* architecture

architectural studies, 13, 25, 127n14
architecture, 1–12, 16–21, 109, 121n5, 122n13, 124n45, 143n31, 144n48, 146n76; and acoustics, 66–72, 77, 80–82, 85, 125n46, 136n3, 136n6; and climate, 47, 50, 55, 57–58, 132n21; and colonialism, 96–103; distributed, 13–15, 110; and surfaces, 24–26, 29–33, 36–37, 40–42, 45, 121n6, 147n79; and verticality, 88–92, 94–95, 105–9, 143nn25–26, 147n79. *See also* architects
aristocracy, 12, 26, 36, 72, 94. *See also* Borletti, Senatore; Visconti di Modrone family
Aristotle, 27
Arrhenius, Svante, 62, 132n19
atmospheres, 13, 16, 18–19, 46–47, 81, 108, 110; and electricity, 58–65; and morality, 48–49; and science, 49–54, 130n12; and ventilation, 54–58
audiences, 49–51, 56; and acoustics, 66–72, 75–78, 80, 82, 83–86; and architecture, 1, 3–5, 10–16, 19–20, 26; and color, 36–37, 41–42; and illumination, 59–60, 63; and plants, 46–47; and renovations, 104, 107–8; and thresholds, 91, 94; and ventilation, 55–57
auditorium floors, 17, 19, 66, 69–70, 76
auras, 63
Australia, 101
Austrian Empire, 16, 27, 36

Bachelard, Gaston, 3–4, 141n7
balconies, 1, 12, 35, 78, 90, 107
Banu, Georges, 4, 20–21, 122n12, 125n45, 129n54, 142n13, 147nn78–79
Barber, Daniel A., 14
Batchelor, David, 27, 30
Bayreuth Festspielhaus, 4, 10, 19, 66–72, 78, 123n20, 123n23
beams, 11, 89, 97, 101
beauty, 12, 49, 98, 119
Benjamin, Walter, 127n16, 133n35
Beranek, Leo, L. 15, 125n46, 138n26, 145n63
Berlin Staatsoper, 25
Berliner, Emile, 82
Bible, 51, 142n22
Biocene, 47
Birmingham Town Hall, 48
Black, Joseph, 49
blueprints, architectural, 71, 95
blues (color), 28, 35, 37, 39, 63
bodies, 4, 20, 23–25, 28, 41, 49, 68, 74–75, 85, 94. *See also* faces; skins
Boito, Arrigo, 73–74, 76
Borletti, Senatore, 22–28, 31–33, 44, 115–17, 126nn4–6, 127n13
boundaries, 11, 13, 21, 23, 88, 107–9. *See also* thresholds
Boxer Uprising, 44
boxes, theater, 55, 72–73, 75, 105; and architecture, 1–2, 12, 15–16, 105; and color, 33–36; and illumination, 60, 64; and redecoration, 22, 26–28, 116–19; and thresholds, 87, 90–91, 94
breath, 3, 18, 20, 48–51, 55, 71, 85, 88–89, 130n12, 143n22
Britain, 43, 44, 101–3; Glasgow, Scotland, 101. *See also* England
British Parliament, 11, 132n21
British Petroleum (BP), 109
Brückwald, Otto, 4, 68
Bruno, Giuliana, 13
Butler, Judith, 46

Caldara, Emilio, 105
Canada, 101
cantilevers, 107
carbon, 47, 57, 60, 110; carbon cycle, 18, 50–53, 130n12, 131n13; carbon dioxide, 3, 18, 47, 49, 53, 62, 110, 132n19; carbonic acid, 49–53. *See also* emissions
care, ethics of, 46
caricatures, 73, 74, 78, 79, 139n41
Carter, Paul, 96
Caruso, Enrico, 102
Casement, Roger, 102
cassa armonica, 76–77, 81, 138n32
casts (operatic), 105–8
Catholicism, 49, 51, 59
Cavendish, Henry, 49
ceilings, 2–4, 67–68, 90–91, 110, 142n13
cement, 76–77, 81, 109
Chakrabarty, Dipesh, 58
Champ de Mars, Paris, 97–98
chandeliers, 57, 87–88, 91, 142n17
chemistry, 15, 28–29, 39, 41, 44, 49, 62, 105, 131n18, 132n19, 132n21
Chevreul, Michel Eugène, 29, 39–42
children, 11, 25, 27, 49, 88
China, 43–44, 62, 101, 129n61, 129n64. *See also* Qing dynasty
Chopin, Frédéric, 66
chromophobia, 27
Clarke, Joseph L., 4
class, 12, 15, 29, 36, 52, 73, 84, 107, 124n42, 142n17. *See also* lower classes; middle classes
cleanliness, 3, 17–18, 30; and energy, 62–63; and music, 47–49, 54; and ventilation, 54–57, 125n47, 133n30
climate change, 14, 53–59, 62, 65, 103, 135n47. *See also* environmental catastrophe
climate science, 50, 53
climatic conditions, 14–15, 18, 54–55, 101
cochineals, 35, 44, 103
Coen, Deborah R., 50
cognition, 38–39, 49
Colombo, Giuseppe, 19, 60–62, 135n45
colonialism, 18, 20, 31, 44, 96–103. *See also* imperialism
coloration. *See* dyes
colors, 15–17, 26–41, 44, 58, 89, 117–19, 127n22, 133n36. *See also* blues (color); chromophobia; dyes; fuchsin (color); gold; greens (color); reds (color); rose (color); turquoise (color); yellows (color)

INDEX

combustion, 19, 26, 51, 53, 60, 62, 108–9
commedia dell'arte, 12, 90
commemoration, 46–47, 53, 98. *See also* memories
commercialism, 28, 58–59, 82, 84, 92–93, 137n18. *See also* consumption
concert halls, 18, 54, 145n63
conductors, 70, 73, 77–78, 80, 139n36
Connor, Steven, 25, 63
consciousness, 25, 48–49, 64, 68, 90, 143n25
construction, 1–3, 11–17, 107, 109–10, 121n4, 124n45, 125n46; and acoustics, 68–78, 81; and atmospheres, 54, 57–59; and colonialism, 20, 96–98, 101, 103; and surfaces, 33, 36, 42; and thresholds, 88, 90–93, 144n42, 146nn66–67
consumption, 28–29, 37, 39, 43, 47, 52, 58–61, 83, 85, 95, 134n40. *See also* commercialism
corridors, 12, 60, 94, 108
cosmetics, 27, 37, 40
Costanzi, Domenico, 70
COVID-19, 3, 46–48, 53
crimes, 20, 88, 91–92, 94–95
curtains, 3, 12, 33, 34, 36, 57, 107–8, 147n79; fire curtains, 108, 147n78

da Costa Meyer, Esther, 14, 57
damask fabrics, 22, 30, 33, 116–19
dance, 62, 64–65, 89
D'Annunzio, Gabriele, 66–70, 72, 137n9
darkness, 3, 10, 13, 26, 30–31, 41, 67–68, 122n9
Davies, James Q., 18, 48, 54
Davy, Humphry, 50
de la Torre, Blanca, 47
de Reszke, Jean, 84
death, 5, 44, 46–47, 87, 91–92, 102–3
decoration, 13, 17, 22–27, 29, 31–37, 39–44, 91, 98, 110, 115–19. *See also* redecoration
dehumanization, 44
Della Sala Spada, Agostino, 64, 135n53
Descartes, René, 49
Dickens, Charles, 144n37
disease, 18, 28, 44, 55. *See also* COVID-19; public health
domesticity, 12, 30, 46, 48, 58, 94, 97

doors, 12–13, 20, 26–27, 107; and thresholds, 11, 88, 92–95, 97, 103, 143n31
dreams, 3, 21, 62, 67, 89–90, 93, 102
dyes, 14–15, 28, 36, 39–41, 44, 127n23

echoes, 68, 76–77, 80, 90
economics, 18, 44, 58, 104, 129n62. *See also* funding; profits
Eden, 3, 49, 54
Edison, Thomas, 58–60, 82, 110, 135n45. *See also* Società Edison Italiana
Eiffel Tower, 97–98
Eight-Nation Alliance, 44
electricity, 18–19, 26, 58–65, 84, 103, 108, 110, 134n41, 135n44. *See also* illumination; infrastructures
EMI records, 82
emissions, 14, 57, 110. *See also* pollution
emotions, 5, 17, 33, 41, 47, 63, 104. *See also* fear
encores, 78, 80, 108, 147n80
England: Liverpool, 101; London, 58–59, 63, 101, 103; London Coliseum, 107; Royal Opera House, London, 109; Savoy Theater, London, 63. *See also* Britain
environmental catastrophe, 15, 18, 47, 49–54. *See also* climate change
Ercole I d'Este, Duke of Ferrara, 3
ethics, 20, 46, 88, 94–96, 102–4. *See also* morality
ethnicity, 42
Eugénie, empress of France, 28
Eurocentrism, 21, 27, 30, 42
Europe, 18–21, 48, 61, 69, 124n45; and colonialism, 101–2; and color, 28–31, 42–44. *See also* Austrian Empire; Britain; England; France; Italy; Spain
exclusion, 11, 13, 31, 94
extraction, 14–15, 57, 96, 101–3; and color, 28, 38, 41, 44; and musical meaning, 5, 10

fabrics. *See* textiles
facades, 11–12, 19, 96–98, 99–100
faces, 13, 17, 25, 35, 37–42, 44–45
fantasies, 3–4, 25, 54, 62, 65, 85, 89
Fascism, 23, 31, 32, 126n6, 128n33

fashion, 29, 31, 35, 37, 40, 95, 127n27
Favaro, Antonio, 75, 80–81, 85, 138n32, 140n47, 141n58
fear, 25, 27, 32, 52, 60–61, 66, 74, 88, 108, 133n36
fires, 54, 55, 66, 68, 103, 108–9, 121n2, 121n4, 147n78. *See also* combustion; curtains; walls
Fogg Lecture Hall, Harvard University, 74
forests, 52–53, 61, 89, 101–2, 122n17. *See also* plants; wood
fossil fuels, 14, 18–19, 53, 58, 60–62, 109–10
foundations, building, 20, 40, 68, 70, 92, 96–97, 103–4
France, 29, 31, 36, 44; Besançon, 69; Paris, 29, 54, 58, 95. *See also* Champ de Mars, Paris; Eiffel Tower; Gobelins Manufactory, Paris; Paris Exposition Universelle; Paris Opéra
freedoms, 12, 58, 60, 62, 65, 88, 93–94, 104–8
fuchsin (color), 28–29
funding, 16, 26, 72–73, 102, 105, 109–10, 146n69
furniture, 13, 29, 35, 39, 52, 116, 118
futuristic fantasies, 64, 134n53

galleries, 73, 107, 133n30, 146n73
Garnier, Charles, 12, 20, 33, 36, 40–42, 75, 91–92, 97–98, 129n54, 142n18, 144n42
Gatti-Casazza, Giulio, 73, 74
gender, 13, 17, 42, 87, 141n5. *See also* women
geopolitics, 43–44, 60–62
Gesamtkunstwerk, 69
Gilbert and Sullivan, 63
Giordano, Umberto, 5, 81–82, 83
giovane scuola, 5, 81
globalization, 14, 57, 99, 124n37, 145n51
Gobelins Manufactory, Paris, 29, 39
Goethe, Johann Wolfgang von, 38–41
gold, 33–35, 89
governments, 23, 27, 72, 102. *See also* geopolitics; Milan, Italy
Gran Teatre del Liceu, Barcelona, 1–3, 11, 46, 49, 53–54, 55, 65, 121n2
greens (color), 34, 35–36, 38–42, 93

Hall-Witt, Jennifer, 15
Heidegger, Martin, 5, 123n19

Helmholtz, Hermann von, 80, 140n47
hermeneutics, 5, 99, 122n18
Herzog, Werner, *Fitzcarraldo*, 101–3, 145n58
homelessness, 11, 123n25
humanity, 12, 47–49, 50–53, 96, 98, 109

identities, 24–25, 27–28, 42
illumination, 3, 15, 26, 38, 58–64, 103, 110, 133nn34–36, 134n38, 134nn40–41, 136n54, 147n86. *See also* darkness
imperialism, 15–16, 23, 27, 31, 40–44, 50. *See also* colonialism
incandescent bulbs, 58–59, 63, 134n41
India, 101; Bombay, 98
Indigenous people, 102–3
industrialism, 15, 22, 28–29, 53, 62, 72, 95, 109, 126n5, 135n45, 137n18
infrastructures, 50, 124n43; energy, 18–19, 58–62, 65; theatrical, 15, 17, 25, 36, 42, 44, 96–97. *See also* electricity; steam power
Ingenhousz, Jan, 50
innovations, 14, 16–17, 19, 29, 69–72, 78, 139n45
insects, 18, 38, 41–42, 44
installations, art, 1, 3, 11, 46–48, 53–54, 65
interiors, architectural, 2, 13–14, 19, 76, 116, 121n6, 127n14; and atmospheres, 47–50, 55, 96, 108, 132n21; and surfaces, 22, 24, 36–37, 41–42, 129n54. *See also* decoration; redecoration
intimacy, 13, 23, 48, 94
iron, 53, 57, 89, 92–93, 96–97, 101, 142n20, 144n37. *See also* structural metals
Italy, 43–44, 104, 121n3; and acoustics, 66, 70, 81, 84, 139n40, 140n47, 140n52; and atmospheres, 48, 57–58, 61–62; Carrara, 101; Como, 32, 44; and Fascism, 31, 126n6; Florence, 12, 94; Lombardy province, 22; Mantua, 3, 91; Murano, 99; Rome, 70, 98; Turin, 64; Venice, 1, 90. *See also* Milan, Italy; Risorgimento; *individual theaters*

Japan, 43–44, 101, 129n64
Johnson, Eugene J., 90, 121n5, 141n10
Johnson, James H., 15, 26, 127n15
Jourdain, Frantz, 98

Kalba, Laura Anne, 29
Kittler, Friedrich A., 10, 77, 123n20, 123n22
Kreuzer, Gundula, 14, 123nn22–23, 147n79

labor, 14, 46, 68, 77, 105, 107; and colonialism, 99, 102–3; and extraction, 28, 42, 44, 65
Lacan, Jacques, 95
land, 50, 58, 72, 96–97, 104–5
Lavoisier, Antoine, 50
law, 78, 116–17, 119, 126n6, 139n40
Le Corbusier, 30, 31, 128n29
Ledoux, Claude-Nicolas, 69
Leroux, Gaston, *Le fantôme de l'Opéra*, 20, 87–89, 91–95, 141n1, 141n5, 141n8, 142nn17–18
literature, 10, 62. See also novels
Loos, Adolf, 30
Louis XIV of France, 29
lovers, 66, 88–89
lower classes, 12, 29, 35–36, 87

Manaus, Brazil, 11, 98, 101–3
manufacturing, 28–29, 39, 42–44, 92, 96–97, 101–2, 105. See also Gobelins Manufactory, Paris
Mascheroni, Edoardo, 77, 139n36
mass media, 10
materiality, 13–14, 16, 19, 65, 144n45; and acoustics, 5, 10, 67, 75, 80, 85, 90; and atmospheres, 49–50, 52, 57; and electricity, 19, 65; and structural metals, 88, 96, 98–99, 101; and surfaces, 23–24, 26, 38; and thresholds, 92–93, 96–101, 106, 109
Maurel, Victor, 84
mediation (acoustic), 81, 84
Medicis, 12, 94
Melbourne, Australia, 97
memories, 3, 24, 53. See also commemoration
Michiel Theater, Venice, 90
microcosms, teatri all'italiana as, 3, 5, 11, 17, 44, 53, 109–10
middle classes, 15, 26, 29, 36, 107
Milan, Italy, 4, 16–17, 23, 27, 44, 48, 138n21; and civic authorities, 72–77, 105, 107, 146n67; Duomo, 59–60, 61; Istituto Tecnico Superiore, 49, 61, 135n45; Milan Conservatory, 16; Pinacoteca di Brera, 23; Teatro del Popolo, 146n66; Teatro del Verme, 57; Teatro Manzoni, 57, 59. See also Borletti, Senatore; Caldara, Emilio; Società Edison Italiana; Società Italiana di Fonotipia; Società Leonardo da Vinci, Milan; Teatro alla Scala, Milan

minerals, 14–15, 20, 28, 38, 41, 52–53, 96
modernism, 80; and architecture, 29–32
modernity, 10, 18–19, 29, 32, 37, 50, 58, 60, 65, 117, 125n45; and acoustics, 77, 84–85, 140n51; and thresholds, 92, 97, 104, 108–9
Modigliani, Ettore, 22–26, 31–33, 44, 115–19, 126n6
Montecatini, 105
monumentalization, 11, 22, 32, 54, 89, 96–97, 119
morality, 18, 30, 48–49. See also ethics
Mouret, Octave, 58
Mozart, Wolfgang Amadeus, 75
Munich Festspielhaus, 97
Murano, 99
murder, 87, 102
museums, 23, 30
music criticism, 16, 48, 65, 67, 70–72, 74, 78, 79, 139n41, 139n44
music dramas, 4, 10–11, 54, 66–69, 72. See also Wagner, Richard
musicians, 1, 14, 16, 19, 48, 69–73, 76–85, 94, 105–8. See also orchestras; singers
Mussolini, Benito, 23, 31–32, 126n4

nature, 1, 3, 13, 102–3; and atmospheres, 49–54; and naturalization, 11–12, 20, 46, 95, 99; and sound, 47–48, 54, 80–81, 85–86; and surfaces, 40. See also animals; extraction; forests; minerals; plants
Naum Theater, Constantinople, 36
neoclassicism (architecture), 35, 98, 118–19
New World, 5. See also colonialism
Newton, Isaac, 37–38
Nietzsche, Friedrich, 78, 137n9
noise, 10, 68, 77–78, 84, 139n40

novels, 20, 38, 58, 64, 66–69, 93, 134n40, 136n53. *See also* Leroux, Gaston, *Le fantôme de l'Opéra*
novelty, 17, 27, 29, 67, 71, 123n22

Oaxaca, Mexico, 44
obsolescence (architectural), 103, 145n64
Oles, Thomas, 20, 95, 104
ontologies, 3–4, 24
Opium Wars, 42–43, 129n61
oratorios, 48
orchestra stalls, 1, 13, 17, 19, 35, 55, 66, 73, 87, 91, 116, 118
orchestras, 5, 10, 17, 19, 64; and isolation, 77–82, 108; orchestra pits, 19, 66–77, 84–86, 139n41, 139n45
Osterhammel, Jürgen, 14, 99
outdoors, 18, 55, 58, 81, 85

Palazzo degli Uffizi, 12
Paris Exposition Universelle, 97–98
Paris Opéra, 25; and Palais Garnier, 12, 20, 33, 42, 69, 75, 91–93, 98, 100, 107, 142nn16–18, 142n20; and Salle Le Peletier, 15
Pastoureau, Michel, 37
Perkin, William Henry, 28
Peruvian Amazon Company, 103
phenomenology, 4
physics, 38, 74, 81
pianos, 66
Piermarini, Giuseppe, 16, 98, 99, 110, 125n46
pillars, 105–6
plants, 1, 3, 11, 15, 28, 46–48, 50–52. *See also* forests
politics, 18, 20, 36, 43–44, 60–62, 84–85, 104, 138n19, 139n44, 145n66. *See also* Fascism; socialism
pollution, 57, 60, 61. *See also* emissions
popularization, 29, 107
poverty, 60, 87, 130n12
press coverage, 16, 48, 54–55, 57, 65, 67, 70–73, 74, 77–78, 79, 82, 139n41, 139n44, 140n47
Priestley, Joseph, 50
privacy, 12, 27, 40, 139n40
profits, 73, 101, 103

prosceniums, 2, 66, 67, 69–70, 94, 106–8
psychology, 29
public health, 55. *See also* COVID-19; disease
public realms, 12, 48, 49, 85, 94
Puccini, Giacomo, 5, 73–74, 81; "Crisantemi" String Quartet, 1, 46–47; *Manon Lescaut*, 4–5, 6–9
purity, 18–19, 29–30, 33, 48, 57, 63–65, 72, 84–86, 130n12, 132n21, 133n36
Pyne, Stephen J., 108–9
Pyrocene, 108–9

Qing dynasty, 43, 129n61

race, 12–13, 31, 42, 97–98, 126n6. *See also* whiteness
railroads, 96, 101–2
rarefication, 3, 18–19, 36, 48, 54–55, 63, 91, 109
redecoration, 14, 17–18; and Teatro alla Scala, 22–28, 31–33, 35, 40, 44, 128n37. *See also* decoration; renovations
reds (color), 17–18, 28, 33–42, 44, 129n54, 130n69
Reid, David Boswell, 132n21
renovations, 13, 16, 23, 31, 138n31, 145n66, 146n69, 146n73; and retrofitting, 103–10. *See also* redecoration
resonance, 10, 76, 80, 138n33. *See also* reverberation
respiration. *See* breath
reverberation, 4–5, 10, 68, 74–77, 80–82, 93, 122n14, 136n3, 138n25, 140n50. *See also* resonance; vibrations
Ricordi, Tito, 82
Rio de Janeiro, Brazil, 99, 100
Ripolin paint, 30
Risorgimento, 72, 84
roofs, 88–89, 92–93, 106–7, 143n25
rose (color), 40
Rossini, Gioachino, 75; *Semiramide*, 4
Rousseau, Jean-Jacques, 27
rubber, 102–3

Sabine, Wallace, 74–75, 138n25
Scego, Igiaba, 42
Schumann, Robert, 66

science, 18, 37–38, 48–54. *See also* acoustics; chemistry; physics
Sealy, Peter, 93, 143n25
seating, theater, 1, 2, 12, 15, 27, 35, 73, 84, 116–18, 125n48; and atmospheres, 55; and thresholds, 87, 90–91, 94, 105, 107
selfhood, 25, 37, 95
Semper, Gottfried, 97
sensory experience, 23, 94; and architecture, 3, 5, 10, 17, 20, 76, 68; and color, 29, 37–38. *See also* tactility; visuality
Serres, Michel, 24
sex, 5. *See also* lovers
sexuality, 5, 27
Sfondrini, Achille, 70
silence, 67–68, 124n42, 139n40; and audiences, 3, 13, 15, 26, 41, 85, 127n15
silk, 2, 17–18, 93; and decoration, 22, 33, 37, 117; red, 37, 39–42, 44; trade, 43–44
singers, 74, 76, 78, 81–82, 88. *See also* voices
skins, 63, 126n9, 126n11; and architecture, 11, 13, 17–18, 37, 97; and color, 38–42; and surfaces, 23–26, 33
slavery, 44, 102–3
SNIA Viscosa, 23, 126n5
social media, 46
social relations, 26, 47, 87, 104; and architecture, 13–15, 143n25; and color, 28–30, 37, 41. *See also* class
socialism, 84, 104–5
Società Edison Italiana, 19, 59–61, 105, 109–10, 133n37
Società Italiana di Fonotipia, 82–84, 140n52
Società Leonardo da Vinci, Milan, 147n78
Sorba, Carlotta, 15, 121nn3–4
sound recording, 10, 82–85, 140nn52–53, 141n56
South America, 101; Brazil, 11, 98–99, 100, 101–3; Chile, 36; Mexico, 44; Peru, 101; Uruguay, 36
Spain, 44; Barcelona, 1, 46. *See also* Gran Teatre del Liceu, Barcelona
spectrality, 38
SS. Giovanni e Paolo, Venice, 1–2, 12, 94, 121n5
stages, 1–3, 33, 57, 66, 76–77, 91, 94, 104–5, 107

staircases, 13, 107–8, 146n76
standardization, 15–17, 25, 35–36, 40, 69–70, 97, 124n43, 124n45, 144n39. *See also* uniformity
steam power, 96, 101–2
steel, 96, 101–4, 107–9, 145n51. *See also* structural metals
Sterne, Jonathan, 77, 122n17, 139n46, 141n55
stone, 11–12, 14, 19, 53, 68, 90, 92, 94–99, 144n45
Stoppani, Antonio, 18–19, 49–53, 61–62, 130n12, 132n18, 135n45
structural metals, 19–20, 88–89, 92–93, 95–96, 142nn20–21, 144n39; and colonialism, 97–103; and renovations, 103–9, 142n20, 144n39. *See also* beams; cantilevers; iron; steel
studios, 77–78, 84–85, 108, 139n38, 139n40, 141n56
sublime, 65, 80, 109
surfaces, 10, 12–13, 16–18, 22–26, 47, 126n9, 131n12; and acoustics, 68, 74–75, 81, 85, 138n25; and chromophobia, 26–33; and erasure, 42–45; and red, 33–42; and thresholds, 89, 93, 95, 99, 105, 126n7
sustainability, 110

tactility, 13, 23, 37, 60, 68
Taylor, Mark C., 26
teatri all'italiana, 87, 121nn2–4, 124n45, 142n13; and acoustics, 66, 69, 72; and architecture, 1–2, 4–5, 11–13, 15–17, 19–21, 25–26, 54; and atmospheres, 48–49, 54–58; and colonialism, 96–103; and color, 33–37, 40, 42, 44–45; and renovations, 103–10; and thresholds, 88–96. *See also* auditorium floors; beams; boxes, theater; cantilevers; *cassa armonica*; ceilings; cement; chandeliers; corridors; darkness; facades; galleries; illumination; orchestra stalls; orchestras; prosceniums; stages; structural metals; textiles; ventilation; windows; wings
Teatro alla Scala, Milan, 4, 16; and acoustics, 80–82, 84–85, 125n46; and conductors, 73–74, 77, 80, 139n36; and corporate sponsorship of, 105, 110, 146n69;

Teatro alla Scala (cont.)
 and dressing rooms, 106–7; and elevators, 106–7; and Ente Autonomo della Scala, 23, 104–5, 126n5, 146n68; and facades, 98, 99; and fire resistant materials, 107–8, 147n78; and galleries, 84, 107, 146n73; and illumination, 19, 26, 59–62, 134n38, 134nn40–41; and lowered orchestras, 19, 70–80, 139n45; and redecoration, 17, 22–23, 26–28, 31–36, 44, 116–19, 128n37; and renovations, 96, 104–5, 107, 110, 145n66, 146n73; and sustainability, 110; and ventilation, 57, 132n30; and Visconti di Modrone, 72–72, 137n18; and wings, 105–6
Teatro Amazonas, Manaus, 11, 98–99, 101–3
Teatro Beneficente Portuguesa, Manaus, 101
Teatro della Fortuna, Fano, 70
Teatro delle Muse, Ancona, 70
Teatro di Baldracca, Florence, 12, 94
Teatro La Fenice, Venice, 4
Teatro Municipal, Santiago, 36
Teatro Regio, Parma, 70; as Nuovo Teatro Ducale, Parma, 35
Teatro Regio, Turin, 4
Teatro Rossini, Pesaro, 70
Teatro Solís, Montevideo, 36
Teatro Verdi, Busseto, 70
Terragni, Giuseppe, 31, 32
textiles, 2–3, 13–18, 22–44, 91, 93, 108, 110, 116–19, 127n27. See also damask fabrics
textures, 22, 26–27, 33, 35, 37, 39
theater administrators, 71–77, 80, 105, 142n18
theater directors, 22–33, 33, 44, 63, 73, 74, 87, 116–17, 118–19, 135n52
Theatro Municipal, Rio de Janeiro, 99, 100
Thompson, Emily Ann, 81, 122n13, 140n51
thresholds, 11, 16–17, 19–20, 87–96, 103, 106–10, 142n18, 143n26. See also verticality
torture. See violence
Toscanini, Arturo, 73–74, 80, 139nn44–45
Toschi, Paolo, 35
traditions, 16, 24–25, 70, 98, 119

transcendence, 11, 19, 54, 64, 67, 69
transportation, 28, 96, 101–2, 132n26, 134n40
Trélat, Émile, 54–55
Tron Theater, Venice, 90
turquoise (color), 3, 91, 110
Tyndall, John, 62, 140n47

uniformity, 22–23, 29, 33, 81, 117, 119. See also standardization
United States, 14, 43–44, 90; and acoustics, 81, 145n63; Louisiana, 5; New York, 58
upholstery. See textiles

values, 12–13, 22, 98–99, 116, 119; and acoustics, 75, 80, 86; and atmospheres, 18, 49, 54; and colors, 22, 27–28, 33, 36
velvet, 2, 34, 116
ventilation, 3, 18–19, 47–49, 54–58, 92, 132n21, 132n26, 132n30
Verdi, Giuseppe, 77, 139n36; *Aida*, 73. See also Teatro Verdi, Busseto
Verne, Jules, 134n40, 135n53
verticality, 12, 20, 87–93, 104, 106
vibrations, 5, 10, 66, 93, 85. See also resonance; reverberation
Vienna State Opera, 25, 56; as Vienna Court Opera, 55–57, 132n25
violence, 24–25, 42, 102–3. See also abduction; colonialism; imperialism
violinata, 5, 82
Visconti di Modrone, Guido, 72–73
Visconti di Modrone, Uberto, 73, 82
Visconti di Modrone family, 72–73, 137n18
visibility, 20, 37–38, 40–41, 45, 70, 72–73, 80; and invisibility, 12, 19, 66, 68–69, 71, 83–84, 94, 108–9
visuality, 23, 29, 37–39, 60; and acoustics, 66–69, 73, 77–78
Vitruvius, 80, 140n48
voices, 5, 27, 53, 62, 74, 81–85, 110, 139n46; and thresholds, 87, 90, 94–95, 102. See also singers

Wagner, Richard, 10–11, 19, 70, 75, 78, 123n24, 137n6, 137n9; *Der Ring des Nibelungen*, 54, 67–68, 72; *Parsifal*,

4, 68; *Tristan und Isolde*, 66. See also Bayreuth Festspielhaus
walls, 10, 13, 18–20, 60, 109, 123n26, 142n22, 143n26; and acoustics, 67–68, 70–71, 76–77, 81–82; and firewalls, 108–9; and renovations, 104–5, 107–8; and surfaces, 17, 22, 26–27, 30, 33, 35, 38, 41, 44; and thresholds, 43, 88, 92–96, 98
water, 5, 47, 49, 51, 52, 62, 78, 79, 88–90, 92–93, 96–97, 101–2, 108, 139n41
wealth, 36–37, 60, 72, 96, 99, 101–2, 110, 130n12
Wechsberg, Joseph, 67
Weinthal, Lois, 13–14, 127n14
whiteness, 13, 17, 30–31, 33, 34–35, 37–38, 40–42, 97–98

Wickham, Henry, 103
windows, 1, 3, 20, 37, 46–48, 58, 91–93, 97, 106
wings, 105
women, 13, 17, 27, 38, 42, 58, 87–88, 92, 110
wonder, 3, 63, 88–90, 93
wood, 11, 14, 66–67, 76–77, 81, 89, 92, 98, 101, 105, 138n33, 145n51. See also forests
World War I, 37
World War II, 135n53

yellows (color), 34–35, 36, 38

Zola, Émile, 58, 93

www.ingramcontent.com/pod-product-compliance
Lightning Source LLC
Chambersburg PA
CBHW022014290426
44109CB00015B/1163